JOHN BROWN'S SPY

JOHN BROWN'S SPY

The Adventurous Life and
Tragic Confession of
JOHN E. COOK

Steven Lubet

Yale

UNIVERSITY PRESS

New Haven & London

Published with assistance from the Mary Cady Tew Memorial Fund.

Yale University Press books may be purchased in quantity for educational, business, or promotional use. For information, please e-mail sales.press@yale.edu (U.S. office) or sales@yaleup.co.uk (U.K. office).

Set in Century Expanded Roman Type by Integrated Publishing Solutions, Grand Rapids, Michigan.
Printed in the United States of America.

Library of Congress Cataloging-in-Publication Data

Lubet, Steven.
John Brown's spy : the adventurous life and tragic confession of
John E. Cook / Steven Lubet.
pages cm
Includes bibliographical references and index.
ISBN 978-0-300-18049-7 (cloth : alk. paper)   1. Cook, John E. (John Edwin), 1830–1859.   2. Brown, John, 1800–1859—Friends and associates.   3. Harpers Ferry (W. Va.)—History—John Brown's Raid, 1859.   I. Title.
E451.L83 2012
973.7′116092—dc23
[B]   2012019509

A catalogue record for this book is available from the British Library.

This paper meets the requirements of ANSI/NISO Z39.48–1992 (Permanence of Paper).

10   9   8   7   6   5   4   3   2   1

To my extended family:
the Lubets, the Levitts, and the Roses

CONTENTS

CONTENTS

AUTHOR'S NOTE

On October 16, 1859, John Brown and his men took control of the federal armory compound in a town then called Harper's Ferry, Virginia. The same town is known today as Harpers Ferry, West Virginia—the apostrophe having been eliminated in a twentieth-century post office reform, and West Virginia having been admitted to the Union in 1863. Brown was soon captured and taken to nearby Charlestown, which is now Charles Town. For the sake of consistency with primary sources, I have opted to use the original town names—Harper's Ferry and Charlestown—throughout the text, while of course referring to their location as Virginia.

Surnames present a slightly more complicated problem, as they were not spelled consistently even in primary sources. I have thus chosen to use the most common spellings—Cook, Stevens, Coppoc—in the text. I have preserved variations where they appear in original quotes, such as Cooke, Stephens, Coppic, and the like. Other nineteenth-century spellings, capitalizations, and punctuation are also repeated now and then within quotations, and I trust that readers will recognize such antebellum usages as they appear.

Speaking of primary sources, it is worth noting that information on John E. Cook falls into three categories. First, I was able to find a relatively limited number of letters, poems, newspaper articles, and other accounts that were written by and about Cook during the years before Harper's Ferry. These provide the most unfiltered descriptions of his character and activities, as they were unaffected by his later notoriety. A second category of sources consists of contemporaneous reports—mostly in newspapers and court testimony, but also in letters and diaries—of the Harper's Ferry raid and its immediate aftermath, including Cook's involvement. Finally, many of the surviving principals wrote recollections of Cook in the years and decades following their contact with him. The latter two categories, and especially the personal reminiscences, were of course influenced by the writers' attitudes toward Cook (and Brown). Because of these considerations, I have been careful to identify my sources throughout the book, and I have noted the situations where I believe cautious reading, and occasionally skepticism, to be appropriate. That said, the sources of all vintages and origins are nearly unanimous in the assessment of Cook's outlook, motivations, and behavior.

Introduction

John Brown sat on a narrow cot in a Charlestown jail, wondering whether John E. Cook had become a traitor. Less than two weeks earlier Brown had commenced a military campaign to free the slaves of the South by leading a small armed band into the sleeping town of Harper's Ferry, Virginia. Although he commanded only twenty-one men, he believed that his guerilla strike would soon rally hundreds of slaves to his cause, thus placing him at the head of an unstoppable army of emancipation. The first step in Brown's bold plan was to seize control of the United States armory and arsenal in Harper's Ferry, with their vast stores of rifles and ammunition. From there he would repair to the nearby Blue Ridge Mountains, where he intended to establish an abolitionist stronghold. Under the authority of his newly proclaimed "Provisional Constitution," Brown would then embark on a series of liberation raids that would eventually break the power of slavery.

That was the plan. In reality, Brown's force was woefully inadequate to the task. Brown's men did initially succeed in taking control of the federal armory compound, but they were soon surrounded by hundreds of local militiamen who poured fire onto their positions. The abolitionist fighters held out as long as they could, but the arrival of a contingent of United States Marines sealed their fate. Brown's army was thoroughly defeated. Ten of the raiders were killed; five escaped to the north; and seven, including Brown himself, were taken prisoner.

Although badly wounded, John Brown was immediately interrogated by his captors, who hoped that he would reveal the identities of his financial backers and other northern supporters. Brown, however, was steadfast. While he was eager to proclaim the goals of his invasion—harshly condemning the evils of slavery—he drew a firm line at implicating others, and he expected his imprisoned troops to do the same.

Brown and other captured raiders were soon taken to nearby Charlestown, the county seat, where they would be tried for treason and murder. Brown quickly realized that he could transform his trial into a remarkable forum for his crusade against slavery, and that his courtroom speeches could now reach across the country like never before. Disdaining efforts to save his life, he used his court appearances to condemn southern justice while eloquently preaching against the sin of human bondage. And while he claimed to speak on behalf of a broad movement, Brown remained careful never to reveal the names of his backers in the North.

For the most part, Brown's fellow prisoners went along with his strategy, in part because they revered their commander in chief and in part because they had little choice. Unlike Brown, who was the focus of national attention, the other prisoners had only limited access to the outside world, and they were represented by abolitionist attorneys who were not inclined to advise their clients to break ranks.

But there was one worrisome exception. Rumors had been flying around Charlestown—and especially within the small jail—that John E. Cook intended to cooperate with the prosecution by exposing all of the participants in Brown's "conspiracy." Brown had kept most of his men completely in the dark about the details of his plan, but Cook was no ordinary soldier and he had access to information that the authorities were eager to learn. Cook had lived undercover for over a year in Harper's Ferry, providing Brown with intelligence that was critical to the invasion, including maps, building plans, and a census of the local slaves. In the anxious weeks before the attack, Cook had played a key role in calming the nerves of Brown's recalcitrant troops and keeping the small band united. On the night of the raid itself, Cook had been entrusted with a crucial mission, leading a sortie deep into the countryside for the purpose of taking slave owners hostage, among them Colonel Lewis Washington, a great-grandnephew of the first president. Holding the rank of captain in Brown's provisional army, Cook had very nearly been the linchpin of the entire operation. To his credit, Cook had accomplished every task assigned to him, and then he had somehow managed to elude the encircling Virginia militia—only to be captured later by bounty hunters.

Cook was a resourceful and intrepid fighter, and yet there had always been something about him that Brown found disquieting. Cook was a young man of exuberant emotion who—while pledging heartfelt dedication to abolitionism—often seemed to be attracted as much to the romance of the movement as to the antislavery principle itself. While Brown saw antislavery work as strict and exacting, Cook wore his militancy lightly. He was casual in his acquaintances, free with his affections, and constantly talking about his real or imagined exploits. In another age or place, perhaps Cook would have been a footloose adventurer, available for recruitment by any cause that promised moral passion and offered high excitement.

Brown was keenly aware that men like Cook—well-meaning but too easily seduced—had been drawn to almost every revolution or insurgency in history. And Brown realized as well that many such men stayed ever true—honoring their comrades and holding to their promises—while others lost courage in the face of adversity. Brown was seldom an impulsive man, but he considered himself a good judge of character, and he had years earlier decided that Cook was one of the better sort, worthy of his trust and capable of full devotion. He now hoped that he had been right about his spy, but he feared the worst. Brown was ready to face the gallows, but would he have to endure betrayal as well?

※　❀　※

Even as John Brown prepared to confront his accusers in the Charlestown courthouse, John Edwin Cook paced about his own jail cell, trembling as much from uncertainty as from fear. His escape from the debacle at Harper's Ferry had for a time seemed almost miraculous. By purest luck he had been outside the armory compound when the federal troops began their final assault, and he had watched from a distance as his comrades were either captured or killed. Along with four other fugitives, he had somehow managed to reach Pennsylvania's upper Cumberland Valley, but his good fortune ran out when he was captured by bounty hunters and then returned to Virginia in chains. That had been ordeal enough, but soon he would face a new test. His interrogators were demanding that he provide them with the names of John Brown's financial backers, and they offered to spare him from the gallows if he would betray the antislavery cause to which he had devoted so much of his life. Cook's lawyer—a politically ambitious proslavery "doughface" from Indiana—urged him to take the deal. Why should such a young man hang for the sake of some fanatical abolitionists in Boston? The attorney handed his client a sheaf of foolscap and a pen. "Just start writing," he said. "Only a full confession can save your life."

The authorities expected great revelations from Cook, who was known to have been Brown's confidant and spy. Now that they had him in custody, the prosecutors planned to wring out every last bit of information from their prisoner, or hang him. Or both.

Cook was an inviting target for coercion. Short and slight, he had delicate features, full lips, bright blue eyes, and blond curly hair that fell in ringlets about his face. Although he was already thirty years old, he had a markedly boyish appearance that many men considered effeminate—a demeanor sharply at odds with his reputation. During his brief ten days at large—from the collapse of the uprising until his capture in Pennsylvania—Cook had been the most wanted man in the United States, and perhaps the most feared. Rumors had spread across Virginia that Cook was preparing to lead a renewed abolitionist invasion, and they had persisted even when every report proved to be unfounded. But now that Cook was in jail, he seemed small and far from dangerous. Despite Cook's importance as a potential informant, the furious Virginians must have wondered how Brown had come to choose such an unimposing figure for so many important positions in his command.

But first impressions can be deceiving and Cook had most of the attributes of a loyal adjutant and effective spy. He had ridden with Brown in Bleeding Kansas, where he achieved the rank of captain in the antislavery militia. In the running battles with Missouri's "border ruffians," Cook did not once flinch from tough duty. He had helped to chase proslavery settlers from their homes along the Neosho River, freely resorting to violence when he thought it was necessary.

Cook was also affable and outgoing, easy to talk to and quick to make friends. He was well educated and well spoken, and, as one neighbor later put it, "he had all the nice little graces of a gentleman."[1] People always seemed to welcome Cook into their homes, and he would repay their hospitality with exaggerated—or perhaps imaginary—stories of his exploits as a buffalo hunter on the Kansas plains. He also had a gift for rhyme, and he could spin out romantic verses almost endlessly, much to the delight of his friends and companions. As Brown recognized, Cook had no trouble ingratiating himself with strangers, which, of course, made it easier for him to deceive the Virginians of Harper's Ferry.

Such extroversion also had a downside. Cook loved to make himself the center of attention, sometimes boasting well beyond the point of toleration. He wore stylish outfits and carried fancy firearms that he showed off constantly to friends and strangers alike. His comrades laughingly called him a "walking arsenal" and teased him for burnishing his weapons at all hours of the day. Although most people found Cook to be charming and charismatic, some considered him an unbearable loudmouth. One thing is certain: Cook was talkative to a fault. He could not resist playing to an audience, especially when there were women in the room. His impromptu rhymes, usually intended to beguile young ladies, "rippled from his mouth [in a] musical voice."[2]

If Cook's personality was flamboyant, his attitude and appearance were still more distinctive. Surviving accounts make it clear that he radiated an unusual air of sexuality, especially for the mid-nineteenth century. Over and over, Cook's male contemporaries described him in female terms. One newspaper reporter said that he had a "feminine rather than a masculine appearance," and one of Cook's own lawyers said that his "large, soft eyes" were as "gentle in expression as a woman's," and his "slightly bronzed complexion . . . would have well befitted the gentler sex." He composed such florid poetry that it sometimes seemed "to have been written by a female," and he even had a slight lisp.[3]

Although men tended to look askance at Cook's affectations, women reacted far differently to his good looks. Young ladies were eager for his company and receptive to his advances, which appear to have been frequent and indiscriminate. He impregnated at least one woman during his Kansas days, resulting in a miscarriage. He fathered a child with his landlady's daughter in Harper's Ferry, marrying her shortly before their son was born. A third woman claimed to have given birth to Cook's child, and it is unknown how many others shared his bed. One of John Brown's sons jealously called him an "expert getting into the good graces of the girls," and his Kansas comrades once voted to rebuke him "for hugging girls" which, as events demonstrated, was an unmistakable euphemism.[4]

Spying calls for discretion above all else—but there was very little that was discreet about Cook's personal life, from his extravagant choice of clothing, to his well-polished firearms, to his brazen pursuit of lovers. He was a notorious libertine, and the stories of his many affairs were eagerly repeated from Kansas to Virginia. There was certainly no other man among Brown's followers with such a bawdy and irrepressible reputation.

His Virginia jailors may not have realized it, but Cook was a poet, a marksman, a boaster, a dandy, a fighter, a storyteller, and a womanizer—as well as a spy. In a lifetime of only thirty years, he had studied law in

Connecticut, fought against border ruffians in Kansas, served as an abolitionist mole in Harper's Ferry, taken white hostages during Brown's insurrection, and almost escaped to freedom. Now he would face the final test—of courage or collaboration—in the crucible of a Virginia jail.

❊　❂　❊

John Brown achieved his iconic status the hard way, but he did not do it alone. In addition to Cook, another twenty men joined Brown's army for the invasion of Harper's Ferry. Most of them were killed, either by gunshots or on the gallows, and virtually all of them have been overshadowed in history by Brown's incandescent persona. That is regrettable, because many of their stories are remarkable. John Kagi, for example, had been a lawyer, a school teacher, and a journalist, but he quit his professional life in order to serve with Brown in Kansas, where he was imprisoned twice and severely wounded in battles against pro-slavery border ruffians. In December 1858, Kagi was Brown's second-in-command on a daring foray into Missouri, where they freed a dozen slaves whom they escorted to freedom in Canada. For all of his accomplishments and adventures, Kagi was only twenty-four years old when he was shot and killed at Harper's Ferry. Aaron Stevens was the only one of Brown's men with formal military training. A veteran of the Mexican War, he was "a dangerous hothead" who had been court-martialed for mutiny and assaulting an officer.[5] Stevens claimed that the incident was precipitated by the officer's frequent physical abuse of enlisted men, but he was convicted and sentenced to hard labor at Fort Leavenworth. Stevens soon escaped from Leavenworth to join a free-state militia in Kansas. He became closely allied with John Brown and participated in the Missouri slave rescue.

Five of the raiders were members of Brown's own family—his sons Watson, Oliver, and Owen, as well as the brothers William and Dauphin Thompson, whose sister was married to Watson Brown. (A third Thompson brother, who did not go to Harper's Ferry, was married to

Brown's daughter Ruth.) Owen Brown managed to escape safely, but his brothers and both Thompson boys were killed by gunfire. Watson lived long enough following the raid to speak with a southern newspaper reporter. "What brought you here?" the journalist asked. "Duty, sir," Watson replied. The southerner challenged him. "Is it your idea of duty to shoot men down upon their own hearth stones?" In great pain, and with great effort, Watson Brown held fast to his beliefs. "I am dying," he said, "I cannot discuss the question; I did my duty as I saw it."[6]

Most moving are the stories of the African Americans in Brown's party. Dangerfield Newby was a freed slave whose wife and seven children were still the "property" of Jesse Jennings, the master of a plantation about thirty miles from Harper's Ferry. Newby had joined Brown's company in the hope of rescuing his family, but he was one of the first men killed during the fighting. He carried a letter from his wife in his pocket that read, "Oh dear Dangerfield, com this fall without fail monny or no Monny I want to see you so much that is the one bright hope I have before me." Lewis Sheridan Leary had been born free in North Carolina, but he later moved to Ohio where he studied at Oberlin College. Leary left behind his pregnant wife when he departed Oberlin to join Brown's troop, fully expecting to "give my life to free others" and expressing only the wish that his wife and child "shall never know want." Leary was shot and killed trying to escape from the armory, but his last request was fulfilled. His widow—who gave birth to a daughter—later married Charles Langston, one of the leading black abolitionists of Ohio, who raised the child as his own. The young girl grew up and had a son whom she named after her step-father; that child was the poet and playwright Langston Hughes. John Copeland, also a freed slave originally from North Carolina, was recruited from Oberlin along with Leary. Copeland survived the raid, but he was captured by the United States forces and turned over to the Commonwealth of Virginia for trial. Copeland wrote to his parents from his jail cell, urging them not to despair and reminding them that he had given his life to "a holy cause."[7]

In the operatic story of the Harper's Ferry raid, Brown's men have been treated mostly as literal spear carriers. In 150 years, there has been no full biography of any one of them. Their actions—and deaths—have been recounted, and their martyrdom has been broadly praised in the many biographies of John Brown, but they have seldom been described at any length as independent moral actors. In fact, they were not merely virtuous ciphers, and some of them were anything but saints. Aaron Stevens, for example, had a brutal temper that led him to kill an elderly slave owner during the Missouri raid, apparently quite unnecessarily. Stevens himself later regretted the shooting, saying, "I had no business in there, and the old man was right." Lewis Leary, for all of his heroism at Harper's Ferry, did not tell his pregnant wife that he was abandoning her for an adventure. He simply departed Oberlin one night, leaving word for her with others.[8]

John Cook's life—and his engagement with John Brown—tells a story of moral complexity writ large, and his role in facilitating the Harper's Ferry invasion has never been explored in detail. As is almost always the case in warfare, the advance job was essential to the greater campaign. It was Cook's assignment to obtain maps of the town and the surrounding roads, to assess the number of slaves who could be attracted to Brown's rebellion, and to identify prominent citizens who could be taken hostage. Without that critical intelligence about the region, Brown would have been at sea when he arrived in the summer of 1859.

Once Brown had established his headquarters at a nearby Maryland farm, Cook again played a crucial part in allowing the attack to go forward. Only weeks before the insurrection, there was a near mutiny among the men that almost caused the collapse of the entire enterprise. At that critical moment, however, Cook played a decisive role in quelling the rebellion. He strongly endorsed Brown's leadership, and he convinced the most apprehensive raiders to remain in the fold. Without Cook's support, Brown might have seen his twenty-one-man army dwindle away, perhaps requiring him to delay or even cancel the uprising. Cook's deployment was equally important on the night of the invasion. He was the only one of Brown's men who could locate and identify the targeted hostages, and he served as an indispensable guide on the sortie into the countryside to capture Lewis Washington and others.

※ ❀ ※

Recent authors have rightly observed that John Brown "sparked the Civil War," although not through a military victory as Brown himself anticipated. Instead, it was Brown's demeanor as he accepted his fate—resolute, unflinching, and selflessly devoted to the destruction of slavery—that motivated many thousands in the North to embrace his cause. In little more than a year after his death, Union troops were marching to the refrain of "John Brown's Body." By the end of 1861, Julia Ward Howe had added new words and a new title to the song— "The Battle Hymn of the Republic"—including, in the fifth stanza, a poignant evocation that could apply equally to Jesus Christ and John Brown: "As he died to make men holy/Let us die to make men free."

In his lifetime, however, John Brown never gathered more than a few dozen men to his side. Leading abolitionists, such as Frederick Douglass, refused to participate in the invasion of Virginia, as did three of Brown's own sons and several others among his most fervent erstwhile supporters. Of thirty-four black men who endorsed Brown's Provisional Constitution of the United States, only one followed him to Harper's Ferry.

What sort of men did join John Brown? Although he assumed the title of commander in chief of an abolitionist army, Brown was in no position to be selective about his recruits. In the end, he accepted every man who seemed willing to fight, including the reckless and voluble John Cook. The leader of an established army might well have preferred to entrust his most sensitive assignments to someone less impulsive, but Brown had little choice. His necessary reliance on such a mercurial figure gives us much insight into his campaign during the years leading up to John Brown's finest hour.

Despite their many differences in background and temperament, Brown believed that he had no more enthusiastic a supporter than John Cook. Until the day of Cook's confession.

❊ ONE ❊

Kansas

John E. Cook was born in 1829 to a prosperous New England family of old Puritan stock.[1] His parents, Nathaniel and Mary, lived in a sturdy frame house in Haddam, Connecticut, where they held interests in a quarry and several tracts of land, placing them among the small town's more affluent and stable citizens. Although John always had an impetuous side, there was little in his early upbringing that seemed to presage his later exploits with John Brown. As devout Congregationalists, the elder Cooks probably found slavery distasteful, but they were never known to express any abolitionist sentiments.

Nathaniel and Mary Cook had seven children—five daughters and two sons—among whom John was the youngest. Unusually for married women of that era, Mary Cook owned agricultural property in her own name, which provided her with considerable independence and no doubt contributed to her self-sufficient character. Five years older than her husband, Mary was forty-two when John was born, and she quite reasonably turned his care over to her daughters, who doted on the baby and made him the center of attention in a household dominated by strong women. Nathaniel Cook was a hard worker and a good provider, but he was chronically disorganized and given to telling imaginative tales. One neighbor called him the Baron Munchhausen of Haddam and another joked that a "verbal long bow" was the source of his constant exaggerations. In one of his stories, Nathaniel boasted of taking an entire flock of wild pigeons with "only one charge of shot," which made a strong impression on his youngest son.[2]

John followed his father's example in many ways. He began telling fanciful tales of his own—amusing his sisters with jokes and stories, and developing a talent for delighting female company that he would carry into adulthood. At some point he also took up shooting, having been inspired by Nathaniel's account of preternatural pigeon hunting. Soon enough, John became a first-rate marksman, practicing his aim in the expanses of the family quarry.

In his teen years, John did his best to fulfill family responsibilities, working in a neighbor's fields for thirty cents a day, according to Nathaniel's ledger. He also took guests on tours of his father's quarry, once escorting two travelers from Prussia on a "mineral excursion" for an enhanced fee of eighty cents.[3] Young John no doubt entertained his visitors with geological anecdotes learned from his voluble father. He might even have offered to give the curious Europeans a shooting exhibition, although that would not have been recorded in Nathaniel's account book. In one way, however, John improved on his father's example. Nathaniel's accounts were a mess. His books were filled with criss-crossed and undated entries, and his handwriting and notations were sometimes indecipherable. John, however, diligently practiced his penmanship, signing his name over and over in the margins of his father's ledger. John's twin sisters Caroline and Catherine—only two years his senior—practiced writing along with him, thus contributing to the development of his elegant cursive technique.

Along with his sisters, John attended private school at the Brainerd Academy, where his father paid tuition ranging from $5.50 to $6.50 per term. He also attended the Haddam Congregational Church, and he sometimes taught Sunday school classes. As Nathaniel later put it, John had a thorough education "in the principles of religious morality."[4]

Nonetheless, John E. Cook had another side, in which he showed himself to be impulsive and reckless. One Haddam neighbor called him "a raskel," who was "always in some scrape." Another thought that John was a boaster and a coward who narrowly evaded punishment but was surely destined to come to a bad end.[5] Whatever his juvenile misdeeds in Haddam, John Cook retained the love and devotion of his older sisters, who would later stand by him in his darkest days. Nathaniel and Mary also thought well enough of John's prospects to finance his education far beyond the limits of the Brainerd Academy.

※　❋　※

John Cook's shameless storytelling and general audacity apparently led his parents to believe that he had a future as an attorney. He was sent to study law at Yale when he was about twenty, but he left school—without explanation—before graduating. Given his capricious ways, it is certainly possible that John was dismissed either for misconduct or poor performance, or he might simply have wearied of study and discipline.[6]

A college degree was not required for admission to the bar in those days, and Cook soon obtained a position reading law in the Williamsburg, New York, office of a young attorney named John N. Stearns. He got the job with the help of his brother-in-law Robert Crowley, who had married Frances Cook several years earlier, and who operated a thriving needle business in Williamsburg (now part of Brooklyn). Frances—or Fanny, as she was called—was eight years older than John, and she would never stop treating him as her beloved baby brother. She repeatedly called upon her wealthy husband to extend himself whenever John was in need.

Beginning work for Stearns in early 1854, Cook was a competent clerk, so long as his duties were limited to copying (then an important skill) and other simple tasks. His elegant penmanship and "correct orthography" pleased his employer, but otherwise Cook turned out to have little talent for law and even less interest "in its science, its facts and its principles." Rather than study how to draw a complaint or a promissory note, Cook's "poetical infatuations" led him to spend his time writing sentimental verse for his many lady friends. Perhaps also as a means of impressing young women, and certainly to the annoyance of his boss, Cook somehow managed to practice shooting when he should have been working on conveyances or deeds of trust. "The use of guns and pistols was with him a kindred passion to his poetry; as a marksman he was a dead shot." It turned out that Cook was willing to do "anything and everything . . . except to learn law," and his clerkship ended well before he was qualified for admission to the bar.[7]

Fanny came to the rescue, convincing her husband to employ John as the Philadelphia representative of his business. Cook showed somewhat more promise as a merchant than he had as a lawyer. His affability made him an effective salesman, and he successfully expanded Crowley's sales to local shop owners. Cook also enjoyed a rich social life. While boarding at the Union Hotel, he made the acquaintance of many women, young and old, whom he charmed with his usual rounds of poetry and stories. It would not be surprising if he gave shooting demonstrations, and he definitely organized numerous games and parties. But even with a surfeit of off-hours female companionship, the mundane work of selling needles could not hold Cook's attention for long. He returned to Brooklyn and worked briefly in another law office, but to no better result.[8]

By the mid-1850s—spurred by idealism and eager for adventure—Cook had become committed to a militant brand of abolitionism that would consume the rest of his life. There is no precise record of Cook's conversion to the antislavery cause. His Williamsburg boss, John Stearns, was a staunch temperance man, and Cook also embraced "anti-whisky" principles during his clerkship, but he does not seem ever to have had an abolitionist mentor. According to Stearns, Cook never displayed any "special interest in Abolitionism, nor any special sympathy for the colored race." As far as his employer knew, Cook's vivid "poetic imagination" took him only into a "land of dreams." In fact, the restless young clerk was dreaming of something much greater than law practice, and certainly much grander than selling needles to Philadelphia shopkeepers.[9]

Cook was no doubt inspired by the lectures of Rev. Henry Ward Beecher, who was then the minister at the Plymouth Congregational Church in Brooklyn Heights, which has rightly been called the leading Protestant church of the era. Beecher was an ardent abolitionist and a spellbinding orator, whose weekly sermons touched on a wide range of political, cultural, and literary topics. Beecher's speaking style was characterized by "originality, logic, pathos, and humor," and his charismatic personality attracted thousands of congregants and guests. Although Cook often accompanied his sister and brother-in-law to the nearby Reformed Dutch Church of Williamsburg—where Robert Crowley was a member of the consistory—John certainly would have been drawn to the charismatic Beecher who, like Cook, was a Connecticut native and a Congregationalist. Cook would later show evidence of Beecher's influence on matters as diverse as abolitionism, temperance, and even a fascination with the novels of Sir Walter Scott.[10]

Beecher's celebrity status was unmatched in antebellum America, and given the opportunity, virtually nobody passed up the chance to hear him preach against slavery. His services were attended at one time or another by Walt Whitman, Abraham Lincoln, Clara Barton, Horace Greeley, Charles Dickens, Ralph Waldo Emerson, Mark Twain, and almost every other literary or political figure who happened to be passing through New York. Some were motivated by the hope of meeting Beecher's older sister Harriet Beecher Stowe, whose momentous novel *Uncle Tom's Cabin* had been published in 1851, and who was a member of her brother's church. Others were attracted by the many famous guest lecturers, who included William Lloyd Garrison, Frederick Douglass, Wendell Phillips, Sojourner Truth, and Charles Sumner. Most of the attendees, however, came to hear Rev. Beecher's own antislavery message, which was militant and unequivocal.[11]

John Cook was surely also attracted by the social opportunities at Plymouth Church. Beecher did not preach free love (although it turned out that he may have practiced it in private), but his congregation was the best place in New York to meet liberal-minded young women. A common interest in the heady subject of abolitionism would have provided Cook with the perfect opening gambit for a more intimate conversation.

❊ ❀ ❊

Henry Ward Beecher came naturally to abolitionism, having inherited the antislavery sentiments of his father, the famous evangelist Rev. Lyman Beecher. In a pattern that was repeated throughout the antebellum period, the younger Beecher expanded upon and radicalized his father's theology—which stressed holiness and benevolence—eventually calling for active resistance to the slave power in the name of "higher law."[12]

The problem of slavery had always vexed American political, social, and religious life. In the first years following the Revolution of 1776, it was optimistically thought that the spirit of the Declaration of Independence would gradually lead to the voluntary abandonment of slavery. But that naïve expectation was soundly dashed at the Constitutional Convention in 1787, when the southern delegates argued vehemently that recognition of slavery was essential to their acceptance of the new Union. While some northern delegates were personally opposed to slavery, not one had come to the convention "intending to grapple with the social and moral issues of slavery," and most were eager to compromise with southerners for the sake of unity and commerce.[13] At the time, enslaved human beings constituted the second most valuable form of private property in the nation—in the aggregate, only real estate was worth more—and the prosperous men who wrote the Constitution were keenly aware that their own fortunes, in all regions, were closely tied to the fruits of slave labor.

When it came to slavery, the Constitution was a product of southern intransigence and northern concessions. It included numerous protections for slavery, including the three-fifths clause, which gave the slave states disproportionate representation in the House of Representatives and Electoral College, and the fugitive slave clause, which would later be interpreted to deny the ability of free states to protect their own black citizens. Charles Pinckney, a leading delegate from South Carolina, was well satisfied with the result, bragging that the southerners had "made the best terms for the security of this species of property it was in our power to make." Nonetheless, the question of slavery would continue to trouble the new nation. As James Madison observed, the states would continue to be divided "principally from the effects of their having or not having slaves."[14]

Opposition to slavery slowly continued to build in the North, and the peculiar institution became ever more entrenched in the South. The issue occasionally flared—as during the Missouri crisis of 1820—but most national leaders agreed that compromise remained in the nation's best interest, and nobody dared to challenge the existence of slavery where it was already well established. For over forty years, antislavery groups were dominated by "elite white ministers, lawyers, and businessmen" who adhered to a philosophy of gradualism and promoted the re-colonization of freed slaves to Africa.[15]

All of that began to change on July 4, 1829, when a young journalist named William Lloyd Garrison stepped to the pulpit of Boston's Park Street Congregational Church. The Fourth of July had long been an occasion for well-to-do Bostonians to express their sympathy for the downtrodden slaves of the South, and Garrison had been invited by the American Colonization Society to make an afternoon address at the annual meeting. It was expected that Garrison, then only twenty-four years old, would invoke piety and charity, while requesting donations for the relief of "a long divided and suffering people." Instead, Garrison used the occasion to make a radical statement "on the necessity of abolishing slavery in the name of equal rights."[16]

Dressed in a black suit with a fashionably broad, Byronic collar spread over the jacket, Garrison's knees were knocking together in apprehension as he approached the lectern. It was his first major public appearance, and he intended to discomfit the self-satisfied citizens in the pews. He began by denouncing Independence Day as "the worst and most disastrous day in the whole three hundred and sixty five," because it commemorated the "glaring contradiction" between the ideals of the Revolution and the reality of slavery. Garrison declared that slavery was "a gangrene preying upon our vitals—an earthquake rumbling under our feet—a mine accumulating materials for a national catastrophe," and he called for "the liberation of two millions of wretched, degraded beings, who are pining in hopeless bondage." Slavery, he said, was a crime for which even the free states bore the stain of constitutional guilt. Abolition would require "a struggle with the worst passions of human nature [and] a collision, full of sharp asperities and bitterness." Garrison concluded with the prescient observation that it would some day be necessary to contend "with millions of armed and desperate men . . . if slavery does not cease."[17]

Within eighteen months Garrison would launch *The Liberator*, which was the first publication in the United States dedicated to the immediate abolition of slavery. In the first issue, which appeared on January 1, 1831, Garrison announced that he would "strenuously contend for the immediate enfranchisement of our slave population," and he repudiated "the popular but pernicious doctrine of gradual abolition." At that moment, in the words of historian Don Fehrenbacher, opposition to slavery began the transition from a sentiment to "a professionalized movement."[18] The difference was important. A movement could recruit activists—men and women who would make the war on slavery the central purpose in their lives—rather than simply inspire sympathizers.

As Garrison's biographer Henry Mayer put it, the doctrine of immediatism placed the abolitionist movement squarely within the ideal of western Romanticism, animating "the moral landscape as the Romantic poets had spiritualized the natural world."[19] That transition had many consequences as it developed an ever more militant edge, one of which would eventually make abolitionism attractive to men like John Cook. Gradualist abolitionism, with its emphasis on patience and pragmatism, could not hold much allure for young men who were searching for adventure rather than toil. Immediatism, however, held out the promise of excitement and even danger, making it a natural home of thrill seekers as well as do-gooders. If gradualism was the calling of earnest altruists, immediatism would also speak to those who saw themselves as swashbucklers, heroes, risk-takers. Garrison himself was a pacifist, but the logic of the movement he started would eventually lead to calls for active resistance and almost inevitably, though almost thirty years later, to the violent embellishments of John Brown.

John Cook was born only two months before Garrison's stunning address at the Park Street Church, and his life therefore precisely coincided with the development of what historians Timothy McCarthy and John Stauffer have called the "culture of abolitionism." As soon as he became aware of events beyond Haddam, Cook would have learned about the many "antislavery societies, vigilance committees, newspaper presses, petition campaigns, lecture tours, etc., that the abolitionists developed to advance their cause."[20] Although Haddam was far from the front lines of the struggle, at least one important event struck close to the Cooks' home.

In 1841, the United States Supreme Court ruled that the Mende African prisoners from *La Amistad* were not slaves and could not be given over to the control of either the federal government or the Spanish ambassador. They were free, but for the time being they had nowhere to go. During the many months that it took for abolitionists to make arrangements for return of the Mendeans to Sierra Leone, the former slaves were moved from a jail in New Haven to the small town of Farmington, Connecticut, less than thirty miles from Haddam. The thirty-two men and three girls arrived in Farmington in mid-March 1842—shortly before John Cook's thirteenth birthday—and remained there through late November. The presence of the Mendeans was well known in Farmington and its environs. They became fully integrated in the community, and they eventually became comfortable enough to confront a "rascally gang" that had been taunting and harassing them. One of the local toughs struck Cinque, the Mendeans' leader, whose friends responded in kind and routed the rowdy white men. Public sentiment in Farmington was strongly in favor of the Mendeans, and there was a feeling of "deep indignation" against the bullying whites.[21]

News traveled quickly between the small towns of Connecticut, and the presence of the Africans—not to mention their bold acts of resistance— could not have escaped notice in nearby Haddam. The exotic Mendeans were, after all, the understandable objects of fascination and gossip. When sufficient funds were finally raised to finance their repatriation, a "great farewell meeting" was held at Farmington's Congregational Church, attended by an immense crowd. At a time when preaching was a predominant form of public entertainment, the momentous event must have drawn spectators from the surrounding villages, and it would have been the talk of the town from Hartford to Haddam. John Cook and his twin sisters were then students at the Brainerd Academy, where the fate of the *Amistad* Africans was surely the subject of many schoolyard conversations. The celebration of the Africans' release may have been John's first exposure to the meaning of slavery—and to the excitement of liberation.

※　◉　※

John Cook's awareness of slavery could only have been heightened in May of 1854—just as he was relocating to Brooklyn—when President Franklin Pierce signed the Kansas-Nebraska Act. Before then, the Missouri Compromise of 1820 had prohibited slavery in federal territories north of the 36'30" parallel, but the new act repealed the compromise and opened vast new lands to slavery in the name of so-called popular sovereignty. Thus, the local population in Kansas would soon vote on whether to allow slavery in the territory. (Slavery was considered impractical in Nebraska due to the climate.) To many northerners, the Kansas-Nebraska Act constituted a foul betrayal of their earlier compromises with southern slavery. As the conservative New England merchant Amos Lawrence put it, "We went to bed one night old fashioned, conservative, Compromise Union Whigs, and waked up stark mad Abolitionists."[22]

In the words of the Crowleys' pastor, Rev. Elder J. Porter, the Kansas-Nebraska Act "inflame[d] the public mind with diabolical resentments" over the spread of slavery. But while Rev. Porter thought that the reaction was regrettably extreme, prominent clergymen elsewhere added fuel to the fire—preaching mightily against the treachery of the southern states—with Brooklyn's Rev. Beecher leading the call to arms. Many young men, including the impressionable John Cook, found it impossible to ignore such challenges to their consciences. Because fewer than a thousand settlers lived in Kansas at the time, it was obvious that the slavery question would be resolved by new arrivals or emigrants, and Cook decided to join the campaign.[23]

At first it seemed that the "Slave Power" would easily prevail in Kansas. Missouri and its 90,000 slaves lay just across the state line and its political leaders—including the rabidly proslavery Senator David Atchison—were eager to spread their peculiar institution to the west. Atchison openly urged his constituents to cross the border, if only briefly, in order to elect proslavery delegates to the territorial legislature. "What is your duty," he asked rhetorically, "when you reside within one day's journey of the territory, and when your peace, quiet, and property depend upon your action?" Other Missourians put it even more bluntly. General B. F. Stringfellow advised his followers "to enter every election district in Kansas . . . and vote at the point of the bowie-knife and revolver."[24]

Abolitionist leaders, however, had other ideas. New York Senator William Seward spoke for many when he accepted the challenge from the "gentlemen of the slave states." He announced on the Senate floor that "We will engage in a competition for the virgin soil of Kansas and God give the victory to the side that is stronger in numbers, as it is in right."[25] Within months, plans were under way "to literally transplant as much of New England to the plains as possible" by supporting the emigration of free-state settlers. John Greenleaf Whittier provided the movement with music, adding new words to the tune of "Auld Lang Syne":

> We crossed the prairies as of old,
> Our fathers crossed the sea.
> To make the West as they the East,
> The homestead of the free.[26]

Leading the effort was the New England Emigrant Aid Society, which began enlisting settlers almost immediately. The first pioneer colony left Boston in July 1854, and others would soon follow. One of the foremost recruiters for the society was the Unitarian minister Thomas Wentworth Higginson of Worcester, Massachusetts, a prominent abolitionist who played a key role in opposition to the Fugitive Slave Act and who later led an African-American regiment during the Civil War. Higginson organized several parties of emigrants from New England, providing them with "rifles, revolvers, and camp equipage" so that they could fight their way into Kansas if necessary. One company was composed entirely of Maine lumberjacks who initially impressed Higginson with their strength yet worried him with their poor discipline. "I never saw thirty men of finer physique, as they strode through Boston in their red shirts and rough trousers," he said in admiration, adding that they were the "hardest to manage" and constituted from the start a "thorn in the flesh" of the organizers. Higginson's concerns were valid, as the men of the Maine contingent were unruly from the moment they reached Kansas.[27] One of those fractious lumbermen was Charles Plummer Tidd, who would join John Brown in both Kansas and at Harper's Ferry, and whose blustery temperament would have a disastrous impact on the life of John Cook.

Both sides in Kansas were heavily armed from the outset. Rev. Beecher

famously raised money to send rifles—Beecher's Bibles—to the free-
staters, and he encouraged young men to take up the cause. Cook was
within earshot of Beecher's call, and when the inevitable fighting broke
out he quickly abandoned his legal career to head west, departing
from New York in September 1855. He would later say that "my poor
dear Mother implored me on her knees not to go." That was probably
true. Few mothers are eager to see their rash sons depart for war, and
Cook was more impulsive than most. His father called him "wild, wayward, and self-willed," which was no exaggeration. As described somewhat more forgivingly by his pastor, Cook was "young, sentimental,
visionary, and adventurous" when he set out to join the battle against
slavery.[28]

Arriving by rail in St. Louis, Cook then took a steamboat up the
Missouri River to Leavenworth, where he spent a few weeks outfitting
himself with frontier tackle, including "a brace of Colts Army revolvers
and a 14 inch Bowie knife [and] a Twenty-two shooting rifle." According
to Cook, he devoted the remainder of the fall enjoying "a wild pleasure
in hunting the Buffalo and the Elk," before repairing to the settlement
of Lawrence for the winter.[29]

By spring, Cook had joined one of the many free-state militias. He
served with flair, impressing his colleagues as "ingenuous, fervid, [and]
passionate." He had "a good horse, handsome clothing, and a brilliant
array of weapons on his person" that included two ivory-handled and
silver-mounted Colt revolvers. Cook claimed to have secretly infiltrated
the proslavery Kickapoo Rangers, "the most desperate gang of ruffians
and murderers ever spewed out [of Missouri] over Kansas," only to be
discovered and threatened with death. According to Cook, he found
himself in "a terrible situation . . . a hopeless prisoner, to all human appearances, among thirty enemies." He managed to save himself only by
racing to the nearest door, "his revolver cocked, and a bowie knife in his
left hand," where he overpowered the guard and made a bold escape.[30]

It was a remarkable, and questionable, story. The Kickapoo Rangers were the most dreaded of all the Missouri militias, infamous for burning the homes of free-soil settlers and attacking their victims with hatchets. The Rangers led the assault on the free-state capital of Lawrence, after which Missouri Senator David Atchison exulted, "Boys, this day I am a Kickapoo Ranger, by God! This day we have entered Lawrence with Southern Rights inscribed upon our banner. . . . We have entered that damn town, and taught the damned abolitionists a Southern lesson that they will remember until the day they die. And now boys, we will go in again . . . and teach the Emigrant Aid Company that Kansas shall be ours."[31]

Atchison urged the Rangers to act courteously toward women, but only to a point. "When a woman takes upon herself the garb of a soldier, by carrying a Sharpe's rifle, then she is no longer worthy of respect. Trample her under your feet as you would a snake." When a Leavenworth editor later wrote that the militia had marched on Lawrence with the intent to "ravish the women, and kill the children," the Rangers retaliated by burning the newspaper office and destroying the press.[32] Was it really possible that a well-educated Connecticut Yankee had passed himself off as a fierce Missourian, even for a short while?

Like many inveterate storytellers, Cook was not always entirely convincing. Some listeners, impressed by his charisma, would accept his tales at nearly face value, while others were more skeptical. Thus it was natural that not all of Cook's Kansas comrades immediately believed his account of astonishing derring-do. It seems, however, that he eventually persuaded even the skeptics by revealing the details of the enemy's plans, which "removed the doubts about him." Cook went on to distinguish himself for his recklessness and bravery, but he continued to brag about his exploits, both real and exaggerated. Not everyone cared for Cook's talkative company. To at least one of his comrades, he seemed like "a desperate fighting dog [who] barked like a King Charles poodle." In general, however, the "reckless, egotistical and querulous" Cook was held in good, if mixed, regard by his comrades. As Salmon

Brown put it, "Cook was brave, conceited, boastful [and] a magnificent shot—a shot like buffalo Bill."[33] That was a fitting description, and it would explain much of what was to follow over the next several years.

For the rest of his life, Cook would relate his adventures to anybody who would listen. In one tale he lost all of his belongings while "swimming my horse across Stranger Creek when closely pursued by about 30 Border Ruffians." On another occasion he bragged that the proslavery forces had offered "a reward of eleven hundred dollars . . . for his scalp." In a third story he saw a friend murdered by Missourians and failed to avenge him only because his own rifle misfired. Cook's tales often began with truth, but he could not resist embellishing them for effect, as John Brown would eventually discover at Harper's Ferry.[34]

※　❋　※

Cook first met John Brown in his camp at Middle Creek, Kansas, in early June 1856. A little more than one week earlier, Brown and his men had conducted one of the most horrific operations of the Kansas war—the Pottawatomie Massacre—as an act of revenge for a series of killings and assaults by proslavery forces. Brown's fury had been building all year, and it came to a head on the morning of May 22 when he learned that border ruffians had sacked Lawrence the previous day, destroying the offices of two antislavery newspapers, burning and looting houses, and razing the Free State Hotel with explosives and canon fire. Later that evening, news reached Brown's camp that Charles Sumner, the abolitionist U.S. senator from Massachusetts, had been beaten nearly to death by a slaveholder while he sat at his desk on the Senate floor. Sumner's offense had been an impassioned speech titled "The Crime against Kansas," in which he insulted the aged and infirm Senator Andrew P. Butler of South Carolina as having taken as "a mistress . . . the harlot, Slavery." Butler's young cousin, Congressman Preston Brooks upheld his family's southern honor by attacking Sumner while he was seated and caning him unconscious before he had a chance to stand up.[35]

Brown's response to the Slave Power atrocities was absolute rage. According to one of Brown's sons, he "went crazy—*crazy*," when he heard the news. We must "fight fire with fire," he declared, and "strike terror in the hearts of the proslavery people." When another son urged caution, Brown retorted, "I am eternally tired of hearing that word caution. It is nothing but the word of cowardice." He vowed to bring "Southern tactics to the Northern side" by taking his own murderous revenge on the banks of Pottawatomie Creek.[36]

On the night of May 24–25, Brown and seven others, including four of his sons and a son-in-law, set out to commit their own atrocity. Under cover of darkness, they surrounded the cabin of James and Mahala Doyle. James Doyle was not a slave owner, but he was a known member of the proslavery Law and Order Party, and that was enough to cost him his life. At gunpoint, Brown ordered Doyle and his two oldest sons out onto the prairie on the pretext that they were under arrest. Only two hundred yards from the cabin, however, Brown's men attacked the Doyles with broadswords, literally hacking them to pieces. Once the gruesome murders were completed, Brown himself fired a shot into the lifeless body of the elder Doyle.

The killing party next headed to the nearby home of Allen Wilkinson, another proslavery settler. Wilkinson, too, was dragged from his home and stabbed to death. Crossing the Pottawatomie, Brown led his men to a third cabin where they found their final victim, William Sherman. Brown's real target was probably William's brother, "Dutch Henry" Sherman, whose eponymous tavern was a notorious meeting place for border ruffians and proslavery militias. But Dutch Henry could not be found, so William was slaughtered in his place. By then it was after midnight, and Brown decided that enough blood had been spilled. Leaving the five mutilated bodies to be discovered in the morning, he ordered his men to clean their weapons and return to their camp for the night.

The Pottawatomie killings enflamed all of Kansas, and Brown's involvement—if not the precise details—quickly became common knowledge. Proslavery newspapers called for the arrest of "Brown and his banditti with the blood of the murdered [settlers] not yet cold upon his hands" and denounced Brown as an assassin. The reaction among free-staters, however, was mixed. Most of the antislavery leaders condemned Brown as a provocateur, if not a barbarian, even while noting that the retaliation had "given an immediate check to the armed aggressions of the Missourians."[37] Two of Brown's sons—John, Jr., and Jason—were so aghast at the killings that they left his camp and fled to their homes in a settlement called Brown's Station. Brown's other sons remained with him, including Frederick, who would be murdered later that summer by Missourians, and Owen, who would be the only one of the Browns to come away alive from Harper's Ferry.

Brown had clearly changed the terms of the battle for Kansas by meeting southern aggression with abolitionist violence. In the process, he moved from the periphery of the struggle to its very center. Brown had not previously been an important figure in the abolitionist movement in Kansas, but after Pottawatomie he came to be regarded, at least among southerners, as a leader of the free-state movement in Kansas. As one Kansan observed, "There is no one for whom the ruffians entertain a more wholesome dread than Captain Brown. They hate him as they would a snake, but their hatred is composed nine tenths of fear."[38]

Not every southerner was afraid of John Brown. Captain Henry Clay Pate, an aggressive leader of the Missouri state militia, reviled Brown as the commander of "an organized band of Abolitionists armed and equipped to thieve, murder, and resist all law," while vowing to bring him to justice. A Virginian by birth, the twenty-four-year-old Pate had long hair, an aquiline nose, and pinched, piercing eyes. His Westport Sharpshooters had scourged Kansas free-staters, frequently taking prisoners and destroying their camps. In early June he set out with a band of about sixty men to capture John Brown, or perhaps to lynch him. Brown, however, was forewarned. On June 2, commanding only about twenty-five troops, he staged a pre-dawn attack on Pate's position near the Black Jack Bog. Although they were outnumbered more than two-to-one, Brown's men routed the Missourians, killing four and taking twenty-three prisoners, including Pate himself. "I went to take Old Brown," Pate later said, "and Old Brown took me."[39]

Cook had taken no part in the Pottawatomie slaughter, but he surely knew about it when he rode into Brown's Middle Creek camp in early June 1856, shortly after the victory at Black Jack. At a time when most Kansans were either frightened or appalled by Brown, Cook was actually drawn to his banner. Whatever he thought of the Pottawatomie murders, he was clearly fascinated by violence and attracted by the promise of reprisal and adventure. Although he arrived too late to take part in the battle, Cook was in time to help guard Brown's prisoners (who were later released unharmed). He was also able to show off his skill with firearms. "Cook was the best pistol shot I ever saw," recalled Salmon Brown. "When the ducks and geese flew over us on the road he would always bring one down with his pistol."[40]

At Brown's direction, Cook spent the rest of the summer and early fall raiding along the Neosho River as part of a continuing effort to frighten proslavery settlers into leaving Kansas. The "Freestate Marauders," as they were sometimes known, would descend on isolated cabins late at night, waking the Missouri homesteaders and threatening them with hanging if they did not abandon their homes. According to one witness, "it was not the intention to murder anybody, but to create a sort of terror which would run off the 'proslaveryites.'"[41] On September 16, 1856, however, murder was indeed the result.

Shortly before midnight, Cook's gang surrounded the home of Christian Carver, a proslavery settler from Missouri, and called for him to come out. By moonlight, Carver could see about a dozen menacing men in his yard, all armed with rifles. As he attempted to light a lantern so that he could load his own rifle, he heard the sound of staves breaking in his door. His pregnant wife Sarah, only sixteen or seventeen years old, lay in bed, trembling in fear. Sarah's younger brother, John Van Gundy, who was only ten years old at the time, was living with his parents in another cabin on the river. He later described the events at the Carvers' as they had been told to him:

> Mrs. Carver had raised up and was sitting on the bed close by an opening between the logs, used as a window. A man outside, poked a gun through the opening nearly against her and fired. She cried out at once, "I am shot! I am killed!" [W]ith loud profanity, several men crowded into the house. . . . One man dipped his hand into a pan of honey that set on the table and exclaimed, "Boys, here is some honey, let's eat it." At this instant one raised a gun at Carver and said, "D—— him and his honey too," but another stopped him and said, "Let him alone now, we will be back in three days and if he is not out of the country then, we will hang him."

Perhaps in horror of having shot such a young girl—she cried out desperately, begging the raiders not to kill her husband as well—Cook and his men left the Carver cabin, but they continued to raid the homes of other proslavery settlers. Cook probably did not know that Sarah Carver died in her mother's arms four days later, but the lesson was not lost on those who lived in the Neosho valley, many of whom took to hiding in the woods at night for fear of attack. Shortly after Sarah's burial, a train of eighteen wagons departed for the safety of Fort Scott, while others, including some free-staters alarmed by the violence, fled toward Topeka.[42]

As it turned out, the Van Gundys' neighbors could have remained in their homes. The abolitionist marauders disbanded by the following month and fighting ceased for a time in the territory. Brown headed back east on a fund-raising mission, while Cook remained in Kansas. He worked briefly as a teamster, hauling goods by day from Nebraska City to Lawrence, while swapping stories at night by firelight with other drovers. While Cook mostly told tales of his own heroics, he was not above joking about his misadventures on the plains. In one story, he told of hunting a panther at midnight—tracking the animal by its "wild piercing shriek like that of a woman in mortal agony"—only to take several foolish shots at a gnarled tree limb that he had somehow mistaken for a crouching predator.[43]

❋　❀　❋

Cook settled in Lawrence for the winter, where he rented a room next door to the journalist Julia Louisa Lovejoy, whose letters describing life in Kansas appeared frequently in New England newspapers. Lovejoy was impressed by Cook's fine clothes and polite manners, describing him as someone "who has been accustomed to good society." Nonetheless, she was alarmed by his recklessness. As the mother of young children, Lovejoy was dismayed that Cook spent so much of his free time practicing pistol skills in the yard next to her house. He shot "at targets so near our dwelling I was often fearful that some mischief might be occasioned by his carelessness."[44]

Lawrence had been rebuilt following the sack by the Kickapoo Rangers, and Cook may have planned to settle there permanently. He speculated in real estate for a while, opening a partnership with a man named Bacon. But even in times of relative peace, Cook remained ready for combat. In the offices of Cook & Bacon "the chief furniture . . . consisted of weapons which were conspicuously displayed on the walls and in the corners." It was common for men to be armed in Kansas, but Cook managed to stand out even in that environment, always carrying ornate pistols and rifles as he tended to business. In addition to land speculation, Cook worked for a free-state newspaper, and he even attempted to rekindle his legal career. On a brief return trip to Connecticut he introduced himself as "a lawyer from Lawrence, Kansas."[45]

Life was certainly easier in Lawrence than it was at the militia camps on the prairie, and Cook was especially drawn by the prospect of female companionship. He had developed quite a reputation among the women of the territory, and his comrades later teased him "for hugging girls" at which he apparently excelled. In Salmon Brown's envious opinion, Cook was "just as much of an expert getting into the good graces of the girls . . . as he was in shooting ducks. He would have a girl in a corner telling them stories or repeating poetry to them in such a high faluting manner that they would laugh to kill themselves. He paralysed the girls with his wit and audacity."[46]

Cook seems to have successfully concealed his illicit courtships from his neighbor, the prim and pious Julia Lovejoy, who reported later that "he appeared to us as a young man of good morals."[47] Then again, she may have intended to refer only to proper appearances, as many of Cook's assignations had become well known by the time she wrote about him.

Cook corresponded with at least two Lawrence women after he left Kansas, and there were probably others. His romances no doubt played a part in Cook's attachment to Lawrence, which he proclaimed in a poem that he published in a local newspaper:

> This our home; and Kansas sod
> Free from slavery's stain shall be.
> Here the tyrant's chast'ning rod,
> Bows no neck, nor bends no knee.
>
> This our home; and we'll never
> Leave a land we so much love,
> Till life's ties shall sever,
> And we seek a home above.
>
> Here, on Kansas' wide-spread plains,
> We shall dwell, through weal and woe;
> Keep it pure from slavery's stains,
> Till life's fountains cease to flow.[48]

❈　◉　❈

By the autumn of 1857, Brown had returned to Kansas and he invited Cook to join his company with the rank of captain. Despite his fierce reputation, or perhaps because of it, Brown always had difficulty attracting men to his side. His largest command the previous summer had numbered only a couple of dozen, and now he was starting again from scratch. Brown therefore asked the genial Cook to help his recruitment, and Cook eagerly agreed. He assisted Brown in assembling a handful of young abolitionists—including Charles Tidd, Aaron Stevens, and seven others—who believed they had enlisted for further battles in Kansas, perhaps with forays into Missouri. Brown, however, had other ideas. In fact, he was already secretly gathering an army for the invasion of Virginia.[49]

Brown did not reveal his true plans until he had gathered his troops in Tabor, Iowa, where the men expected to spend the winter months in training. At first, Brown's soldiers were stunned when he announced that they would be heading east. They had signed on for the purpose of fighting proslavery aggression in Kansas, not to begin a new war in Virginia. Cook at first protested vigorously, by then reluctant to leave the ladies of Lawrence behind. He exchanged sharp words with Brown, but "after a good deal of wrangling" Cook and the others consented to go on. Cook later rationalized that he had no real choice in the matter as he lacked sufficient funds to return to Kansas, but in any case he accompanied Brown when the group departed Tabor on December 4, 1857, purportedly headed for a new training camp in Ohio. Wintertime travel was hard going, and the group got only as far as the Quaker colony of Springdale, Iowa, before they were compelled to make camp until the weather improved. Brown himself soon departed for the east and another round of visits to his financial backers. He left his son Owen to look after Cook and the other men, who were expected to occupy themselves with an improvised regimen of military training and intellectual debate. As it turned out, Cook was frequently absent from camp—often for several days at a time—claiming that he was lecturing "in the different school districts" in the vicinity of Springdale.[50]

It may be that Cook really was teaching children here and there, but he also used his trips away from camp to court his students' older sisters and other single women in the nearby Quaker communities. Cook was constantly flirting with the girls in and around Springdale, and the "simple-minded young Quaker ladies" were all impressed by his polished etiquette and refined manners. One young woman wrote to her friends that Cook's "fair complexion, blue eyes and long curling hair made him handsome, and his being so agreeable socially made him all the more attractive."[51]

Cook was intimate with at least one Quaker woman, resulting in a pregnancy and then a miscarriage or a stillbirth. He "righted it as far as he was allowed to," offering to marry the girl, but for reasons now unknown "he was not permitted to do so." Once the pregnancy ended, the young woman's parents might have objected to her marriage to a transient adventurer. And indeed, Cook was gone from Iowa soon afterward, leaving all of his sweethearts behind. His close brush with parenthood, however, does not seem to have changed his ways, as he continued to pursue women wherever he went. Cook's Springdale lover, grieving the loss of her child and her almost-fiancé, could not get over the relationship nearly so easily, and she seems to have lamented his departure to her friends. Two years later, another Springdale girl—evidently a confidant of Cook's abandoned paramour—expressed disappointment when she learned that he had married someone else.[52]

Cook was not the only one of the recruits who revealed his essential character during the winter in Iowa. Charles Tidd displayed his petulant temper, and Owen Brown demonstrated his skill as a peacemaker. The irascible Tidd quarreled with several of the men over their use of tobacco in close quarters. He was trying to quit smoking, and he curtly demanded that everyone else "keep their pipes and smoke entirely out of his way" so that he could avoid temptation. The others agreed for a while, but they soon resumed their habit, which threw Tidd into a rage. He resorted first to threats, and then he set out to "destroy all the pipes which belonged to anyone in the house." The smokers retaliated by defiantly lighting up in Tidd's presence, which of course aggravated the tense situation as the stocky lumberman became increasingly angry over each new cloud of smoke.

Owen Brown recognized that there was fault on both sides, but by then the conflict had nearly spiraled out of control. Eventually, Tidd decided to depart the camp "on account of the bitter feeling against him," and he left temporarily to find work on a nearby farm. It took all of Owen Brown's ability as a negotiator to keep Tidd from abandoning the group completely. "I labored with him as thoroughly as I was capable of," he said, "to persuade him and get him reconciled to remain with us."[53] Tidd returned, but that was not the last time he would have to be coaxed back into the abolitionist army. John Cook was not involved in this particular contretemps—he might have been away at the time on one of his amorous expeditions—although it remarkably presaged his later interactions with the fatally irritable Tidd.

※　◉　※

Brown returned to his men in April 1858, having again changed his mind about their destination. Rather than proceed directly to Ohio, Brown took them instead to Chatham, Canada West (now Ontario), where he convened a convention for "true friends of freedom." Chatham was home to a large population of fugitive slaves and free blacks, quite a few of whom had become well established and prosperous. The community was fiercely supportive of abolitionism, and Chatham served as a major terminus of the Underground Railroad. Many Chathamites had "boldly gone back from their Canadian homes, and guided kinsmen or friends on the way to freedom."[54]

It is quite possible that John Cook had never gotten to know any black people before he arrived in Canada. Only a small number of free blacks lived in Connecticut when he was growing up, and probably only one "colored" family lived in Haddam. There was a significant African-American presence in Brooklyn, where he served as a law clerk, but it does not appear that he ever sought out, or even met, any of its members. Kansas was yet another story. For all of their antislavery fervor, many of the free-soilers were anti-black as well. They opposed slavery because they wanted to maintain the territory as a haven for white people and free labor, not because they favored racial equality. Consequently, there were few blacks in the free-state militias, and again there is no record that Cook ever worked or fought alongside anybody who was not white. Cook would later write passionately about his hatred of slavery and his determination to see "the millions . . . cast aside the fetters and the shackles that bound them," but his dedication—at least until the spring of 1858—was more the product of theory than experience.[55]

In Chatham, however, Cook boarded for nearly a month with James Monroe Jones, a black man originally from North Carolina. A slender man with effusive muttonchops and bushy eyebrows, Jones was an accomplished gunsmith and engraver who operated a profitable shop in the center of town. Jones was also well regarded for his education, having graduated from Oberlin College before emigrating to Canada, and he served as a justice of the peace in his adopted home. United by their love of firearms, Cook and Jones spent many days together during Cook's stay in Chatham, "cleaning and repairing the revolvers and other arms belonging to the [Brown] party."[56] Cook carried a fancy rifle and a pair of engraved revolvers to Harper's Ferry, and it is possible that he obtained them at Jones's shop, or that he at least polished and inscribed them with the help of his first black colleague.

Brown had great expectations for the Chatham conference, planning to use it as a rallying point and springboard for the invasion of Virginia. He invited many of the most famous stalwarts of the abolitionist movement—including Harriet Tubman, Gerrit Smith, Wendell Phillips, and Frederick Douglass—but none of the notables were willing to attend. The actual turnout was sparse. Only thirty-four blacks attended (all from the Chatham environs), along with twelve whites (all from the Springdale camp, including John Cook). Undaunted, Brown used the occasion to announce his goal of establishing a provisional government in the mountains of Virginia, where escaping slaves could find freedom, equality, and self-sufficiency.

The convention ratified a forty-eight article "Provisional Constitution"—covering everything from the branches of government to the sanctity of marriage—under which Brown was named commander in chief and John Kagi was appointed secretary of war. Many other officers were nominated—including a president, cabinet secretaries, and congressmen—from among Brown's black and white supporters. Most were elected by acclamation, although the office of president remained vacant and a special committee (including Cook) was chosen to fill it at a later time. At the close of the conference, it was proposed that the delegates swear allegiance to the provisional government, but Brown vetoed the idea because he had a religious objection to swearing oaths. Instead, every attendee simply pledged his "parole of honor," affirming that he would not "divulge any of the secrets of this Convention, except to the persons entitled to know the same, on pain of forfeiting the respect and protection of this organization."[57] The promises were no doubt sincerely made at the time, but the forfeiture of respect would later prove an insufficient sanction for enforcement when push came to shove in Virginia.

Although Brown's presentation at the conference included the broad outline of his plan—he intended to create a mountain colony populated by northern abolitionists and runaway slaves—he did not reveal the site or the extent of the proposed invasion, even to his most ardent backers. With one exception.

Only John Cook was fully let in on the secret of the destination. Following the Chatham conference, Brown detailed Cook to Harper's Ferry with instructions to spy on the locals in preparation for the coming raid. It would be Cook's job to obtain maps of the town and the surrounding area, to assess the number of slaves who might be attracted to Brown's rebellion, and to identify prominent citizens who could be taken hostage. Brown had other plans that prevented him, for a while, from re-connoitering the area himself, but he needed detailed information as soon as possible if his campaign was to succeed.

John Cook was an odd choice for such a sensitive mission. Although the assignment called for exceptional discretion, Cook was flamboyant and impetuous. His cheerful disposition allowed him to make friends easily, but he was talkative to a fault, often known to rattle on about himself to anyone who would listen. At least one of his colleagues complained to Brown about Cook's "indiscreet talking," and Brown's daughter would later describe him as "impulsive and indiscreet." Cook also had a short temper; he exchanged harsh words with Brown on more than one occasion, and he quarreled with several of his companions in the Springdale camp, trading "ugly words [and] much swearing."[58] Among all of Cook's acquaintances, the single word used most often to describe him was "reckless."

Then there was the matter of womanizing. Brown's rigorous Calvinism made him more than a prude in sexual matters. Although he led a vigorous connubial life—fathering twenty children with two wives—Brown strongly disapproved of sex outside marriage. A man of almost no humor and "moral to the point of prissiness," he abhorred ribald behavior and "coarseness absolutely repelled him." In fact, Brown's Provisional Constitution prohibited "indecent behavior, or indecent exposure of the person," and it strictly banned "unlawful intercourse of the sexes." Cook, however, was an utter libertine, whose promiscuous ways were notorious among his friends. As Salmon Brown sardonically put it, "I never thought he was overstocked with morality."[59] Or discretion.

Even as Cook was conferring with Brown about his mission to Virginia, he wrote overheated letters to several young women whom he had known in Iowa, perhaps including the mother of his stillborn child. In one letter he sent his love to at least nine women—Phebe, Sarah, Agnes, Esther, Elvira, Laura, and Eliza, as well as two or more unnamed "dear sisters"—while mentioning no men at all. He asked the recipients to keep his whereabouts "a secret from all," but the admonition to so many people was obviously futile, and the letters were in blatant violation of Brown's stern order to remain absolutely incommunicado.[60] Although Brown probably did not know the extent of Cook's forbidden correspondence, he must have been aware of Cook's multiple relationships with the Quaker women of Springdale.

It is therefore puzzling that John Brown selected the volatile, loose-lipped, libidinous John Cook to act as his clandestine agent. Other, more trustworthy men were available for the job, including any of Brown's many sons. Cook later claimed that he had wanted to go back to Kansas, but that Brown considered him too notorious there and sent him to Virginia instead. Years later, however, Brown's daughter insisted that Cook had lobbied heavily for the posting to Harper's Ferry, and that Brown, troubled by Cook's volubility, had agreed reluctantly. That may have been the case, as Cook was certainly known to prefer the comforts of town—with the promise of romantic attachments—to the exclusively masculine rigors of training camp. Brown might also have been influenced by Cook's own boasts about successfully spying on the Kickapoo Rangers, or perhaps Brown was simply weary of Cook's constant talking and thus thought it preferable to send him on a solo assignment where extroversion might actually be an asset.[61]

Cook remained in Chatham for a few weeks following the conference and then departed for Cleveland where he did nothing to justify Brown's confidence. According to Richard Realf, the secretary of state of Brown's provisional government, Cook conducted himself in Cleveland "in a manner well calculated to arouse suspicion." In an apprehensive letter to Brown, Realf complained that Cook

had stated in his boardinghouse that he was here on a secret expedition, and that the rest of the company were under his orders. He made a most ostentatious display of his equipments—was careful to let it be known that he had been in Kansas—stated among other recitals of impossible achievements, that he had killed 5 men; and, in short, drew largely on his imagination in order to render himself conspicuous.

Almost needless to say when speaking of Cook, there was also at least one woman involved. As Realf cautioned Brown, "He found out and called upon a lady friend whom he knew in Conn.—talked a great deal too much to her." Despite his longstanding friendship with Cook, Realf feared that "our chief danger will accrue from him, and his dreadful affliction of the 'caocethes loguendi,' which rendered into English means 'rage for talking' or 'tongue malady.'"[62]

Brown dispatched Cook to Harper's Ferry despite Realf's warning—and despite everything he knew about Cook's louche morality—although he did appear to have serious misgivings up until the last moment. Cook later recalled Brown's emphatic admonition when he took leave, "*He gave me orders to trust no one with our secret*, and to hold no conversations with the slaves."[63] As Brown should have realized at the time, Cook would not follow either instruction.

❦ TWO ❦

Harper's Ferry

Harper's Ferry was far from the heart of Virginia's agricultural slave country. Located at the confluence of the Potomac and Shenandoah Rivers—about 165 miles from Richmond and 65 miles from Washington, D.C.—the town was primarily a manufacturing and transportation center for rail, canal, and river traffic carrying passengers and freight between eastern cities and the western frontier. Most important to the local economy were the federal armory and arsenal, where thousands of rifles were manufactured and stored for use by the United States military. The small urban black population included domestic servants and a significant number of free black people who worked for the hotels, railroads, and factories. There were also numerous small farms and some larger plantations in the surrounding countryside where, as throughout the South, much of the labor was provided by slaves.

John Cook arrived in Harper's Ferry in early June 1858, taking a room under his own name at Mrs. Mary Ann Kennedy's boardinghouse in the adjacent village of Bolivar, less than a mile from the heart of town. Originally called Mudfort, Bolivar had been renamed in 1825 in honor of Simón Bolívar, the South American freedom fighter. Few, if any, Virginians appeared to appreciate the irony of naming a municipality after a man who had called for the elimination of slavery throughout the New World. It is possible that Cook was attracted to the town because of its nominal association with abolitionism, although he was probably more attracted by Mrs. Kennedy's comely daughter.[1]

The gregarious and well-educated Cook had no difficulty ingratiating himself with the locals, and he easily found a series of jobs as a school-teacher and private writing tutor. He was also employed as a lock tender on the canal at the north end of the United States armory grounds, which allowed him to acquire extensive knowledge of the layout of the compound. Always using his real name, he sometimes worked as a traveling map peddler and book agent, making calls on farms and settlements throughout the area while surreptitiously gathering information that he conveyed to Brown through intermittent correspondence. The spy often wore an impressive brace of ivory-handled revolvers under his coat, which he could not always resist displaying for effect. Cook spoke freely of his days as a free-state fighter in Kansas, bragging to the wife of the local schoolmaster that he had "seen blood flow like water." He was "known to be anti-slavery, but not so violent in the expression of his opinions as to excite any suspicions." Notwithstanding his open abolitionism, Cook apparently made a favorable impression on his new neighbors, no doubt because he "spoke so fluently and intelligently" with cultured grace and fine manners.[2]

Despite his many friendships and acquaintances in and around Jefferson County, Cook's understanding of the populace remained shallow, and his occasional reports to Brown seemed strongly affected by some combination of self-aggrandizement and wishful thinking. In one letter, Cook informed Brown of an upcoming election in Maryland and suggested, with characteristic exaggeration, that afterward "we will get some of the candidates that will join our side." There was never a chance that any Maryland political figure—whether Republican, Free-Soiler, Know-Nothing, or renascent Whig—would join Brown's army. Brown's plan depended heavily on attracting local slaves, free blacks, and abolitionists to his cause, and Cook's imaginative predictions evidently contributed to Brown's own visions of popular support. To the very end, Brown expected to be joined by hundreds of slaves—"the bees will begin to swarm," he explained to Frederick Douglass—although of course that never happened. Brown was later said to complain bitterly that Cook had deceived him into thinking that the slaves were "ripe for insurrection."[3]

Cook's undercover work still allowed him plenty of time to seek the favors of local females. He kept track of attractive women in Jefferson County, and he expressed regret when Eugenia Mauzy—whom he called "a great favorite in town [and] a beautiful young lady"—married an Englishman. Cook was especially attentive to his landlady's daughter, eighteen-year-old Virginia Kennedy, and he probably romanced others. Virginia (or Jenny, as she was sometimes called) was "an attractive young woman, large, regular featured, blonde in complexion [and] quiet in manner." The journalist Richard Hinton, one of Brown's admiring biographers, later described Virginia as always having been "blameless in life" and "innocent of the world," but that account of her chaste character was more defensive than accurate. In fact, it seems that Virginia had a somewhat questionable reputation in straight-laced Jefferson County (which was no doubt easily acquired), and at least one officious neighbor expressed surprise that a girl of her sort could attract a gentleman like John Cook. Another resident, albeit one with a grudge, was even more harsh, saying that "her record was bad and that she was beyond her old mother's control, and used vile language home and abroad."[4]

But whatever her past indiscretions (if any), Virginia was seduced by Cook's charms as other women had been before. The couple made love, and this time there were lasting consequences. Cook impregnated Virginia in the fall of 1858, causing a small scandal among the townsfolk who muttered in private about the danger of "free love" and expressed their dismay that a child had been "conceived in sin."[5]

Domestic life in the Kennedy home had been in disarray for much of the previous decade, and Virginia's pregnancy only made it worse. Virginia's father, an armory worker named John P. Kennedy, had died when she was about three years old, leaving his widow alone to support Virginia and her younger brother James. Boarders came and went over the years, and some stayed longer than others. By the late 1850s, another man was living in the Bolivar rooming house with Mary Ann—claiming to be the stepfather of her children—although they do not appear to have married. That man, who sometimes called himself Mr. Kennedy, angrily confronted Cook when he learned about Virginia's pregnancy—which of course had become visible—and the ensuing argument nearly became violent. It was evident that the two men could not continue to live in the same house, and Mrs. Kennedy preferred her daughter's lover to her own not-exactly second husband. She had taken a strong liking to Cook, who had a way with ladies of all ages, and she would later treat him as though he were her son. Mary Ann's own unsettled relationships might have led her to appreciate the importance of encouraging a stable marriage for her daughter despite its promiscuous start. For whatever reason, she sided with the young couple in the dispute and threw the faux Mr. Kennedy out of the house.[6]

Mary Ann Kennedy's tolerant approach certainly seemed at the time to be in her daughter's best interest. A local minister married John Cook and Virginia Kennedy in an outdoor ceremony on April 15, 1859, temporarily quieting tongues and calming tempers. Their son John, Jr., was born the following month. Proper decorum was thus maintained. Even after Cook was exposed as spy and insurrectionist the southern press remained circumspect, reporting only that Cook had been "introduced into society, which resulted in his courting and marrying a Miss Kennedy of South Bolivar."

For a short while, John and Virginia Cook enjoyed a close and comfortable domestic life. John recited poetry for his poorly educated wife, and he read aloud to her from Shakespeare's sonnets and the novels of Sir Walter Scott. Both parents delighted in the arrival of their son, who was a bright and energetic child. John Cook seemed to have made a fine home in the Kennedy boardinghouse, but because of his secret mission the idyll could not last long.[7]

When did Virginia learn about Cook's double life, and how much did he tell her before they were married? Cook had never concealed his antislavery views or his "identity with the Kansas free-state cause," so he had no doubt wooed Virginia by regaling her with stories of his battles against the Missouri ruffians. He surely showed off his ornate firearms—which would have been impressive to a naïve town girl—and he probably bragged about his friendship with famous abolitionists. Virginia's family was proslavery, but she claimed always to have been an "abolitionist at heart." That may or may not have been true—what could a southern teenager truly understand about abolitionism?—but Virginia's professed sympathy would naturally have prompted Cook to share his ideals with her. Even after the marriage, Cook continued to write letters to his lady friends in Iowa in which he condemned "the whipping slave lash" and boasted of the "part allotted to me in the great mission now before us."[8] He no doubt expressed the same thoughts to his wife, either cryptically or forthrightly.

Cook had no choice but to confide in Virginia as the date for the insurrection approached. Brown had ordered Cook to say nothing to his wife about the looming raid, but that was obviously impossible as a matter of both character and logistics. Cook was nearly incapable of discretion, especially while sharing a bed, and in any case he had to explain the presence of Brown and the other mysterious northerners who kept showing up at the Kennedy boardinghouse. As Virginia later put it, "a northern man was in appearance the most conspicuous object imaginable" in Harper's Ferry, so it was inevitable that she would question her husband about her suspicions.

By early summer 1859, perhaps a month after their child was born, Cook had revealed to Virginia that "the purpose of the party was to free the slaves," while stressing that "her life depended on her fidelity to the secret." Even then, however, she did not fully understand what was going to happen, and she never could have imagined the magnitude of the events that would follow. Cook later denied that either his wife or mother-in-law knew anything about his mission in Harper's Ferry, although by then he was anxious to protect them. In fact, both women had known all along of Cook's connection to John Brown and the shadowy strangers who surrounded him, even if they were unaware of the details.[9]

In his own way, Cook returned the love of his new family. He was, by all reliable accounts, an honorable husband and a devoted father, but his allegiance to John Brown would soon cause terrible hardship to his wife and son. In turn, his family obligations would complicate, if not compromise, his mission.

While Cook was busy collecting intelligence and courting his shotgun bride, Brown continued his efforts to raise funds and drum up support for his plan. It was not easy. "Men are afraid of identification with me," Brown lamented, "though they favor my measures."[10] He was at least half right. Many abolitionists were definitely wary of associating too closely with the ultra-militant Brown, but even his closest friends and key financial backers (including the self-named "Secret Six") were hesitant about his plan to forcibly free slaves in the South. And among those who most strongly favored Brown's measures, there was still considerable doubt about the viability of his plan. There had been numerous successful slave rescues in the North over the previous decade—from Boston to Milwaukee—but those usually involved individual runaways who had been recaptured by slave hunters, only to be freed by hastily organized abolitionist mobs. There had been many fewer attempts over the years at organized large-scale rescues in the South, and most of those failed.

Harriet Tubman's work was the great exception. "The General" (as Brown called her, in recognition of her great skill as a field commander) had made numerous forays into the South, escorting some three hundred slaves to freedom in Canada. More typical, unfortunately, was the attempt of the Edmonson family—slaves who worked in the homes of wealthy families in Washington, D.C.—to organize the escape of seventy-seven slaves on the Potomac River schooner *The Pearl*. The plan was well executed, but it was foiled at the last minute when shifting winds prevented the ship from making its way into Chesapeake Bay. The slaves were captured and the ship's captain and pilot were prosecuted and sentenced to prison. Jonathan Walker was likewise caught when he attempted to smuggle seven slaves out of Florida aboard his fishing boat. Walker, too, was convicted, and he was sentenced, barbarically, to have the palm of his hand branded with the letters *SS*, for "slave stealer." Walker became a hero to northern abolitionists—the subject of John Greenleaf Whittier's poem "The Man with the Branded Hand"—but his story, and others like it, stood as a grim reminder of the great difficulty and risk involved in rescuing slaves from the South.

There was yet another impediment to Brown's plan. One of his erstwhile comrades—Colonel Hugh Forbes, a British soldier of fortune who had earlier signed on as Brown's drillmaster—had leaked details of the plot to several eastern political figures, including Horace Greeley and Republican Senators Charles Sumner, William Seward, and Henry Wilson (whom he approached on the floor of the Senate). That made it necessary "to delay further action *for the present*," as Brown explained to his son Owen. Even after Cook arrived in Virginia, Brown realized that he would first need to carry out a diversion (distracting attention from Forbes's traitorous revelation) and a demonstration (proving to skeptics that he could operate effectively in slave country). He concluded that both goals could be achieved by returning to Kansas. As Cook later put it: "There was a lack of confidence in the success of his [Virginia] scheme. It was, therefore, necessary that a movement should be made in another direction, to demonstrate the practicability of the plan."[11]

Brown traveled to southeastern Kansas under the name Shubel Morgan, determined to prove that he could successfully bring slaves out of the South. He struck on the evening of December 20, 1858, riding with twenty men into Vernon County, Missouri. Brown's troops raided the farms of three slaveholders and liberated eleven slaves, while also taking several horses, mules, and wagons and killing one of the slave owners who appeared to resist. Thus began a very public journey of over a thousand miles, taking Brown and his company through Kansas, Nebraska, Iowa, Illinois, Indiana, and Michigan. As he escorted the former slaves to freedom, Brown abandoned his alias and dared the authorities to attempt to arrest him. Missouri Governor Robert Stewart and President James Buchanan offered cash rewards, and Brown was pursued across Kansas by both proslavery posses and federal troops. Brown, however, made good the claim that he could not be taken, at one point routing a large contingent of United States cavalry at the Battle of the Spurs. The entourage reached Detroit in late March 1859, where Brown placed his liberated traveling companions—who now numbered twelve, a child having been born en route—on a ferry to Canada.

Now able to boast that he had actually freed slaves from bondage, Brown was at last ready to implement his great plan. His financial backers were elated at the success of the Missouri rescue, and they were even more impressed by Brown's ability to defy federal authorities. Where funding had previously been scarce, enough money was now available to move arms and other matériel to a staging point in Chambersburg, Pennsylvania, including rifles, revolvers, ammunition, and over nine hundred specially manufactured pikes that Brown believed would make perfect weapons in the hands of freed slaves. Gathering troops, however, was another matter. Harriet Tubman and Frederick Douglass both declined to join the invasion force, as did many others whom Brown attempted to enlist. In the end, Brown would recruit only twenty-one men for his liberation army—including John E. Cook, who was already stationed at Harper's Ferry.

※ ❀ ※

Now traveling under the name Isaac Smith, Brown arrived in Harper's Ferry in early July 1859, meeting briefly with Cook in town and probably learning for the first time about his spy's wife and newborn son. There is no record of Brown's reaction to this news, or how soon he realized that the wedding had narrowly preceded the birth. But Brown badly needed Cook to continue scouting the armory and arsenal grounds, so any scolding or recrimination must have been restrained. Nonetheless, Brown mistrusted the young mother, and "he impressed on Cook very urgently that he must tell [her] nothing" of their mission. Beyond that, Brown never showed any interest in Virginia and her child. He would shun them until the week before the raid, when their inconvenient existence could no longer be ignored.[12]

Brown's first order of business was to locate a secluded base of operations, and for that purpose he soon rented a small farm in Washington County, Maryland, from the estate of Dr. Booth Kennedy (who was unrelated to Virginia Kennedy Cook).[13] At first, Brown was accompanied only by his sons Owen and Oliver and one other man from Kansas, but additional recruits arrived slowly over the following six weeks. Eventually, Brown would gather twenty-one men to his side, sixteen whites and five blacks. The free African Americans included Lewis Sheridan Leary and John Copeland from Oberlin, Ohio, and Osborne Anderson, who had lived most recently in Chatham. Dangerfield Newby was a freed slave from Virginia who hoped to rescue his wife and children who were still enslaved on a nearby plantation. The fugitive slave Shields Green, a companion of Frederick Douglass's, chose to join Brown even when the famous black abolitionist declined. Barclay and Edwin Coppoc, young Quakers from Springdale, Iowa, arrived in late summer, as did several Kansas veterans, including John Henry Kagi, Brown's second-in-command, the drillmaster Aaron Stevens, and Maine lumberjack Charles Tidd. Three additional members of Brown's family—his son Watson and sons-in-law William and Dauphin Thompson—completed the fighting complement. The last man to arrive was Francis Merriam of Boston, who was physically unfit for combat but who brought with him a much needed $600 in gold.

Life on the Maryland farm was extremely stressful for the small army. The crowded farmhouse was ill equipped to feed and shelter so many people. There were no beds for the men and only a table and a few chairs in the dining room, although the lack of basic furniture was more than counterbalanced by the presence of "unmercifully numerous" fleas.[14] Making matters worse, Brown insisted that the men stay concealed during daylight hours, to avoid inviting attention from the outside world. Brown's daughter Anne and his daughter-in-law Martha, both teenagers, arrived to assist with chores, such as cooking and cleaning, and they alone were allowed to interact with the neighbors.

Brown attempted to enforce an embargo on written communication, but the men, with so much idle time on their hands, naturally turned to writing letters. Many of them wrote to friends and family, explaining that they had embarked on an abolitionist expedition to Virginia. Some were even more dangerously explicit than that. In Springdale, the Quaker patriarch Moses Varney learned that Brown was planning to liberate the slaves of the South by raiding Harper's Ferry, where he intended to "arm the negroes and strike the blow." Varney even knew that Brown had one of his "leading men (a white man) in an armory in Maryland." Although he situated the armory on the wrong side of the Potomac, Varney was otherwise remarkably accurate (and he likely mistook the site of the armory for the location of the farm). The old Quaker never disclosed the source of his intelligence, but it might very well have been John Cook in a characteristic fit of "caocethes loguendi." Like several of the other raiders, Cook had remained in regular contact with the Springdale community, and he had been close, in one way or another, to Varney's daughter Emlen. Varney definitely knew that Cook was in Harper's Ferry "quietly taking observations preliminary to the attack," which was the sort of information that would have come from the spy himself.[15]

Letters aside, most of the men remained caged under Brown's strict regime, although some occasionally refused to follow orders. Several of the most troubling incidents involved John Cook. One afternoon, when Cook was visiting the farm, a neighbor lady arrived for an unannounced visit. Anne saw her coming and signaled to the men to hurry upstairs and hide. The others obeyed instantly, but Cook audaciously remained standing in plain sight. "As it was too late for him to go upstairs," Anne frantically hustled him into her own ground floor bedroom. While Anne made a commotion to distract the visitor, Martha helped Cook slip out of the window to escape. The contrived "rumpus" was probably unnecessary, as Cook was already adept at silently climbing in and out of bedroom windows, but Anne Brown was not inclined to take chances with her father's mission.[16]

A few of the other recruits also resorted to defenestration, although in less dramatic circumstances, occasionally sneaking away from the farm for a brief respite from close quarters. At least two of them paid unauthorized visits to Cook in town, which apparently upset Anne and Martha. Interviewed by the radical clergyman Thomas Wentworth Higginson shortly after the failed raid, the young women stressed that they always lacked "confidence in Cook because 'he was not a man of principle.'" Anne knew virtually nothing about Cook's personal background, later writing, "I knew very little of the past lives of the men, as I never asked any questions concerning their affairs." Thus, her assessment of Cook's character must have been based on his behavior—and the behavior he encouraged in others—at the farm.[17]

The constant confinement was hard on the "invisibles," as Anne Brown called them, but they were even more troubled by the absence of information about Brown's plans. Almost until the last day, they were never told the date, the exact place, or any of the important operational details of the coming insurrection. Many of the men believed that they were simply going to liberate slaves, carrying them away to the free states as Brown had done in Missouri, although on a much larger scale. Thus, it came as a great shock when Brown selectively began to reveal that he intended to seize the federal armory in Harper's Ferry. In fact, the revelation led to a small rebellion at the farm, with many of the men arguing that such a raid would be virtually suicidal. Others, including John Cook and John Kagi, always "favored the plan of taking the town [and] government buildings" and attempted to restore discipline in the ranks. Cook himself had made "many visits to examine and report on the Government buildings [including their] weak or strong points," so his backing for Brown carried great weight among his comrades.[18]

Charles Tidd became so disaffected that he stormed away from the farm, just as he had angrily departed the training camp in Iowa two years earlier. This time, he went to stay for a week with Cook and his wife in Bolivar. Tidd was a strapping man with high cheekbones, a brooding complexion and a trim beard. He was not fainthearted—he had participated in Brown's Missouri rescue the previous year—but he had profound doubts about Brown's leadership. Most historians have attributed Tidd's departure simply to his need to "let off steam" before he returned to the fold, but there may have been far more to it than that. Tidd did not merely stamp away in an impulsive fit of anger. Rather, he brought along his heavy trunk, including all of his keepsakes and important belongings. That was the act of a man who intended to leave town permanently, not merely to spend a few days allowing his temper to subside.[19] But something appears to have changed Tidd's mind during his stay at the Bolivar boardinghouse, and it was almost certainly related to Cook's unremitting enthusiasm for the Harper's Ferry plan. Tidd ended up returning to the Maryland farm after about a week, although he left his trunk behind in Bolivar, suggesting that he was still contemplating a getaway.

Unlike Tidd and most of the others, Cook strongly agreed with Brown's far-fetched belief that the Harper's Ferry armory would be an "impregnable position when once in their hands," and he used his considerable powers of persuasion to assuage his doubting comrades.[20] In the disastrous aftermath of the invasion, Tidd would naturally second-guess his decision to rejoin Brown's army, and he would angrily recall Cook's role in convincing him not to return safely to Maine.

※ ❀ ※

For all of his insistence on secrecy, Brown himself did not join the sequestration. Although he was surely the most recognizable man in the group, he traveled freely around the area, often stopping at neighboring farms where he helped tend to ailing livestock. He also visited "Dunker" churches in the area, worshipping alongside members of the pacifist antislavery sect and occasionally delivering sermons. He made a point of reconnoitering Harper's Ferry in person, familiarizing himself with the layout of the streets, bridges, and trestles, as well as the locations and entranceways of important buildings.

If Brown did not trust his troops to show their faces after sunrise, he did, perhaps out of necessity, trust Cook to continue his surveillance. The two men boldly met in broad daylight on Shenandoah Street in the center of Harper's Ferry. Cook was well known in town, having lived there for a year, and he was easily recognizable by any of the scores of people with whom he had worked or socialized. Brown, by that time, had grown the heavy white beard by which he is now usually characterized and which was distinctive even in 1859. The meeting between Cook and Brown may not have drawn any special notice that summer, but it was far from circumspect. At either that meeting or another, Brown instructed Cook to intensify his intelligence gathering, tasking him with making specific plans for the capture of prominent hostages.

Thus, Cook connived to make the acquaintance of Colonel Lewis Washington, an important landowner and slaveholder in Jefferson County. Washington was the great-grandnephew of President George Washington, to whom he bore a striking resemblance, and Cook decided that the most famous resident of Harper's Ferry would also make the most valuable hostage. One afternoon in early September, as Washington walked past the armory, Cook approached the gentleman and addressed him by name. "I believe you have a great many interesting relics at your house," said the spy, "could I have permission to see them if I should walk out some day?" Believing Cook to be one of the armory workers, Washington agreed to extend an invitation, little suspecting that Cook had fingered him as a future prisoner.[21]

About a week later, Cook called at Washington's home, a 670-acre plantation known as Beall-Air, about five miles outside Harper's Ferry. Cook inquired again about the heirlooms Washington had inherited from his famous uncle, and the trusting landowner proudly displayed "the sword presented by Frederick the Great to General Washington," as well as a pistol that had been given to Washington by the Marquis de Lafayette. Cook angled for an opportunity to handle General Washington's gun. He had always been fascinated by fine weapons, and besides, firing the gun would provide an occasion to step outside and take a look around the grounds. Cook therefore asked how recently the old weapon had been used, hoping that might lead to a test firing. Washington, however, explained that he had only fired the pistol once, eight or ten years earlier. "I had merely tried it, and cleaned it, and put it in the cabinet," he said, and "it would never be shot again."

Still needing an excuse to see more of the estate, Cook engaged Colonel Washington in a discussion of firearms. He told Washington that he "belonged to a Kansas hunting party, and found it very profitable to hunt buffaloes for their hides." Perhaps Cook was intentionally tempting fate by mentioning his days in Kansas, but Washington's suspicions were not aroused and the friendly conversation continued. Then Cook unbuttoned his coat and revealed his two silver-mounted revolvers. Washington was much surprised at the display of weaponry. Harper's Ferry was not on the frontier, and visitors did not often arrive so extravagantly armed. Cook, however, concocted a story about needing the guns for his work as a buffalo hunter, explaining that he planned to return shortly to Kansas. Washington expressed surprise that someone would risk hunting buffalo with side arms, but Cook replied that "he had his horse so trained that there was no danger." He was now wearing the guns "to accustom his hips to their weight," because he had recently been weakened by a fever. Cook asked if Washington would like to try his large army-style pistols, and Washington took the bait. He agreed to take Cook outside for some target practice.

The two men set up a target under a large tree in front of Washington's house. They fired twenty-four shots between the two of them, although it is not recorded who had better aim. Strangely, Cook had not until then introduced himself, but Washington noticed that one of the pistols had "'John E. Cook' engraved on the breech of it on a brass plate." He asked the visitor if that was his name, and Cook replied that it was, adding that "I engraved that myself; I borrowed the tools from a silversmith . . . and thinking I could do it better myself, I did it." The silversmith in the story was no doubt James Monroe Jones, of Chatham, but Cook prudently refrained from telling Washington about his friendship with the black artisan.

At the end of the shooting match, Cook invited Washington to return the visit. As Washington later explained, "He told me that he had a rifle . . . that he would like me to look at, as he saw I had some fondness for fire-arms. He said to me, 'When you come down to the Ferry, if you will call, I should like you to see it and try it.'"

Ensnaring Lewis Washington was not Cook's only conspiratorial project in preparation for the Harper's Ferry raid. Brown was certain that many slaves would spontaneously join his uprising once the news had spread, so he assigned Cook to assess the strength of the expected reinforcements by counting all of the male slaves within a distance of eight or ten miles. It was a touchy job, as too many inquiries about slaves—especially from an outsider—would surely attract unwanted attention. Until the last minute, Brown had qualms about entrusting Cook with the mission, due to his well-known loquacity. Brown's daughter later recounted that her father "lived in constant fear" all summer

that Cook would slip up and give away their plans. Brown was especially worried that Cook would say something to his wife's family—not
because he was disloyal or lacked good intentions, but rather because
he was naturally "very impulsive and indiscreet."[22]

In fact, the talkative Cook had already hinted among "the Quaker
and Dunker farmers of that section [that] there might be 'disturbances'
or 'active uneasiness' among the 'darkies.'" In the end, however, Brown
had no real choice. His entire strategy depended upon an ingathering
of slaves, and for that he needed accurate information. Of all his men,
only Cook was familiar with the environs of Harper's Ferry, and only
Cook had "made himself acceptable" among the local citizens. For his
part, Cook was enthusiastic about the assignment, even proposing "to
go about among the slaves on the plantations and form secret societies"
to let them know "that there was a project on foot to help them to their
liberty." Cook argued that the forewarned slaves "would be ready and
in a measure prepared" to join a rebellion. But Brown did not think the
slaves could be trusted, and he "positively forbade" Cook from spread-
ing the word. Nonetheless, and perhaps against his better judgment,
Brown sent Cook out to conduct his census.[23]

But how to do it without arousing too much suspicion? Cook hit upon
the device of pretending to gather statistics for a book about the "relative number between the whites and slaves" in the area, while also
settling a wager about the total number of slaves. He began by in-
quiring at the Jefferson County clerk's office about the number of free
blacks in the area, and he then expanded his search to the outlying districts. Cook covered the region well, traveling almost all the way to the
county seat of Charlestown, eight miles southwest of Harper's Ferry,
and beyond. Among others, he visited the property of a slaveholder
who lived about fifteen or twenty miles from Harper's Ferry, where he
"went all over the plantation, conversed with the negroes, and finally
stayed overnight." Cook's ruse was so successful that he even gained
entry to the home of Andrew Hunter—a well-connected lawyer who

would later lead the prosecution of Brown and others—where he was given full details about the makeup of the household.[24]

True to form, Cook could not completely resist sharing his secret. At one point along the road he encountered a "party of four negroes— two free and two slave," and he asked "if they had ever thought about their freedom." The two slaves replied that they wanted to be free, but doubted that they ever would be. Cook told them that freedom would arrive before long, and he encouraged them to "look for the good time coming."[25] If the four black men understood Cook's cryptic message, they did not reveal it to anyone.

❋　◉　❋

Finally, in early October 1859, Brown told Cook to pull up stakes. Brown must still have been wary of Cook's tendency to talk, because his written instructions, as Cook recalled, included multiple warnings to make the move in absolute secrecy:

> *Dear sir,*—You will please get every thing ready to come with your wife to my home this morning. My wagon will wait for you. I shall take your wife to Chambersburg, and shall start early to- morrow morning. Be as expeditious as possible. Be very careful not to say or do anything which will awaken any suspicion.
>
> You can say your wife is going to make a visit to some friends of her's in the country. Be very careful that you do not let any of our plans leak out.[26]

Oliver Brown picked up the Cook family on the evening of October 6, driving them to the Maryland farm house where they spent the night. The next day after dinner, in the middle of a driving rain, Brown and his son Watson escorted Virginia Cook and baby John to Chambersburg, Pennsylvania, where they would remain until after the raid. Brown's treatment of Virginia Cook was thoughtless at best, verging on heart- less. Only a week earlier, he had sent his own daughter and daughter-in-law to his farm in North Elba, New York, where they would be sheltered by other family members. There was no reason that Virginia and her child could not have accompanied the two other young women, rather than be cast loose in Chambersburg on only one day's notice. For reasons of his own, however, Brown was less concerned about the welfare of Cook's wife and son. Perhaps that reflected his disdain for the couple's promiscuity, or perhaps he merely balked at imposing two more needy souls on his hard-pressed family in North Elba, whose resources were already stretched thin. Then again, Brown would soon prove willing to risk the lives of his own sons, so perhaps he considered Virginia and her baby as simply two more expendable casualties in the war of liberation.

Upon returning from Chambersburg, Brown assured Cook that he had secured lodging for Virginia at Mary Ritner's rooming house, "and that she liked her boarding place very well." In fact, the baby had cried during the entire trip, and Brown had not bothered to see whether the child settled down after Virginia was shown to their room next to the first floor parlor. Perhaps Virginia truly did like the accommodations, but she must have been worried about much more than the quality of quarters. "Rustic and ignorant" of the outside world, she had never before traveled from Harper's Ferry. She could only have panicked when she realized that she and her nursing infant had been marooned penniless among strangers. Although she had a warm place to sleep for the time being, it appears that Brown had prepaid for no more than two weeks' lodging in Chambersburg.[27]

Mary Ritner was Brown's favorite innkeeper for good reason. As the daughter-in-law of former Pennsylvania governor Joseph Ritner, who was "a sturdy man of anti-slavery sentiment," she was sympathetic and hospitable to the abolitionist movement. Her late husband had been a conductor on the Underground Railroad (and also on a real railroad). Ritner's guests had often included Brown himself, as well as his sons and supporters, although she would set firm limits later that month by refusing to shelter fugitives when Brown's raid failed. In early October, however, Ritner's was the logical place for John Brown to house Virginia Cook. John Kagi was briefly staying there at the time, and he helped keep Virginia relatively calm in her strange surroundings. Unaware that her hometown was about to be invaded by her husband and his friends, Virginia was under the impression that she would soon be joining an emigrant party on the way to Kansas. Perhaps she suspected by then that she had become entangled in a much more dangerous plot, but it is not known whether she protested the sudden change of circumstances for herself and her child. If Virginia complained to her husband, neither one of them ever mentioned it afterward.[28]

Cook's disappearance could not remain entirely unnoticed, given how many places he had frequented in and around Harper's Ferry. Lewis Washington attempted to find him, hoping to take up the earlier invitation to try out Cook's rifle. Washington, however, was not troubled when he was informed that Cook had left town. "I supposed, in all probability, he had gone to Kansas, as he told me he intended to go in a few days."[29] Washington would not see Cook again until the night of the insurrection.

❉ THREE ❉

Insurrection

It was only on Saturday, October 15, 1859, that John Brown announced to his twenty-one followers that they would begin the war on slavery the next night. Until then, six or seven of the men had never been informed of the full scope of the plan, still believing they were about to participate in another lightning raid to bring slaves to the North, rather than an extended guerilla campaign in Virginia. Only on Sunday morning was the Provisional Constitution read to them, after which Brown distributed printed commissions to those "who were to hold military positions in the organization." Brown then "offered up a fervent prayer to God to assist in the liberation of the bondmen in that slaveholding land," and he obtained a promise of allegiance from each of his men.[1]

As one of Brown's few confidants, Cook had already known most of the details. An enthusiastic supporter of the plan, he was eager to get it under way. Before they could start, however, Brown had a final admonition for his soldiers,

> And now gentlemen, let me press this one thing on your minds, you all know how dear life is to you, and how dear your lives are to your friends; and in remembering that consider that the lives of others are as dear to them as yours are to you; do not, therefore, take the life of any one if you can possibly avoid it; but if it is necessary to take life in order to save your own, then make sure work of it.[2]

Late on Sunday evening, October 16, Brown and eighteen of the men (three, including his son Owen, had been left behind to guard their weapons cache) began their attack. The five-mile march from their farmhouse to the Potomac River was uneventful, making it the most completely successful phase of the entire operation. Cook and Charles Tidd were in the vanguard, tasked with cutting the telegraph wires linking Harper's Ferry to the outside world. Brown and the rest of the company then silently crossed the bridge from Maryland into Virginia. Once on the Virginia side, Brown divided his command, sending small squads to guard the Potomac and Shenandoah bridges, and leading his main force to seize the different buildings comprising the federal armory compound. At first they met little resistance, and all of their objectives were easily secured.

Cook and five others—two white men and three blacks—were sent into the countryside to capture Colonel Lewis Washington and other slave owners and to liberate their slaves. Cook was not nominally in command of the small detachment—that honor fell to Aaron Stevens—but he was clearly the actual leader of the expedition. Only Cook was familiar with the roads around Harper's Ferry, and only he could reliably locate and identify Colonel Washington and the other targeted prisoners. Without Cook as a guide, Stevens and the others would have found themselves wandering in the darkness, with scant likelihood they could complete their urgent assignment by dawn. Time, however, was of the essence. Brown intended to hold the slave masters hostage, and he believed that their freed slaves would be only the first of multitudes to rally behind him at morning light. The overnight kidnapping of Colonel Washington—carried out in part by black men—was therefore crucial to the mission, as it represented Brown's intended assumption of the mantle of the American Revolution. Cook was under special instructions to retrieve Frederick the Great's sword, which Brown prized for its symbolic value.

Arriving at Washington's house after midnight, Cook and his comrades battered in the rear door with a fence rail. Washington was asleep in bed, but he was awakened when they entered the building and called his name. Standing in his nightshirt, Washington confronted the armed men. In his own self-aggrandizing version of the events, Washington was remarkably fearless, given that he was facing intruders waving rifles and pistols. First he belittled the gunmen—"You are a very bold looking set of fellows, but I should doubt your courage; you have too many arms to take one man." And then he taunted them—"I believe with a pop-gun I could take either of you in your shirt tail." The raiders apparently remained silent through all that, as Washington continued to demand an explanation. Then, by the light of a flambeau, Cook confirmed Washington's identity and the raiders made him a prisoner, although a very calm one. "The only thing that astonished me particularly," Washington later said, "was the presence of this man Cook, who had been at my house some three or four weeks before that."[3]

As a witness at Brown's trial, and again at an 1860 hearing before a U.S. Senate investigating committee, Washington testified that the raiders were after more than slaves and symbolism. In addition to announcing their intention to free the slaves of the South, they also attempted to steal his silver tea service and his watch, but he bravely resisted their demands. "You have set yourselves up as great moralists and liberators of slaves," he rebuked the would-be thieves. "Now it appears that you are robbers as well," he said, while staunchly refusing to surrender his watch. That scolding appeared to chasten the intruders, at least in Washington's account of his own undaunted courage. He was, in fact, a man of powerful bearing—with chiseled features and a fierce moustache—obviously accustomed to intimidating those who did not share his "enormous superiority of lineage."[4]

According to one member of the raiding party, however, Washington was not nearly so bold. Osborne Anderson—a free black who joined Brown from Canada—said that Washington "cried heartily" and "begged us not to kill him." Far from fearlessly defending the sanctity of his pocket watch, Washington frantically attempted to negotiate for his freedom. "You can have my slaves," he implored, "if you will let me remain." The raiders refused the offer, and the slave master "stood as if speechless and petrified." Then Washington was compelled to deliver the famous sword of Frederick the Great to his captors, and he was visibly shaken when Anderson—a black man—stepped forward to take it from him.[5]

Whatever the state of Washington's composure, Cook and company bundled their hostage out to his waiting carriage and escorted three of his male slaves to the accompanying farm wagon. After some difficulty getting the harnesses straight, they departed the plantation with Washington firmly wedged next to Cook on the carriage's back seat. Cook acknowledged that Washington had politely received him only a few weeks earlier, and the kidnapper apologized for making a prisoner of his former host. Cook disingenuously claimed that he was only obeying his superior officer, although it had actually been his own idea to include Washington among the hostages.

The next stop was the farmhouse of John Allstadt—Washington's neighbor and fellow slave owner—where they arrived at about 3:00 a.m. As they had at Washington's, "they bursted the door open with a rail." Roused from his bed by the banging, Allstadt attempted to push the door shut, but the raiders threatened to burn down the house if he failed to open it. The fearful Allstadt complied, and three armed men entered the house while three others, all holding rifles, remained outside. Informing Allstadt that they intended to free the country of slavery, the intruders ordered him to get dressed. Ignoring the cries of Allstadt's terrified daughters, they asked if there were any other men in the house.[6] By that time, Allstadt's eighteen-year-old son had come down from his upstairs bedroom, only to be seized by the collar and roughly held until his father finished dressing.

The two Allstadts, père and fils, were hustled out into their yard, where they saw that their seven male slaves had already been assembled. The senior Allstadt recognized Colonel Washington's carriage, but he was not given an opportunity to speak with his friend. Instead, he was seated in the farm wagon, along with his son and all of the slaves. Allstadt later implied that Cook had been among the three men who entered the house and took him captive, although Cook claimed that he had waited in the carriage to guard Colonel Washington. In either case, Allstadt never saw Cook after the wagons left his farm.

With the white prisoners under guard and the newly freed slaves now armed with pikes, the small procession continued on its way to meet John Brown at Harper's Ferry. John Cook could be proud that his mission had thus far been accomplished almost without complications. The same could not be said for long about Brown's end of the operation.

※ ◈ ※

After crossing the river in near silence, Brown led the main contingent of his force toward the federal compound. Finding only token resistance, they quickly took control of the major buildings, including the arsenal and armory, while taking additional hostages from among the workers and unlucky passersby. Two men—one of them Brown's son Oliver—had been left behind to guard the bridge and railroad trestle, and they proved to be unfortunately quick on the trigger.

At around midnight, while Cook and company were taking Colonel Washington into custody, a night watchman approached the two raiders on the bridge. Oliver Brown tried to grab the man, but he broke free and began to run toward town. Brown fired, wounding the watchman slightly and setting off the chain of events that would eventually raise a countywide alarm. A little over an hour later, an eastbound train slowed to a stop before crossing the trestle, and the conductor and another man got out to investigate the unusual absence of lights on the bridge. They were met by gunfire from Oliver and his companion. That drew other railroad workers to the scene, including Hayward Shepherd, a free black man who worked as the baggage master. Determined to hold the bridge, the two raiders continued their panicky firing, hitting Shepherd in the back. Shepherd would die later that morning, making a free black man the first casualty in John Brown's war of liberation. The shooting awakened more citizens, including Dr. John Starry who attempted to tend to Shepherd's mortal wound just as Cook was breaking in the door at the Allstadt property.

Cook knew nothing about the shooting on the bridge as he continued to bring his prisoners toward town. They arrived at the armory some time before dawn, where the hostages were introduced to their captor. "This is John Brown," they were told. And to make sure there was no mistaking his identity or his cause, Brown himself added, "Ossawatomie Brown, of Kansas." Brown still did not know how badly his position had already deteriorated, and it would soon become much worse. For the time being, he gathered his hostages in the armory engine house, making a point of placing them under the charge of a black man, Shields Green. Washington later complained of Green's impudence, but all of the hostages were treated well during their imprisonment. Brown explained to Washington, "I wanted you particularly for the moral effect it would give our cause, having one of your name as a prisoner."[7] To emphasize the point, Brown took the sword of Frederick the Great and continued to wear it until he was subdued the following day. (Cook had retained Lafayette's pistol without Brown's knowledge; it would later cause him much misfortune.)

Cook remained at the armory compound only long enough to warm himself by a fire in the engine house. As the sun rose on the chilly morning, Brown sent him into Maryland—along with Charles Tidd and William Leeman, and four recently liberated slaves—on a two-part mission. First, Cook was ordered to capture the brothers James and Terrence Byrne, who were prominent slave owners, while freeing—or, more accurately, commandeering—their slaves. It was the Byrnes' bad luck to live near Brown's hideout in Maryland, and Cook had no doubt counted their slaves when he conducted his census. Brown assumed that the Byrne slaves would be eager for their freedom, but he had never actually determined whether they wanted to serve as laborers for the second phase of Cook's operation. After capturing the Byrnes, and with the assistance of their slaves, Cook was next supposed to return to the Maryland farmhouse to gather Brown's weapons cache and move it to a schoolhouse nearer to Harper's Ferry. Brown's ultimate plan was to retreat to the schoolhouse, where he would retrieve his rifles and pikes before establishing his redoubt in the mountains. It was a complicated assignment, but Cook carried it out diligently—until the rapidly unfolding events made it impossible.

Detaining the Byrnes was not hard to accomplish. Terrence happened to be out for a horseback ride early on Monday morning when, just after daylight, he encountered "a wagon on the road, driven by a colored man." A voice called out for him to stop, and Byrne recognized John Cook, whom he had met several times before. Byrne reined in his horse, assuming that he was about to have a friendly conversation.

"I am very sorry to inform you that you are my prisoner," said Cook.

Smiling at the absurd idea, Byrne replied, "You are surely joking."

"I am not," said Cook, now waving a rifle.

William Leeman then moved closer to Byrne and made the threat explicit. "No parley here, or I will put a ball in you," he said. "You must go with us to your place; we want your negroes."[8]

The bewildered Byrne had no choice but to lead the party back to his house, where his brother was sitting on the front porch. Byrne whispered "servile war," to his brother, as the two men were ushered into the sitting room. Byrne's sister and a female cousin were also in the house, and the family was made to sit silently while the garrulous Cook delivered a speech on the subject of slavery and equality. Once that was finished, they demanded the Byrnes' slaves.

"Captain Cook," came the reply, "you must do as I do when I want them—hunt for them." As was common in the Upper South, the household slaves had been given the day off on Sunday to visit their wives on other plantations, and they had not yet returned by Monday morning. With only one wagon and much more to accomplish that day, Cook could not afford to spend any time tracking down the slaves. Instead, he and another raider stayed in the Byrne farmhouse, keeping the family under guard, while their comrade and the Washington slaves continued on to Brown's headquarters, a mile and a half distant, to pick up the hidden rifles and pikes. That operation took about an hour, during which the ever-talkative Cook explained to his hostages that Brown's men "had possession of the armory, railroad bridge, and telegraph, and before night would have the canal; that Colonel Washington was a prisoner at Harpers Ferry, and that his fowling-piece was carried by one of the negroes."[9] After the wagon returned, the entire group—including the Byrne brothers and five or six slaves—departed for the schoolhouse as planned.

Schoolmaster Lind Currie was stunned when the heavy farm wagon rolled up to the door of his one-room schoolhouse. Class had already convened for the day, and the thirty children—including boys and girls, ages eight to sixteen—were frightened by the sight of so many armed men, not to mention the prisoners and the pike-carrying slaves. Cook entered the building at the head of the party, wearing two revolvers and a large Bowie knife in his belt and carrying a rifle. He demanded possession of the schoolhouse, informing Currie that the intruders "intended depositing their arms and implements of war there." As the black men unloaded the many boxes of weapons, Cook earnestly told the schoolmaster of his intention to free the slaves, while offering protection to those slaveholders who complied voluntarily.[10] It was typical of the voluble Cook that he attempted to explain himself even to the people he detained, including Currie and the Byrne brothers. Although his comments may have sounded like warnings—or at best, high-handed speeches—to his captives, Cook was sincere in his convictions and had always been open about his beliefs. He apparently thought that he could persuade even hostile southerners, whom he tried to befriend at the same time he was forcibly confining them.

After the arms were deposited, Cook's fellow raiders departed in the wagon, taking most of the slaves and the Byrne brothers to join the other hostages at the armory, with Cook and one slave remaining at the schoolhouse to guard the weapons. Leeman would stay in Harper's

Ferry, and die there, while Tidd took the wagon back to the Maryland farm, planning to move another load of weapons.

By this time Currie's students had become panicky. A new father himself, Cook had sympathy for the children and he attempted to calm them as much as he could. When that proved impossible he agreed to dismiss them. One of the youngest boys, however, was so distraught that he could not be sent home alone. Currie asked for permission to accompany the boy home and Cook agreed, extracting the teacher's promise to come back afterward.

Currie kept his word, returning to the schoolhouse after about an hour. He found Cook sitting there with one slave. Shots could now be heard from the direction of Harper's Ferry, and Currie asked Cook what was happening. "Well," Cook replied, "it simply means this: that those people down there are resisting our men, and we are shooting them down." Although Cook did not yet know it, most of the firing was in the opposite direction. Brown had been surrounded by local sharpshooters who were raking his positions with deadly effect. As the constant shooting continued, Cook must have realized that something disastrous was happening to his comrades—hundreds of guns were being fired, but Brown's contingent at the Ferry numbered no more than sixteen. He thought about joining the others at the armory but, as he later reflected, "My orders were strict to remain at the school-house and guard the arms, and I obeyed the orders to the letter."[11]

※　❀　※

Despite their overnight successes, daylight had brought nothing but bad news for Brown and his men. The shootings at the railroad trestle had attracted attention and given away his plan. As news of the invasion spread through the surrounding region, armed militia members began arriving in small groups. Dr. Starry, who had attempted to save Hayward Shepherd's life, had taken the initiative to alert the local militia by asking the Lutheran church sexton to ring his bell as an alarm.

By mid-morning on Monday, October 17, while Cook was anxiously sitting at the Maryland schoolhouse, Brown and the others were besieged by a dozen militia companies and scores of outraged civilians, taking fire from all sides.

The first of Brown's men to fall was Dangerfield Newby, who had come to Virginia hoping to free his wife and children. Newby was shot in the neck at about 11:00 a.m., dying almost instantly, but his quick death was not a sufficient punishment to satisfy the outraged townspeople. His corpse was beaten with sticks, stabbed, and mutilated, his ears and genitals cut off as souvenirs. Newby's body was then thrown to rooting hogs that dragged the intestines from his wounds. A ghoulish Maryland journalist later wrote that the incident "could not fail to improve the . . . value of pork at Harper's Ferry next winter."[12]

One by one, Brown's men were picked off or taken prisoner throughout the day. They fought back, attempting to hold their positions on the bridges and at several government buildings and killing several Harper's Ferry citizens including Mayor Fontaine Beckham. Brown eventually withdrew his forces to the armory's sturdy brick engine house, taking special care to protect his many hostages. He made several attempts to negotiate a cease-fire, offering the freedom of his hostages in return for safe passage out of Virginia, but his messengers were either captured or shot and killed even when showing a white flag. One of the captured raiders was later murdered by the militia-mob, taken to a railway trestle, and used for target practice until his body fell into the river below. The corpse "could be seen for a day or two after, lying at the bottom of the river, with his ghastly face still exhibiting his fearful death agony."[13]

※ ❀ ※

As afternoon approached, Cook realized that no one would ever come to retrieve the weapons and that it was pointless to hold to his orders. Schoolmaster Currie, who had been forcibly detained the entire time, asked permission to go home. The now dejected Cook allowed him to leave, but exacted Currie's promise not to reveal what had happened at the schoolhouse. Remarkably, Currie again kept his word, although by then there was not much of a secret to maintain. Brown's invasion had already all but collapsed, and Cook would be gone from the schoolhouse soon after Currie departed.

After releasing his hostage, Cook left the schoolhouse and briefly considered trying to join Brown's men in an attempt to save his comrades. He got as far as a canal lock, about a mile outside town, where he learned from a black woman that "our men were hemmed in and that several of them had been shot." He also met the lockkeeper's wife, whom he knew well from his year as a spy, and whose husband was among Brown's hostages at the armory. The woman realized that Cook was somehow connected to the insurgents—he had, after all, never concealed his abolitionist activities in Kansas—and she begged him to try and get her husband released from the engine house. Cook agreed, and continued toward the Ferry, rifle in hand.

About a half mile farther, Cook encountered two boys who informed him that Brown's men were now encircled by troops from Charlestown, Martinsburg, Hagerstown, and Shepherdstown and, more alarmingly, that the militia would be "coming up the road after us soon." Nonetheless, Cook pressed on, climbing a steep hill "in order to get a better view of the position of our opponents."

Prepared as he was for the worst, Cook was still distraught by what he observed. "I saw that our party were completely surrounded [and] I saw a body of men on High street firing down upon them." Abandoning any hope of joining his friends, Cook decided to see if he could divert the militiamen by drawing their fire upon himself. He held onto a tree branch to maintain his footing on the hill, and, as he later recounted, "I therefore raised my rifle and took the best aim I could and fired." Cook's tactic worked, if only momentarily, as the snipers immediately turned toward the hill and began shooting at Cook's position. Cook fired several more rounds, causing many of the Virginians to flee for cover, as though "they had important business to attend to elsewhere."[14] Judge Richard Parker would later claim that one of Cook's bullets hit and killed a Virginian named George Turner, but that crime was never specifically charged or proven.[15] In any case, the militiamen continued to fire at Cook until one of their shots severed the branch he was holding, sending him falling fifteen feet down the hillside. Severely bruised, and with his "flesh somewhat lacerated," Cook finally decided that it was time to make his own escape. He continued to the bottom of the hill and began walking down the road away from Harper's Ferry.

After only fifty yards, Cook passed a store where he saw "several heads behind the doorpost looking at me." Alone and frightened, Cook cocked his rifle and "beckoned to some of them to come to me." After some tense hesitation, two youngsters emerged from the store. Recognizing both of them, Cook demanded to know if there were any armed men in the building. The boys swore there were none, satisfying Cook that he was safe for the time being. Unsure of what to do next, Cook headed for the canal lock, perhaps intending to inform the keeper's wife that his rescue mission had failed. Instead, he ran into one of the canal workers, William McGregg, whom he questioned at length. Cook learned, more or less accurately, that "the bridge was filled by our opponents and that all of our party were dead but seven—that two of them were shot while trying to escape across the river." It is unlikely that McGregg was an abolitionist sympathizer, but he evidently regarded Cook as a friend. He made a point of telling Cook about the location of hostile troops and advised him to leave the area immediately.

Accepting McGregg's obvious good judgment, Cook "bid him goodnight and started up the road at a rapid walk." He reached the home of an Irish family where he was provided food and coffee, along with the inaccurate news that Brown had been killed earlier in the day. Believing the rumor to be true, and with no clear idea about what to do next, Cook returned to the weapons cache at the schoolhouse, which he found shuttered as he had left it. Hoping that some of his comrades might have decided to use the school as a rendezvous point, he cautiously entered the building with his rifle cocked and his revolver drawn. He called out for friends, but no one answered. Striking a match, he searched the dark building and confirmed that no one was there. He then tried calling in the woods surrounding the schoolhouse, but again he got no response. That left him no real alternative other than return to Brown's hideout in Washington County, and he began the five-mile walk.

Somewhere along the road, Cook saw a group of men walking toward him. When they had approached within about fifty yards, he warily raised his rifle and ordered them to halt. As it turned out, however, Cook had encountered friends—raiders Charles Tidd, Owen Brown, Barclay Coppoc, Francis Merriam, and one of John Allstadt's freed slaves—who were making their own way from Brown's rented farmhouse toward Harper's Ferry. Cook shared the shattering news that he had learned that afternoon, including the inaccurate information that Brown had been killed.

Tidd was despondent, perhaps recalling his missed opportunity to decamp from Harper's Ferry two weeks earlier. He had voiced severe misgivings about Brown's plan until the last possible moment on Sunday night—even making one final effort to call off the operation before crossing the bridge to Harper's Ferry—and he was in no mood for suicidal heroics. "The fact is, boys," he said, "we are used up; the best thing we can do is to get away from here as quick as we can." Owen Brown at first rejected the idea of "deserting any friends who might want to escape with us," and for a while the men argued among themselves while standing on the road. As darkness approached, both Cook and Tidd insisted that it would be sheer madness to attempt a rescue of any survivors. Owen only reluctantly agreed, finally allowing that "we might have shown our good-will by killing one or two of the enemy; still it would have surely cost our lives." The five men decided instead to return to Brown's Maryland house, where they could make plans for their escape to the north.[16]

The fugitives stopped at the farmhouse only long enough to gather some food, ammunition, blankets, and other supplies for their flight before heading on to a wooded mountainside where they made an uneasy bivouac. It was now late on Monday night, and rain was falling as the men lay down for their first sleep since Sunday morning. Their rest did not last long. At "about 3 o'clock in the morning," according to Cook, "one of our party awakened and found that the negro had left us." The slave had prudently determined that he had no future with the hunted white men, so he quietly slipped away to return to his master. Correctly fearing that the slave would give away their location—he did in fact inform the authorities where the refugees were hiding—Cook and company concluded that they had to move their camp before daylight. They climbed to the summit in the darkness and then slept for the few remaining hours until dawn. At daylight Tuesday they "passed over to the other side of the mountain" where they again waited until dark before "cross[ing] the valley to the other range beyond."[17]

* * *

Late on Monday night, October 17, Colonel Robert E. Lee arrived in Harper's Ferry, at the head of a detachment of United States Marines. The regular troops took up positions surrounding the armory, replacing the militia men, many of whom had become drunk on both liquor and hatred. By nightfall Monday, most of the abolitionists in the Harper's Ferry armory had been killed or severely wounded, including Brown's sons Oliver and Watson.

Early Tuesday morning, Lee sent Lieutenant J. E. B. Stuart to the armory gate to demand Brown's surrender. Brown refused and attempted to negotiate safe passage. Instead of continuing the parley, Stuart gave the command to storm the compound. Wearing George Washington's dress sword, Brown bravely attempted to rally his men—Lewis Washington would later call him "the coolest man I ever saw in defying danger and death"—but Stuart's troops quickly subdued the few surviving raiders. Although badly wounded, Brown was taken alive, as were four of his comrades. The death toll at Harper's Ferry stood at fifteen—ten raiders, four townspeople, and one of Stuart's men who was killed during the assault—but more lives were yet at stake.

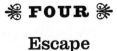

❋ FOUR ❋

Escape

It would be a long time before Cook and his fleeing companions fully learned what had happened to John Brown at the siege of Harper's Ferry. At the very time when J. E. B. Stuart's men were taking control of the armory, the five fugitives were huddled anxiously on a mountainside and wondering how they could escape to freedom. Maryland was hostile territory and southern Pennsylvania was not much better. The nearest refuge was probably close to one hundred miles away by road in western Pennsylvania, but of course they could not take to the roads. Their ultimate objective, the Western Reserve of northeast Ohio, was hundreds of miles farther still.[1] It was all but impossible for them to imagine how far they would actually have to walk over the rough, densely wooded terrain. With only the provisions they could carry on their backs, they braced themselves for a cold, wet, desperate, and dangerous march.

More than any of the others, Cook understood that he was a wanted man. He was familiar to many citizens of Harper's Ferry, and he could be named—and identified—by Lewis Washington, Terrence Byrne, Lind Currie, and most of the other people he had encountered along the canal on Monday afternoon.

In fact, Washington provided Cook's name to the authorities immediately after his rescue on Tuesday. The following morning, Wednesday, October 19, Washington executed an affidavit in which he swore "that a certain John E. Cook" was part of the kidnapping party, "affiant having distinctly recognized him when he was seized and robbed of his property." Washington added that Cook "is now a fugitive from justice [and] he is fleeing and attempting to escape in the state of Maryland, Pennsylvania, or New York." A warrant for Cook's arrest was issued on the strength of Washington's affidavit, and Governor Henry Wise promptly issued a huge $1,000 reward for Cook's capture. Handbills were distributed in three states, and newspaper reports were published across the country, giving Lewis Washington's unflattering description of Cook: "Five feet four to six inches high; weighs 132 pounds; walks with his breast projecting forward, and his head leaning toward the right side; has light hair, with a small growth around the upper lip, is of sallow complexion, and has a sharp, narrow face."[2] It is possible that the odd details about Cook's gait and mien were meant to suggest a delicate or effeminate appearance. That would be consistent with almost every other contemporary description of Cook, especially from men, and none of the other fugitives were ever described in anything approaching a like manner. But if that was the intended implication, the innuendo has been lost in the passage of time.

Most of the details about Brown's army were still unknown. Cook was variously thought to be Brown's second-in-command, his aide-de-camp, or even his son. It was rumored that he was lurking on the outskirts of Jefferson County at the head of a large group of runaway slaves, and an even more outlandish story had Cook threatening to "march an army of several thousand men" to retake Harper's Ferry. In one fevered report, Cook was said to be "murdering the whites" in the nearby village of Sandy Hook. The local militia promptly sallied out to investigate but the alarm proved false. More realistically, although also untrue, Cook was spotted in towns as far away as Greencastle, Pennsylvania, and Hagerstown, Maryland. A telegraph line repairer near Martinsburg claimed to have been "shot at by Capt. Cook himself," and several citizens in Mechanicsburg thought they saw Cook "with his hat drawn down over his eyes" (although the man was described as weighing between 180 and 190 pounds, which was at least fifty pounds heavier than Cook himself). One newspaper wryly reported that "the mysterious and elusive Cook has been seen and recognized and traced by pretty much everybody between Harper's Ferry and Chambersburgh."[3]

Cook's name had become so well known that witnesses later imagined they had seen him almost everywhere during the insurrection (and during incidents both before and after). The Harper's Ferry night watchman, for example, thought that he had been taken hostage by Cook on Sunday night, although he had actually been seized by Oliver Brown. Slave owners throughout the region soon reported, although without meaningful details, that their "negroes . . . had been tampered with by Cook," and a clerk at the Wager House Hotel said he had once seen Cook conferring with "one of our colored servants." More provocatively, it was said that Cook "had an improper connection with a negress, Betsy, in Bolivar." The young black woman was arrested, but a magistrate's investigation quickly debunked that particular tale. Two other black women were also briefly arrested for supposed connections to Cook, including the possession of a suspicious supper basket that was falsely thought to have been prepared for his escape. As late as October 23, fully a week after the outbreak of the raid, Cook was sighted in the mountains near the Ferry, including an alleged face-to-face encounter with a woman who claimed to be a relative of his wife.[4]

For a short while, John Cook was one of the two most famous militants in the country, second only to John Brown himself. The *Richmond Enquirer*, for example, immediately blamed the insurrection on "the scoundrels Brown and Cooke," with the latter identified as "Brown's chief aid." In a speech in Richmond on Friday, October 21, Governor Wise described Brown's defeat in great detail and singled out Cook's involvement. Wise mentioned Cook five times (more than any of the other known raiders, save Brown), accurately describing his spying mission, his census of slaves, and his surveillance of the armory. Wise even accused Cook of murdering a slave who "attempted to escape from him."

Virginia Senator James Mason issued a similar statement the same day, mentioning Cook three times and naming no other member of Brown's army.[5]

Cook's sudden infamy also prompted some tentative statements of support from his friends in the East. His former employer, Brooklyn attorney John Stearns, published a long letter in the *New York Times* in response to reports that Cook had been a leader of the Harper's Ferry raid. Stearns believed that his impressionable apprentice must have been "a subject of *fanaticism* in this matter [rather] than the monster of crime which the fears of Virginians have painted him." After outlining Cook's distinguished family history, Stearns opined "that this Harper's Ferry rebellion was an incident of special temptation that crossed his path, rather than the result of a long-settled and matured purpose." Should Cook be arrested, Stearns concluded, a fair trial would surely "separate his acts from the *fears* of the people, and lead to a charitable judgment of the condition of mind that has induced" his regrettable actions.[6]

The authorities eventually realized that other raiders had escaped, but only Cook could be identified. Under interrogation, Brown had admitted that "three white men [had been] sent away on an errand" and thus were not captured or killed, but he had refused to disclose their names. Consequently, the first reward announcement named only Cook, while referring to another three unknown white men; it did not identify Barclay Coppoc, Charles Tidd, Francis Merriam, and Owen Brown. Other early accounts of the raid, including Robert E. Lee's initial report to the War Department, listed only "Capt. John E. Cook of Connecticut" as having escaped. Perhaps their own anonymity brought some small comfort to the other four refugees, who realized that Cook alone was known in Harper's Ferry.[7] As it was, however, they also knew that they were being hunted, and that it was worth their lives to remain out of sight.

In fact, the fugitives probably could have been captured quickly following the raid, but, fortunately for them, neither the Virginia nor Maryland authorities took effective pursuit. The local militia men had mostly gotten drunk on Tuesday, following Stuart's successful operation, and their revels continued all day Wednesday. Lee's regular troops were more disciplined, but they had their hands full maintaining order in the town and preventing a lynching. Governor Wise was busy interrogating the captured Brown, anxiously trying to determine the likelihood that more armed abolitionists were about to descend on Virginia. It took the rumor of an atrocity to get the manhunt started, when a hysterical story spread that the village of Pleasant Valley, Maryland, had been attacked by Cook's men, and that a white family had been massacred in their cabin. Colonel Lee was skeptical, but he could not ignore the frantic stories of "cries of murder and screams of the women and children." Refugees from outlying towns were pouring into Harper's Ferry, fleeing from imaginary abolitionist marauders, so Lee decided to investigate the reported attack. He led a detachment of two dozen men to the "outraged hamlet, four or five miles away" and found the local residents quiet and unharmed. There had never been any danger of a further abolitionist attack, but, in fact, Cook's party was at that very time hiding on the outskirts of Pleasant Valley, quite unknown to Lee. They were close enough to hear the hoof beats of the federal troops "which made them wrongfully believe that they were discovered," but the soldiers rode past them in ignorance, while the five frightened raiders hid silently in the brush.[8]

❁ ◉ ❁

Cook's university studies and his work as a Brooklyn law clerk had not prepared him for endless tracking through the wilderness—nor had his comfortable year at a Harper's Ferry boardinghouse—but at least he was in good health and he had been hardened by his service in Kansas. Three of his comrades were in worse shape; Brown had left them behind to guard the farmhouse because they were the least physically fit of his soldiers. Their various disabilities would cause many difficulties as they tried to escape from Maryland to the North.

Owen Brown was the third of John Brown's many children. Like the other boys, he resembled his father, although his complexion was ruddy and his unkempt beard was rufous red. Owen's most noticeable feature, however, was his crippled arm, which he injured as a young child. The injury had not kept Owen from serving with his father in Kansas and participating in the Pottawatomie massacre, but his limited range of motion did prevent him from undertaking the most strenuous physical tasks. Fortunately, Owen's lame arm would not greatly interfere with his ability to hike over mountains, and perhaps (as he later claimed in his memoirs) he was even able to carry a full "fifty pounds of provisions on his back." In worse shape was Barclay Coppoc, an Iowa Quaker whose brother Edwin had been captured at the armory. Coppoc was "touched with consumption" that taxed his endurance and often made it difficult for him to walk. Still, he managed to keep up with his friends, never complaining about the hardship. Francis Merriam had lost an eye as a youngster, but that was the least of his problems. He was the "frail scion of upper-class Boston," a wealthy young man who was considered erratic and unbalanced even by his friends. His initial attempt to join up with Brown was rejected because of his infirmities, but he was later accepted (virtually at the last minute) when he contributed substantial financial resources at a time when Brown was desperate for money. Merriam was useless for combat, which is why Brown would not allow him to participate in the raid. To the dismay of Owen Brown and the other fugitives, Merriam also turned out to be nearly incapable of escape, needing constant assistance to make his way through the thickets and streams. Although he did his best, his comrades "were gravely handicapped by [Merriam's] weakness and inability to go more than a mile or so without resting."[9]

Charles Tidd was easily the strongest of the fugitives. The former lumberjack from Maine had broad shoulders, sturdy legs, and muscular arms. Unfortunately, there were intense personal difficulties between Cook and Tidd that caused greater problems than any of the other men's physical shortcomings. They had been assigned to work together during most of the raid—first cutting the Harper's Ferry telegraph lines, and then kidnapping Washington, Allstadt, and the Byrnes—but that did not mean they could easily cooperate as fugitives.

True, the two men had known each other in Kansas. They had also spent the winter together at Brown's camp in Springdale, where they stayed up playing cards until midnight with no evident animosity, but familiarity does not always breed friendship. Tidd often sought the favor of young women in the Iowa Quaker communities, but his approach had been far less refined than Cook's. In one instance, Tidd had apparently attempted to seduce a girl named Elizabeth Varney, who resisted his advances (or so she told her parents). But whether or not he managed to have his way with her, Tidd boasted to his friends about his sexual encounter with Elizabeth. Salacious gossip quickly spread around the camp and eventually got back to the pious Varneys, causing them great unhappiness.[10] Cook was in no position to criticize someone else's trysts, but he was too much of a gentleman to respect anyone who bragged about it afterward. If nothing else, he surely disdained Tidd's churlish treatment of women.

Nonetheless, the two men were close enough that Tidd retreated for a week to Cook's house in early October after quarrelling with Brown. That was probably the origin of their antagonism. Tidd had once been on the verge of quitting Brown's army, and in the desperate aftermath—freezing, hungry, and hunted—he must have regretted heeding Cook's plea to rejoin the conspiracy at the Maryland farm. Tidd also believed that Brown and the others might have avoided being surrounded at the armory if they hadn't spent so much time carrying out "all of Cook's romantic notions [such as] the taking of George Washington's sword and pistols."[11] One can imagine the recriminations that followed, with Tidd silently faulting (or perhaps loudly rebuking) Cook for the disaster that had befallen them. Seething with resentment, Tidd did not realize that Cook's embellishment of the mission had probably saved his life. If it had not been for the additional time spent in the excursion to Colonel Washington's, he might well have been trapped inside the armory when the Virginia militia men arrived.

The situation was not helped by the clash of the two men's temperaments. College educated and proudly commissioned as one of Brown's captains, the "bold, fiery, quick-thinking" Cook believed that he should be the refugee group's leader, and he wanted the men to risk traveling by road—and even to steal horses—in order to make more rapid progress toward safety. The ponderous Tidd—who was one of the few privates in the small army—wanted to stay as much as possible in the mountains, where he believed the crags and laurel bushes would discourage pursuers. In short order, the disagreement became bitter, as Tidd was not impressed by Cook's schooling, rank, or arguments. A much larger and slower man than Cook, Tidd was not afraid of a fight, but he was extremely cautious and he was shocked by Cook's appalling braggadocio during the first days of their flight. Both men were known for their tempers, and they might have come to blows, or perhaps parted ways, had not Owen Brown intervened in favor of following the mountain ranges rather than the roads. Even so, it took all of Owen's negotiating skills to hold the small band together. He had once before, in Iowa, managed to calm Tidd's temper, and now he succeeded in doing so again in far more parlous circumstances. "It was not easy work to separate Cook and Tidd," Owen later recalled, but he succeeded in persuading them to wait "to have it out [until] they could do it without endangering others."[12]

It turned out that Tidd was right. When the first posses were finally organized to chase the Harper's Ferry fugitives, they kept entirely to the roads and were therefore relatively easy to evade. Some of the militias later rationalized the failure to find their quarry by blaming it on Cook's superior knowledge of the terrain, but that only shows how quickly his myth had developed. In fact, it was believed that Cook had many armed men under his command, and the pursuers were evidently wary of encountering them in the isolation of the mountains.[13]

Sticking to their plan, the five raiders hid "by day in the thickets on the uninhabited mountain-tops." Doing their best to avoid all human contact they spoke only in whispers and shunned "all traveled roads at all times, except as we were obliged to cross them in the night."[14] They waded through streams in order to throw bloodhounds off their trail, and they refrained from lighting campfires for fear of being discovered. Their provisions—mostly dry biscuits and sugar—ran out after only a few days, and they were eventually reduced to scavenging fields and orchards for whatever crops remained standing in late October, or stealing food from unattended farmyards and henhouses.

❋ ❋ ❋

At Cook's insistence, the group headed almost due north in the direction of Chambersburg, Pennsylvania. There were good reasons to go to Chambersburg, and also good reasons to avoid it. The population of Franklin County, where the town is situated, was almost evenly divided on the politics of slavery, with slightly more Republicans than southern-oriented Democrats. "The undertow of anti-slavery conviction was stronger" than political affiliation, however, and many of the Democrats were also sympathetic to fugitive slaves. Chambersburg was therefore an important station for runaway slaves, who followed the Underground Railroad from Virginia, through Hagerstown, Maryland, and into Pennsylvania. Even the local judges, though sworn to uphold the Fugitive Slave Act, were known as willing to "feed the trembling sable fugitive, hide him from his pursuers, and bid him Godspeed on his journey toward the North Star."[15]

Because of Franklin County's well-known resistance to the Fugitive Slave Act, it must have seemed that other antislavery fugitives could find shelter there as well. On the other hand, Chambersburg was such an obvious destination that it was certain to be among the first places any bounty hunters would search for the Harper's Ferry escapees. As one citizen observed, it was clearly "the most inviting refuge for the fleeing insurrectionist."[16] And, in fact, reward notices for Cook were circulated in Chambersburg almost immediately following the raid.

It might therefore have made more sense to travel more sharply northwest toward Ohio, steering clear of the most obvious route, but Cook's wife and child were in Chambersburg, and he was determined to go there. Owen Brown objected to Cook's proposal, worrying that it crossed far too many valleys and roads. He knew what he was talking about.

Unlike the others, Owen had once before made the trip between the Maryland farmhouse and Chambersburg on foot. The previous August, Owen had accompanied his father to Chambersburg for a meeting with Frederick Douglass. Although Douglass had refused to join the Harper's Ferry conspiracy, his factotum Shields Green accepted the invitation. Green was an escaped slave from South Carolina who had lived for a time at Douglass's home in Rochester, and he was willing to return to slave country for the purpose of insurrection. According to Douglass, Green declined the option of returning safely to upstate New York, saying, "I b'l'eve I'll go down wid de old man."[17] Transporting a fugitive slave from Pennsylvania through Maryland, however, was not a simple endeavor, and Brown feared attracting attention by bringing black men to his headquarters in daylight. Brown therefore entrusted his son Owen with the job of bringing Green to the Maryland farm in secrecy, with instructions to travel only at night.

Owen Brown and Shields Green began the trip in a covered wagon, but they were forced to abandon it south of Hagerstown when they were confronted by a band of potential slave catchers. From that point, Owen and Green made their way by foot, fording rivers and climbing mountains for several days and nights. Owen's later account of the journey included some highly improbable episodes. He said that he tumbled forty feet down a hillside while maintaining his grip on a jug of lemonade. Even more implausibly, he claimed to have built a make-shift raft, which he then pushed across a deep river, plunging himself into the water but nonetheless keeping the frightened Green perfectly dry.[18] There is no doubt, however, that Owen had successfully guided Green to the safety of the farmhouse, where he was greeted with warm cheers.

Despite Owen's experience, the others all deferred to Cook. He was the only married man in the group, and they were sympathetic to his hope of finding his family. Owen, too, finally consented to head toward Chambersburg rather than strike off on his own. At age thirty-five he was the oldest man in the party, and he realistically considered himself the best woodsman among them. He firmly believed that his friends could not survive without his constant supervision.

Like so many memoirists, Owen Brown was the hero of his own story. He was the oldest of Brown's sons to join the Harper's Ferry raid—his elder brothers, John, Jr., and Jason, had refused to participate because they were "sick of fighting and trouble" after their experiences in Kansas—and he therefore felt a special responsibility to his father. Owen himself suffered "nervous fever" following his involvement in the Pottawatomie massacre, but he resolved his guilt by rededicating himself to the antislavery cause. He eventually became the staunchest defender of the Harper's Ferry plan, both within the family and among outsiders, and he often served as a bridge between the old commander and "the hesitant young men" who made up the tiny army. As the only member of the Brown family who survived the insurrection, he would spend the next three decades dwelling in the heroic past. He devoted the rest of his life to safeguarding John Brown's legend—and inciden-tally attempting to develop his own.[19]

Owen often marked his belongings with the initials O. X., explaining that was easier to write than O. B. According to Anne Brown, John Cook used to tease Owen about his quirky signature, telling everyone at the Maryland farm "that O. X. stood for Oxentricity, his proper name it ought to be."[20] The nickname was humorous, but the description was accurate. Owen had his share of odd habits—including shabby dress and celibacy—that must have seemed inexplicable to Cook. Nonetheless, the two men got along well, perhaps because the temperaments complemented one another. Owen was reticent and taciturn, and Cook was brash and outgoing. Owen shied away from female company, which was the exact opposite of Cook's approach. And unlike many other men, Owen never seems to have been jealous of Cook's successful romances.

According to his no doubt exaggerated account, Owen's mature guidance and unfailing good judgment proved essential to everyone's survival. He sometimes had to restrain Cook and Tidd from continuing their feud, or from hunting game within earshot of roving posses. He had to prevent his comrades from lighting fires at night, and he had to caution everyone to remain still and hidden during the daytime. Despite his lame arm, he claimed to have carried Merriam on his back when the others were willing to leave him behind, and he once carried Cook across a wide creek while also shouldering "two bundles, four guns, revolvers, and ammunition." He seldom complained about the burdens of leadership, although he did grow weary of keeping his eyes fixed on the North Star. "Looking up in that way night after night," he said, "guiding the party, got to be very painful indeed." Owen accomplished all of that during weeks on the run, while also mending the men's clothes and boots, preparing their meals, and occasionally stealing chickens, milk, and apples. Regarding the latter, he later explained, "I am not in the habit of stealing . . . but antislavery men would have been glad to give what little we needed to the cause, and proslavery men certainly owed it that much."[21]

Owen's misgivings about the trip to Chambersburg proved to be well founded. As he had warned his friends, the route took them through the Cumberland Valley, where they had to cross the well-traveled and much-patrolled road between Hagerstown and Baltimore. After nearly a week of travel—they did not know the precise date as they had "no time-piece in the party" and had lost track of the days—they approached the perilous gap in the mountains, only to see that "horsemen were scampering hither and thither on the highways, and the whole country, it seemed, was under arms." They heard the constant baying of bloodhounds, and they saw the alarm fires of the bounty hunters. As Owen observed, "there was nothing like safety for us till we should get across that pike." Their first forays failed because the constant presence of armed men and dogs stopped the fugitives from getting anywhere near the road. Finally, at about midnight, they found a seemingly deserted stretch of the pike and decided to make a dash for it. Fearing for their lives if caught, they somehow managed to reach the hills on the other side, eventually crossing into Pennsylvania. "Nothing but the excitement of this fact enabled some of us—especially Merriam—to accomplish what we did that night," Owen later said.[22]

Entering Pennsylvania did not bring safety. The terrain was dangerous and so were many of the people. Cook tripped on the first night after crossing the state line, falling down a steep, rocky gorge. Owen heard something "snap when he fell, and thought it was his leg," but it turned out to be only the limb of a tree. Cook was severely bruised, and he limped badly for days afterward. More treacherous than the ravines, however, were the proslavery citizens of Pennsylvania's South Mountain region, many of whom supplemented their incomes by hunting fugitive slaves. More than a few of them would later fight for the Confederacy, and two of them would soon come face-to-face with John Cook.

Finally, after hiking more than one hundred miles across mountain trails, the party approached within fifteen miles of Chambersburg.[23] Tidd and Owen Brown decided to scout ahead for the best route through the next valley, while the still-injured Cook remained behind with Merriam and Coppoc, hiding in the thick woods. Tidd and Owen advanced about a mile and half when they saw a farmhouse in the distance. Sneaking to within two hundred yards of the homestead, they were overcome by "the smell of something like doughnuts cooking." Tidd had remained stoic through the long days and nights of hunger and exhaustion, but now the smell of distant cooking made him stagger. He "vowed he wouldn't go a step farther without food," and he told Owen that he was going to head for the farmhouse. "It is just as well to expose ourselves one way as another," he said.

Owen was certain that the bedraggled Tidd would immediately be suspected as a Harper's Ferry fugitive, and that the stolid lumberjack would never be able to bluff his way out of trouble if he were questioned about his identity. Sending Tidd to the farm would be tantamount to surrender. Owen therefore pleaded with him to return to the others, promising to devise a plan to obtain some food. Back at camp, everyone agreed—despite Owen's lingering reservations about the wisdom of the entire venture—that Cook should be the one to go after provisions. After all, "he could wield the glibbest tongue, and tell the best story."[24]

※　❈　※

John Cook was almost glib enough. He had always been able to make friends with strangers—as he had so easily during his year as a spy in Harper's Ferry—and the farm family in the valley proved no exception. They readily accepted Cook's story that he was a member of a hunting party that had gotten lost in the hills, and they invited him to stay for an early afternoon meal. The splendid visit, as Cook put it, lasted several hours, and he afterward returned to his friends bearing "a couple of loaves of bread . . . some good boiled beef, and a pie" that he had purchased at the farm. The half-starved fugitives feasted on the supplies, enjoying their first real meal in over a week. Owen Brown, however, was apprehensive that Cook's successful foraging expedition would only encourage greater risk taking in the future.

Owen soon had more to worry about. Perhaps giddy on a full stomach, Cook revealed that he was carrying Lafayette's "old-fashioned, one-barrel" pistol, which he had stolen from Lewis Washington and surreptitiously withheld from John Brown. He began firing the gun at random in what he claimed was an effort to carry out "the story of our being hunters." For Tidd, that was almost the final straw. He had been upset from the start by Cook's impulsiveness, and he was now enraged at the sheer foolishness of attracting attention with unnecessary gunfire. The farm family had never questioned the existence of a hunting party, so there was no reason to keep up any pretense, and nothing good could happen if anyone else decided to investigate Cook's gunshots. Tidd brusquely demanded a stop to the firing, but Cook refused, saying "he knew what he was doing and would not take orders." The quarrel became nasty as the two strong-willed men exchanged increasingly hostile threats and recriminations. Fearing that a fistfight—or even a gunfight—would break out, Owen rushed to get between them. With Coppoc's assistance, and with Merriam lying helplessly on the ground, he finally separated the two belligerents, but only for the time being. Tension simmered between Cook and Tidd, and Owen feared that "one or both of them would . . . have been killed in this feud" if it continued to boil.

Things were not much better the next day, October 26, as the group continued toward Chambersburg. Owen was in a hurry to get as far as possible from the place where the ill-advised gunfire had occurred, and he was therefore willing to risk traveling by daylight. All through the morning, Cook continued to complain about Tidd, reviving the quarrel and making renewed threats against his companion. In calmer moments, Cook expressed happiness about his "prospective meeting with his wife and boy in Chambersburg," but his anger at Tidd was never far from the surface. Owen was not sure which of Cook's moods was more dangerous. The bickering with Tidd threatened the group's fragile cohesion, but any attempt to visit Cook's family was likely to draw the attention of bounty hunters. Owen presciently warned Cook that "his imprudence would be so great that he would never see his wife and child again," but there was really nothing he could do to improve the increasingly parlous situation.[25]

At mid-afternoon the party stopped to rest by a clear spring. Remembering the previous day's meal, Coppoc volunteered to go on a search for more provisions and the others readily agreed. Owen again failed to dissuade them. Realizing that the frail Coppoc was poorly suited to the task, Owen said that "Cook was the man most fitted to the mission." Cook had no objection, eager as he was to get away from Tidd. Taking several dollars from Owen, and carrying only a revolver hidden in his waistband, Cook departed from the group "between three and four o'clock in the afternoon."

The hungry fugitives expected Cook to come back in a few hours, as he had the day before, but he had not yet returned by dusk. They waited until dark, and then "till nine o'clock, till midnight, and still he did not come." Hoping that Cook had only gotten lost, they "lingered about, calling and watching for him till at least two o'clock in the morning," before accepting the reality that Cook would not be returning. Now fearful for their own safety, the men broke camp in the middle of the night. Tidd gathered up a few of Cook's belongings, including Lafayette's single shot pistol. Owen considered such sentimentality a little odd on the part of the missing man's "mortal enemy," but he surmised that it might have been Tidd's way of making amends—retrieving a small reminder of Cook out of remorse for their now pointless squabbles. But the rest of Cook's gear—and more—had to be abandoned. Owen Brown's later bragging notwithstanding, the loss of Cook left the group with only one fully able-bodied man. Neither Coppoc nor Merriam was strong enough to handle an extra load, and there was a limit to how much Tidd could carry. Reluctantly, the fugitives hid some of their heaviest supplies, including rifles and ammunition, and continued their trek northward.[26]

❖ ✸ ❖

Cook was confident, brave, and capable—he was "the quickest and best shot with a pistol" that Owen Brown had ever seen—and he was no doubt unafraid when he walked down the mountainside in search of food. He was certain that he could talk himself out of any trouble that arose, and if need be he could also shoot his way out of a tough spot. Unfortunately for him, Cook "walked into the hands of the only man in Franklin County who combined with the courage and skill the purpose to capture him."[27]

There were two Logan brothers, Daniel and Hugh, living in southern Franklin County between Chambersburg and the Maryland border. The Logans were "shrewd, quiet, resolute men, both strongly Southern in their sympathies . . . and both trained in the summary rendition of fugitive slaves without process of law." They had ample opportunities to ply their trade, as it was "common for slaves to escape from Maryland and Virginia into the South Mountain" district, which had thus become "the favorite retreat of the fugitive slave." Rather than form their own hunting parties, aggrieved slave owners would circulate handbills describing the fugitives and offering rewards for their capture and return. The Logan brothers were able to make a solid living tracking runaways, and they were not always scrupulous about statutory requirements. "Many fleeing sons of bondage were arrested by them and quietly returned to their masters," with no regard paid to the formalities of either a warrant or a hearing.

Daniel Logan was the younger and more intelligent of the two brothers. He was exceptionally "silent, cunning, tireless, and resolute," and he was known for his size and his strength. Daniel was also a "born detective" who seldom failed in his work. Although he reveled in winning his "crude contests with fugitive slaves," he was a mercenary at heart with no deep principles on the subject. Unlike his older brother, who would fight for the Confederacy in the Civil War, Daniel Logan "did not believe that either slavery or freedom was worth dying for." He was, however, always ready to collect the bounty on a fugitive or an occasional outlaw, whether his quarry was black or white.[28] It was Cook's miserable luck to walk from the forest into an open field in the borough of Mont Alto, where Daniel Logan was standing with a group of iron workers from the nearby forge.

Emerging from a thicket, Cook was ready with the practiced story that he was a lost hunter in search of provisions. He should have known better than to step into the middle of a work party, but he had already hiked several miles and he did not want to return to his friends without food. He was probably also reluctant to face Tidd empty-handed. With typical nerve and in this instance true carelessness, Cook approached the laborers and asked where he could "replenish his stock of bread and bacon."

Daniel Logan, however, was not as naïve as had been the farmers the previous afternoon. "It had been known for some days . . . that Captain Cook was at large . . . and a minute description of his person had been published" far and wide. The bounty hunters of the Cumberland Valley were therefore on the constant lookout, anticipating that Cook would retreat in their direction and turn up somewhere in their hills. They intended to be ready for him. According to the handbills, Cook was "a man of desperate courage [and] a rare expert in the use of pistol and rifle; and his capture alive was not expected." But Logan was not intimidated. Keenly aware of the value of the Harper's Ferry fugitives, he was always well-informed and fearless at his work. As he watched the ragged man step out of the woods, Logan whispered to Cleggett Fitzhugh, the manager of the iron works, "That's Captain Cook; we must arrest him; the reward is $1000."

Slyly, Logan invited Cook to accompany him to a nearby—though actually nonexistent—store for supplies. That was Cook's last opportunity to run for his life, but Logan had "disarmed suspicion . . . by his well-affected hospitality," and Cook did not realize that he was being flanked by the two bounty hunters. With Logan and Fitzhugh on either side of him, the unsuspecting Cook began to walk toward town, only to be roughly seized by the arms "and held . . . as in a vice," making it impossible for him to reach his pistol. He probably still could have broken free from either one of his captors alone, but it was "one small, starved man against two strong mountaineers," and he could not escape from both. After a brief and hopeless struggle, the smaller Cook was over-

powered. "Why do you arrest me?" he asked, both fearing and expecting the answer. "Because you are Captain Cook," said Logan, to which
the despondent prisoner had no ready reply.[29]

Cook was taken to Fitzhugh's nearby home, where he was "stripped
of his weapons" and given a cold meal. A search of the captive's person
turned up several incriminating documents, including a printed commission, marked number four, as a captain under Brown's "Provisional
Government" that left no doubt about his identity:

HEAD QUARTERS—WAR DEPARTMENT
Near Harpers Ferry, Md
Whereas: John E. Cook has been nominated a captain in the
Army established under the provisional government. Now, There-
fore, in pursuance of the authority vested in us by said Constitu-
tion, we do hereby appoint and commission said John E. Cook,
captain.
Given at the office of the Secretary of War, this day, October 15th,
1859.
John Brown, Commander in Chief
J.H. Kagi, Secretary of War

The bounty hunters also found two receipts in Cook's pocket book,
both bearing his signature in a "bold, legible hand." Equally damning,
although more circumstantial, they recovered a small piece of parch-
ment with a string tied on one end, with the handwritten inscription:

One of a pair of pistols presented by Gen. Lafayette to Gen. Washington, and worn by Gen. W. during the Revolution—descended
to Judge Washington, and by him bequeathed to George C. Washington, and by him to Lewis W. Washington, 1854.[30]

That was not quite the smoking gun itself, which Cook had left in a car-
petbag on the mountain, but it was certainly enough evidence to claim
Governor Wise's reward.

Cook was bundled into Fitzhugh's open buggy for the trip to Chambersburg. Logan did not bother to tie his prisoner's hands, informing him instead that he would be shot if he attempted to escape. Cook "did not need an extended acquaintance with his captor to assure him[self] that what he threatened he would certainly perform."

It was a twelve-mile ride to Chambersburg, which gave Cook ample time to try to talk his way out of the jam. He engaged his captors in constant conversation, and at one point Logan remarked that he was interested only in "the reward or its equivalent." That broad hint gave Cook hope, as he realized that he might be able to negotiate his way to freedom.

"You will get a reward of one thousand dollars for me, you say?" asked Cook.

"Yes, a thousand dollars."

"They will hang me in Virginia, won't they?"

"Yes, they will hang you," replied Logan unemotionally.

"Do you want to have me hung?" asked Cook, searching for a way out of his predicament.

"No," said Logan. It was strictly a business proposition for him, and he was quite open to alternatives.

"Then you want only the reward?"

"Yes, that's all."

Cook jumped at the opportunity to ransom his life. He came from a well-to-do family, and two of his sisters had married even more affluent men, one of whom had recently been elected governor of Indiana. He told Logan that $1,000, or even more, would not be hard to raise, if only he could get in touch with his brothers-in-law in Indiana and New York. Logan was wary of being duped, naturally distrusting Cook's story "of high dignitaries and large fortunes." He was unwilling to release the prisoner on his word, and he insisted on some "practical way to make Cook's credit good enough" to trust. After some discussion, Logan proposed to contact Colonel Alexander McClure, "a Republican and law-yer," to act as Cook's counsel and to secure the deal. Logan offered to take Cook directly to McClure's office "without revealing his identity to any others." Then, if McClure guaranteed payment of the ransom, Logan would simply walk away and leave Cook to go free.[31]

❧ FIVE ❧
Jailed

Although he was only thirty-one years old, Colonel Alexander Kelly McClure was already one of the most prominent antislavery men in Franklin County and probably the person most willing and able to make the needed arrangements for John Cook. Originally a Whig activist, McClure had been awarded an honorary military title when he served on the staff of William Johnson, the first Whig governor of Pennsylvania. He was later appointed a deputy federal marshal by Millard Fillmore, the last Whig president of the United States. Like many northern Whigs, McClure had opposed the Compromise of 1850 with its enhanced Fugitive Slave Act. The 1851 Christiana slave rebellion near Philadelphia—in which a Maryland slave owner was killed while attempting to capture several runaways—convinced McClure that the recovery of fugitive slaves was morally repugnant in the North, and that the slavery issue would eventually "either disrupt the Union or involve the country in fraternal war." McClure was further outraged by the Kansas-Nebraska Act of 1854, which threatened to extend slavery into previously free territory. The slave power, he believed, had become "violently aggressive," and he identified strongly with the free-state men who resisted the Missouri invaders. As a lawyer, he was perhaps most deeply offended by the *Dred Scott* decision of 1857, in which the United States Supreme Court observed that a black man had "no rights which the white man was bound to respect." That infamous decision, he believed, so advanced the slave power that it "practically made freedom sectional and bondage national." In consequence, that "deepened and intensified the convictions of the North, and compelled them [*sic*] to gird their loins and be prepared for the inevitable conflict."[1]

When the Whig Party collapsed over the issue of slavery, McClure became one of the organizers of the Pennsylvania Republican Party, motivated by "the intense resentment of the people of the North against the encroachments of slavery." He served as a delegate to the Republicans' first national convention in 1856, and the following year, at the age of twenty-nine, McClure was elected to the Pennsylvania House of Representatives from a district that had long been held by the Democrats. He was reelected twice to the state house and then to the state senate in 1859. He was also the owner and editor of the *Franklin Repository and Transcript*, one of the most influential newspapers in the region, which he used as a platform to attack slavery (and to engage in a running debate with the proslavery *Democratic Valley Spirit*).[2]

McClure would later play an important role in Republican Party and national politics. As a delegate to the 1860 Republican Convention in Chicago, he was instrumental in swinging Pennsylvania's votes away from favorite son Simon Cameron (whom McClure considered intolerably corrupt) in favor of Abraham Lincoln. That fall, he campaigned vigorously for Lincoln and helped the Republicans carry the crucial Keystone State while winning reelection himself as a state senator. At the outbreak of the Civil War, McClure became the chairman of the Pennsylvania senate's Committee on Military Affairs, and he helped to organize a conference of the "Loyal War Governors of the North" at a time when Lincoln needed all the political support he could muster. Lincoln later appointed McClure an assistant adjutant general, in which capacity he supervised the draft in Pennsylvania and enlisted seventeen regiments for the Union Army—more than any other single recruiter, according to McClure. He remained in Chambersburg during most of the war, but he did not escape the hostilities. Confederate troops occupied Chambersburg three times, taking McClure prisoner in 1863, at which time he briefly met with Robert E. Lee. In 1864, during the third occupation, the rebels targeted McClure's estate for destruction before sacking and burning the entire town.[3]

In late October 1859, however, McClure was still primarily a local figure and the lawyer to whom Chambersburg abolitionists frequently turned for assistance. Only a few weeks earlier he had drawn up a will for Francis Merriam—then on the penultimate leg of his journey to Harper's Ferry and, of course, staying at Mary Ritner's boardinghouse—in which the wealthy young man devised the bulk of his substantial estate to the Anti-Slavery Society of Massachusetts.

The selection of Merriam's attorney was likely dictated by John Brown himself. Brown usually did his own reconnoitering and he had often visited Chambersburg in the summer and fall of 1859, having chosen the town as the staging point and matériel depot for his invasion of the South. Brown was traveling incognito, under the name of Isaac Smith, on the pretense that he was a businessman investigating mineral deposits in Maryland, which gave him plenty of opportunity to learn about members of the Chambersburg bar. As an avid newspaper reader, Brown could not have missed the many stridently antislavery articles that had appeared in McClure's *Franklin Repository* in 1859, including several that praised the Oberlin fugitive slave rescue, in which scores of white and black Oberliners had forcibly intervened to release a captured runaway from slave catchers. Brown himself had closely followed the rescuers' indictment and trial in Cleveland the previous spring, visiting several of them in jail and ultimately recruiting two of their number—John Copeland and Lewis Sheridan Leary—to join his army. Thus it would not have escaped Brown's notice that the *Franklin Repository* took a strong side "in this war now waging for freedom [against] the slave power" and condemned slave hunting as "the highest crime known in barbarous or civilized, in savage or Christian society."[4]

McClure later realized that he had, in fact, seen Brown "nearly every day for several weeks in the crowd that usually assembled about the post office before the arrival of the evening mail," and that he had spoken with Brown several times as they passed on the street. The two men might once have been in the same room, attending Frederick Douglass's public address in late August. Brown and Douglass had arranged a secret meeting at an abandoned quarry outside Chambersburg, where Brown made one final attempt to persuade Douglass to join the raid. Douglass declined, however, warning Brown that he would be walking into a "perfect steel-trap" from which he would never get out alive. As cover for his presence in Chambersburg—which could hardly be concealed, given his fame as the nation's leading black abolitionist—Douglass also arranged to present a lecture at the town hall. An unsigned article in the *Franklin Repository* reported quite favorably on Douglass's speech, noting that his theme was "the wrongs of race" which he addressed "in a style which would have been creditable to many, very many of our white orators." The editorialist was probably Alexander McClure, and it is entirely possible that Brown was quietly standing in the back of the hall. In any case, Brown would not have missed the local newspaper articles about Douglass, who was his good friend and almost co-conspirator. He had to be pleased by the favorable treatment that Douglass received in the *Repository*, especially in comparison to the condescending and offensive remarks published in the proslavery *Valley Spirit*.[5] And it was widely known in Chambersburg that McClure had either written or approved of the *Repository*'s report.

Merriam was shepherded to McClure's office by John Kagi, who was using his usual pseudonym, John Henry (or J. Henrie). Kagi was evidently under orders not to let Merriam out of his sight; the two men shared a room at Ritner's, registered under Kagi's phony name, and they stayed so closely together that witnesses later confused their descriptions. Mentally challenged as he was, Merriam's role in the insurrection was above all else as a financier, and it was up to Kagi to ensure that Merriam's funds were appropriately directed. Thus Kagi rather pointedly refused McClure's request to witness the will after Merriam had executed it, insisting that both witnesses (two were required under Pennsylvania law) had to be from Chambersburg.[6] Kagi and Brown evidently recognized that none of their comrades were likely to pass that way again soon, in either life or death, and they obviously wanted to ensure that young Merriam's assets would be put to the right use.

Although Merriam did not fully comprehend the situation, his hatred of slavery was profound and sincere. Little realizing how much danger he was about to face, and why he suddenly needed a will, he told McClure only that he was a traveler from Boston who was going on a journey to the South. It was a questionable story that a curious lawyer might not have swallowed at the time—why would a wealthy Bostonian impulsively decide to write a will in remote Chambersburg?—but McClure convinced himself there was nothing in Merriam's request "to indicate anything at all out of the ordinary." Other Chambersburg citizens were in fact suspicious of Merriam, who made constant use of the telegraph office and sent one message for the astronomical fee of six dollars. Even so, McClure deliberately chose not to make any "inquiry into the plans or purposes of the testator."[7]

It was Logan who proposed involving McClure in the negotiations for Cook's freedom, although the bounty hunter was doubtless unaware of the previous contact between the lawyer and the Harper's Ferry raiders. Cook might possibly have known about Merriam's will, depending on how much he had learned about Brown's dealings with the abolitionist community in Chambersburg. But even well apart from his mysterious probate client, McClure was in every way the obvious conduit to Cook's friends or allies in the outside world.

※　❂　※

Logan and Cook arrived in Chambersburg slightly before sunset on October 26, both men eager to locate McClure and to consummate their arrangement. Without revealing his purpose, Logan took a room at a

local hotel and sent a messenger to McClure's office. The lawyer, however, could not be found. McClure had chosen that afternoon to walk to
the outskirts of Chambersburg to inspect some real estate in which he
was interested. On his way back to town, he stopped at a small store to
chat with friends about local politics.

Upon learning that McClure's office was empty, Logan had messengers search the town, looking in every place where the lawyer was
known to stroll in the evening, but without success. As McClure later
explained he was enjoying the end of the day in "an out-of-the-way
place, and among the last that would be thought of in deciding to look
for me."[8]

Logan grew anxious as darkness fell. His ongoing search for McClure
had drawn attention—as does anything unusual in a small town—and
he feared "the discovery or suspicion of the identity of his prisoner."
Logan finally decided that he had waited long enough, and rather than
risk having his furtive deal exposed, he figured that he was better off
simply collecting the reward. He sent for a constable and started with
his prisoner for the office of Justice of the Peace Samuel Reisher to
deliver Cook to the custody of the law.

The courthouse was in the center of Chambersburg, several blocks
from the hotel. As Logan and Fitzhugh marched their prisoner down the
street, they could not help attracting far more notice than they wanted.
By the time they arrived at the courthouse, a crowd had gathered, following the captors and captive all the way to the building's door. The
small courtroom quickly filled, as Logan and Fitzhugh apprised Judge
Reisher of the situation. Reisher then convened an impromptu hearing,
which he began by admonishing Cook that "he was not obliged to say
anything which would criminate himself."

The prisoner wisely replied that he chose "to remain quiet, and
not answer any questions," but his silence had come far too late to
do himself any good. He had already spoken freely to the two bounty
hunters, both of whom were now ready to deliver him up and collect

their reward from the Commonwealth of Virginia. The judge turned first to Fitzhugh, who testified about the arrest, including the prisoner's attempts to break free when he was recognized as Captain Cook. Fitzhugh also testified to Logan's conversation with Cook—including the proposed bribe, which he characterized as a feigned act of friendship that had been intended only to elicit an admission that they had the right man. Logan told the same story, although he appeared shamefaced when he explained that his offer to let the prisoner "skeet" had been a successful ruse. He quickly added that Cook had freely acknowledged his identity during the conversation and confessed having been at Harper's Ferry. To prove his point, Logan produced the documents he had seized from Cook, including the printed commission signed by John Brown.[9]

By then McClure had arrived back in town. As he was walking homeward following his leisurely afternoon in the country, he noticed the commotion outside the courthouse. He was surprised to learn that one of the Harper's Ferry fugitives was inside, and he immediately pressed his way into the building. Although the room was crowded, McClure had no difficulty approaching the bench. He was a stout man of considerable physical presence—having grown up on a farm, he had the physique of a laborer—and his broad face and jutting chin made him instantly recognizable. Nor had McClure ever hesitated to assert himself. His relentless feud with the proslavery *Valley Spirit* had been conducted in the sharpest terms. McClure accused his adversaries of "mingled imbecility and malice" and other assorted foul deeds and dishonest, unscrupulous, and malignant representations—and then he sued them for libel.[10] Thus, it was completely in character when he barged to the front of the room and interrupted Logan's testimony with an immediate objection.

Although one observer believed that McClure had spoken disrespectfully to the witness, Logan actually seemed relieved to see the lawyer. He had clearly been embarrassed by his admitted betrayal of his prisoner, and he apparently wanted to make at least a show of good faith.

"My God, Colonel McClure! Where have you been?" exclaimed Logan. "I have been hunting you for more than an hour. That's Captain Cook, and I had agreed to bring him to you."

McClure had already realized the gravity of the situation. He signaled to the justice of the peace, who then turned to Cook. "Here's your counsel now," said the judge, although the crucial evidence had already been received.

It had been Cook's bad luck to stumble across Logan in the Mont Alto field, and even worse luck that McClure had tarried in the countryside that very afternoon rather than keep his usual business hours. If McClure had gotten back to his office even thirty minutes earlier he might have been able to negotiate Cook's immediate freedom. But now, standing in the courthouse, in the presence of a judge and surrounded by gawking townsfolk, it was obviously far too late to present a defense, much less to negotiate with Logan for a payoff. As a lawyer, however, McClure was ready to do what he could for his new, and desperate, client. He took Cook into a corner, where they could have at least a brief private conversation. "I am Cook," said the prisoner, "there is no use denying it." "I had expected to meet you at your office and escape this misfortune," he added. "What's to be done?"

That was a good question, but McClure did not have a good answer. Escape might have been a possibility under other circumstances. Justice Reisher had once declined to serve as a federal fugitive slave commissioner, and he had no stomach for turning prisoners over to Virginia, whether they were white or black. He "would have been quite content had Cook been able to bounce through the window and escape," but that could not be done in front of so many witnesses. Nor was any legal defense available, given that Cook's identity had already been established by two witnesses and the incontrovertible documents. McClure therefore turned to the court and said, "There is no dispute as to the identity of the prisoner: a hearing is needless. Let him be committed and await the demand for his rendition."[11]

❊ ◉ ❊

It might have seemed that McClure had capitulated on behalf of his client, but in fact he had a plan, or at least the beginning of one. It was already nighttime, and no extradition warrant could arrive that day from Virginia. It therefore might still be possible to arrange an escape for Cook, assuming that the other local authorities were as potentially accommodating as Judge Reisher.

McClure took leave of the court and accompanied his client and the constable to the town jail, where Cook was handed over to Franklin County sheriff Jacob Brown. Like Judge Reisher, Sheriff Brown was ready to allow Cook's escape, but he first wanted reassurance that no adverse consequences would follow. As McClure later put it, Brown did not conceal "his willingness to let Cook get away if it could be done without official responsibility for the escape; and this he was more than willing to leave me to decide." Sheriff Brown was in a tricky position. He had failed to win reelection on October 11, and his term was going to expire in a matter of weeks. His electoral chances had no doubt been damaged by the fact that there had been six escapes on his watch, leading the public to conclude that there was "no security in the jail." Franklin County had recently been compelled to spend a considerable amount of money remodeling the building to provide better security.[12] Even for a lame duck, an escape on the prisoner's first night in custody would have been both personally embarrassing and politically deadly.

The sheriff's antislavery sympathies also created a uniquely awkward dilemma for McClure, who counted the sheriff among his clients. McClure believed that Sheriff Brown "was more than ready to obey any instructions I might give him to facilitate Cook's escape without legal responsibility for the act," but he still found himself "in the rather delicate position of being counsel for a prisoner whose escape I wanted to effect, and at the same time . . . counsel for the sheriff whose duty it was to prevent him from escaping."[13] McClure's personal ethics apparently permitted him to coordinate a jailbreak in behalf of a noble cause. He had long since chosen his side in the "irrepressible conflict" and had concluded that sending fugitives to the South was a "dead letter" in which he would not participate. But his sense of professional responsibility would not allow him simultaneously to betray another client.

McClure was at best a lawyer of modest ability. He had been admitted to the bar just three years earlier, and he had practiced only intermittently with middling success. He had won a few verdicts, including an acquittal in a murder prosecution in which he was one of three defense counsel, but he had also failed badly in other cases when working alone. McClure's newspaper had predictably praised his eloquence in court, but in truth he was a much better journalist than an attorney, and he would eventually leave law practice in order to devote himself to politics and publishing. Still, McClure understood that he was bound by the lawyer's oath, sworn to by every attorney in Pennsylvania, "to behave himself in the office of attorney according to the best of his learning and ability, and with all good fidelity, as well to the court as to the client."[14]

There was no easy way for McClure to resolve the incompatible demands of abolitionism and professionalism or to decide which client's interests should come first. Instead of making an immediate decision, he asked to be left alone in the cell with Cook, hoping to arrive at a solution to the problem. Lawyer and client spoke for quite a while. Despite Cook's well-earned reputation as a "reckless desperado," McClure found him to be surprisingly restrained. Cook was understandably nervous and impatient, speaking in "quick impulsive sentences" and constantly "repeating that he must escape from prison."

McClure patiently reminded Cook that he could not simply walk out of jail, and cautioned him that "his escape that night, under any circumstances, would be specially dangerous to himself and dangerous to the sheriff." Cook did not share McClure's concern about Sheriff Brown, but he found it more convincing that the jail would be under especially heavy watch on his first night in custody. In any case, McClure was un-

willing to provide any assistance that night, reasoning that "my presence with him in the jail until a late hour and my professional relations
as counsel of the sheriff forbade any needless haste."[15]

There would be time enough, McClure believed, to wait for the right
moment. Cook would be safe in the Chambersburg jail until a formal extradition request arrived from Virginia, and it did not seem as though
that could happen any time soon. McClure "carefully considered every
possible method of getting a requisition for him from Richmond" and
concluded that even if news of Cook's arrest "was telegraphed to Richmond that evening, a requisition by mail or special messenger could
not possibly reach Chambersburg the next day or night." With that
in mind, the lawyer and client decided that the escape should be postponed for a day, so as not to occur immediately following their meeting.
Perhaps the delay would provide only plausible deniability, but that
would still be safer—for both McClure and the sheriff—than having
Cook escape only hours after arriving. McClure assured the frightened
prisoner "that the next night he should have the necessary instructions and facilities to regain his liberty," and he meant what he said.
By the end of the evening, McClure had recruited two accomplices "who
took upon themselves the work of ascertaining just where and by what
means Cook could best break out of the old jail." According to McClure,
the two nameless plotters did their work well. They visited the builder
who was responsible for the recent security remodeling and obtained
"minute instructions as to the best method of making the escape." Mc-
Clure fully expected that Cook would be "following the North Star" by
the end of the next day.

Once the escape plans were confirmed, McClure returned to the jail
for an extended interview with Cook. There was no legal strategy or
testimony to prepare, but the lawyer was fascinated by his client and
wanted to learn as much as possible about the man who engaged in such
daring antislavery exploits. The ever-talkative Cook was more than
ready to oblige. Now confident that he would regain his freedom, Cook
"threw off the cloud of despair that shadowed him in the early part of

the evening" and surprised McClure "with the eloquence and elegance of his conversation." The two educated men discussed poetry and painting and the nature of "the beautiful world." McClure soon forgot that they were sitting in a chilly prison cell and found himself imagining that they were in "the library of some romantic lover of literature and the fine arts." McClure later recalled that Cook was "thoroughly poetic in taste and temperament, with a jarring mixture of wild, romantic love of the heroic."[16]

It was the wild and romantic Cook, far more than the intellectual, who most intrigued McClure. Cook recounted "his hairbreadth escapes in Kansas [and] the price set upon his head." In McClure's eyes, "his whole soul seemed to be absorbed in avenging the Kansas slavery crusades by revolutionary emancipation in the slave states." McClure's several memoirs did not include the details of Cook's stories about his exploits in Kansas, which the prisoner probably embellished to impress his lawyer. Perhaps Cook told of his narrow escape from the Kickapoo Rangers or repeated the improbable claim that he had killed five men, although neither of those incidents would seem to justify Cook's perpetual quest for revenge. In fact, there is only one semi-documented incidence of actual armed combat between Cook and proslavery forces. Shortly after Cook had arrived in Kansas, he and two other free-staters were riding on a routine patrol when they were ambushed by Missouri ruffians. One of Cook's comrades was killed by a shot through the forehead, and the bushwhackers escaped when Cook's rifle misfired. Cook was said to have exacted a terrible—although never specified—revenge for the death of his friend. Whatever the truth of those claims, or any others he made, Cook pledged to McClure that he would continue the war against slavery after his release, vowing that "the battle must be fought to the bitter end; and we must triumph, or God is not just." That was apparently enough for McClure.[17]

To a modern reader, there seems to have been something almost erotic about McClure's encounter with Cook. In one account, the lawyer described his client's "long, silken, blonde hair [that] curled carelessly about his neck," and his "large, soft eyes" that were "gentle in expression as a woman's," while noting that Cook's "slightly bronzed complexion . . . would have well befitted the gentler sex." Another time, McClure called Cook "keenly emotional" and praised his "skin as soft as a woman's, and his deep blue eyes and wealth of blond hair."[18] But perhaps that was nothing more than the florid styling of a nineteenth-century memoirist.

Whatever the nature of their rapport, McClure's feelings toward Cook were complex. The lawyer was appalled by the irrational "desperation of the Virginia insurgent." He attempted to convince his client of the "utter madness of attempting such a revolution," and he was distressed when Cook "rejected all law and logic and believed only in his cause." Although he was impressed by Cook's sense of duty and devotion, McClure could not accept a claim of justice "that had the sanction of a higher law than that of man." On the one hand, McClure rebuked Cook as "a wild fanatic on the slavery question [who] regarded any and every means to precipitate emancipation as justified by the end." On the other hand, McClure was willing himself to break the law—to put the end before the means—by facilitating Cook's escape, and this with full knowledge that Cook was willing "to kill or to desolate homes with worse than death by the brutal fury of slave insurrection."

Ultimately, McClure the abolitionist was most deeply moved by Cook's genuine readiness to die for the cause of freedom, even though McClure the attorney could not justify Cook's crime at Harper's Ferry. John Cook would have many other lawyers in the following months, but none of them would prove nearly as willing as Alexander McClure to accept him as he was, "a sincere fanatic, with mingled humanity and atrocity strangely unbalancing each other, and his mad purposes intensified by the barbarities of slavery."[19]

❖ ❖ ❖

Once Cook had finished telling his story, McClure said good-bye for the night and promised to visit again the next day. Arriving home about an hour before midnight, McClure was surprised to discover his wife

Matilda and her friend Virginia Reilly dressed in their overcoats and carrying a small package. Matilda McClure and Virginia Reilly were young leaders of Chambersburg's polite society. The previous summer, Matilda had organized a concert for the benefit of the public library that drew the "largest and most highly respectable" audience in Chambersburg's recent history. Fifteen young ladies sang at the concert, each one representing a different flower.[20] And just a few weeks earlier, Mrs. McClure had served as a judge in the Household Manufacture competition at the First Annual Exhibition of the Farmers and Mechanics Industrial Association. Virginia Reilly was the daughter of United States Congressman Wilson Reilly, who was a free-soil Democrat. Her brother was a cadet at West Point, and she was engaged to marry Rev. Thomas Orr, the son of another prominent Franklin County family.[21]

It was unusual to see two such respectable ladies about to venture onto the street so late in the evening, and McClure realized they must have had a compelling reason. Both women were "strongly anti-slavery by conviction," and they explained that they were headed to the jail in order to rescue Cook. Their plan was to "dress him in the extra female apparel they had in a bundle, and one of them walk out with him while the other remained in the cell" impersonating the prisoner. Of course, the female faux-Cook could expect to be released the next morning when the ladies' ploy was discovered. It was not an original ruse, having been employed successfully on behalf of other fugitives, most famously in the Michigan case of runaway slave Lucie Blackburn. McClure, therefore, was certain that his wife's proposal was actually workable, but he was still determined to prevent it. He assured the women that Cook would be able to escape the following night without embarrassment to the sheriff or to McClure himself. The two young ladies protested against any delay, expressing their deep apprehension that something could go wrong the next day. McClure held firm despite the women's pleading. "Only when it was peremptorily forbidden as foolish and needless" did the women reluctantly abandon their plan "with tears in their eyes."[22]

That was the second time that Cook "could have made his escape in thirty minutes that night," and both times McClure had prevented it. Nonetheless, he went to sleep quite certain that his client would soon be free. McClure went to his office as usual the following morning, planning to make his promised visit to Cook later that day.

At about noon, however, the sheriff rushed into McClure's office, "wild with excitement and his eyes dimmed by tears."

"Cook's taken away," he cried, sent back to Virginia on the morning train.

McClure was dazed. "A thunderbolt from a cloudless sky could not have startled me more," he later said. How was it possible for an extradition warrant to have arrived so quickly?

The answer was that the ill-fated John Cook had just encountered his third instance of wretched luck in less than twenty-four hours. As it turned out, a Virginia requisition had already been waiting for him at nearby Carlisle, although it had actually been issued by mistake.

Cook and his four companions were not the only raiders who had escaped from Harper's Ferry. Two others—Osborne Anderson and Albert Hazlett—had managed to slip away from the arsenal under cover of darkness and had also headed north to the free states. Rather than take to the mountains, Anderson and Hazlett followed roads and railroad tracks. They therefore traveled much faster than Cook's party—with the advantage that they did not have to carry a frail companion—reaching the vicinity of Chambersburg several days before Cook encountered Logan and Fitzhugh at Mont Alto. By then, however, Hazlett was hobbled by a blistered foot, and he and Anderson therefore decided to split up. As a suspicious looking black man, Anderson wisely chose to remain hidden during daylight, but Hazlett, who was a native Pennsylvanian, risked flagging a wagon ride from a passing farmer, who brought him to within about three miles of town. At that point the wary Hazlett took his leave, explaining that "his business required him to take another road." As Hazlett climbed down from the wagon, however, the farmer noticed that his passenger was carrying a large new revolver. His suspicion aroused, the wagon driver headed straight for Chambersburg, where he alerted friends that they might be able to capture a fugitive and obtain a reward.[23]

Arriving in Chambersburg on foot, Hazlett attempted to find help at Ritner's boardinghouse—where he briefly contacted Virginia Cook—but he was spotted by bounty hunters who frightened him away. Hazlett somehow managed to evade his pursuers as he painfully made his way north toward the town of Carlisle. He was overtaken the following day, arrested after "a violent resistance," and placed in the Cumberland County jail. The bounty hunters had never heard of Albert Hazlett and assumed that their captive was the notorious (and extremely valuable) Captain John Cook. Word was quickly sent to Virginia, and Governor Wise took immediate action. Declaring that "John E. Cook has been guilty of Participating in murder and robbery, and causing invasion and insurrection [and] that he has been arrested in Pennsylvania," Wise issued a requisition seeking his extradition to Virginia.[24]

It soon became obvious, however, that the man in custody was not really Cook. He was younger, heavier, considerably taller, much rougher in appearance, and in other ways did not fit the description of John Cook as "an effeminate looking man." When Virginia Cook was interrogated about the fugitive seen at the Ritner house, she denied that it had been her husband and the authorities evidently believed her. Meanwhile, Hazlett claimed to be named William Harrison—a pseudonym previously used by other militants in Kansas—and denied all knowledge of John Brown. His jailors did not at all believe the latter part of the story, but the extradition proceeding was suspended until they could determine the true name of the prisoner.[25] Wise's valid requisition for Cook remained in the hands of the Cumberland County sheriff.

Thus, when Cook's arrest was announced, it was a simple matter for the authorities to bring Wise's requisition to Chambersburg on the early train from Carlisle. The Cumberland County sheriff, who was closely allied with the proslavery Buchanan administration, arrived in the company of a Virginia lawyer named Douglass and another man named Kimball, who was the brother-in-law of U.S. Attorney General Jeremiah Black. Fearing that the Chambersburg sheriff would attempt to delay or defeat the extradition, the delegation went immediately to the courthouse rather than proceeding directly to the jail. At the courthouse they obtained a perfunctory hearing before the president judge—who rode circuit but happened that day to be in Chambersburg—and presented their papers for his approval.

The documents were clearly in order, and the judge had no choice but to enter his "command for the prompt rendition of the prisoner." With the formalities now accomplished, "the judge repaired to the prison . . . and performed his plain duty under the law by declaring the officer entitled to the custody of Cook." The entire transaction took only twenty minutes, and Cook was removed from the jail before his lawyer even knew about the warrant. Loaded with irons, the prisoner was placed in a wagon and driven to the railroad station to be taken away on the noon train. McClure later lamented that his wife had not acted on her "woman's intuition without waiting to reason with man on the subject." The lawyer's masculine judgment had failed his poor client, and he sorrowfully observed that "no man in like peril ever seemed to have had so many entirely practicable opportunities for escape; but all failed, even with the exercise of what would be judged the soundest discretion for his safety."[26]

※　◉　※

Compounding the pathos, Cook's risky efforts to reach his wife and son in Chambersburg had all been in vain. By the time he was taken prisoner, Virginia and child had fled to the east, although not without great difficulty. Word of the Harper's Ferry insurrection had reached Chambersburg almost immediately, and Virginia would have heard the broad outline of events—and intuited much more—by late Monday, October 17. She soon learned of Cook's escape and the $1,000 price on his head. At that news, according to one of her fellow boarders, she understandably became "terribly distressed and frenzied with grief. Her situation was pitiable in the extreme. She was a total stranger here, with a small young babe, and not a dollar to pay her boarding or assist her to go away."[27]

Virginia's first impulse was to return to Harper's Ferry, where her mother lived and where she might obtain reliable news about her fugitive husband. Using the name Miss Kennedy, she attempted to leave by stage coach on Tuesday, shortly after news arrived in Chambersburg that the insurrection had failed. She was thwarted, however, when "the stage driver refused to take her, saying that he could never get her through alive." Her true identity had already become known, the driver told her, and all "along the railroad route armed men were searching for her." According to another report, she was in fact turned away for lack of funds to pay the fare, but in either case Virginia found herself, as she later put it, "alone with her baby, never having traveled before, knowing herself hunted, [and] half dead with fright."[28]

Virginia returned to the Ritner house on Tuesday, worried and disappointed, but still hoping to be able to get back to Harper's Ferry. She was persuaded by the other boarders, however, that it would be too dangerous for her there, due to "the intense excitement and possibility of her being arrested, harassed or insulted." That was surely the right decision. Tempers were raw in Harper's Ferry in the days following Brown's defeat, and only Governor Wise's stern measures saved the surviving raiders from a threatened lynching. With Brown and the other prisoners safe in government custody, the attention of the enraged militias naturally turned toward Captain John Cook. Vigilantes were on the lookout for Cook in and about Harper's Ferry, and they had little intention of bringing him back alive. As one local newspaper put it, "He is a villain of the blackest hue, and should be placed outside the . . . protection of the law. A court of justice should not be disgraced by the presence of such a black-hearted and atrocious villain." In that violent atmosphere, it was entirely possible that vengeance would be taken on Cook's wife. Even in her absence, the Kennedys' house was thoroughly searched and Virginia's mother and younger brother were interrogated.[29]

Things were little better in Chambersburg. The proslavery segment of the populace was especially furious over the invasion of Harper's Ferry, and vigilante search parties went door-to-door looking for Cook or other refugees. Virginia's presence in town was considered an outrage by the local Democrats, prompting Dr. William Boyle—the owner of the *Valley Spirit* and Alexander McClure's political nemesis—to write to Governor Wise in Richmond with the suggestion that Virginia had "papers in her possession" that could shed light on the insurrection. Boyle believed that Cook was already hiding in Chambersburg, and he emphatically, though mistakenly, told Wise, *"There is no doubt about him being here."* Boyle assured Governor Wise that Virginia Cook's "movements will be closely watched," and he proposed that it would be "of some advantage to send a shrewd officer here to investigate affairs. Much evidence could be obtained."[30]

The Ritner house was in fact kept under constant, if spotty, surveillance. The building was searched and Virginia was questioned by bounty hunters—including at least one reporter for the *Valley Spirit*—after Albert Hazlett was seen lurking outside the window. The interrogation must have been traumatic for Virginia, who was terrified about her future and ashamed of her circumstances. She lied about the date of her wedding, placing it a year earlier in time so that her son would appear to have been conceived after the marriage. The humiliated look on her face, however, must have given her away, as it was reported that she seemed "cunning" when she told the story. Still, the investigators appeared to believe her when she denied all knowledge of her husband's whereabouts, perhaps because she cooperatively confirmed that "John Henrie Kagi had been one of Brown's men in Kansas" and had been one of the last to depart the Ritner boardinghouse earlier that month.[31] They left her alone for the time being, but she had no way of knowing when they would be back.

Although she was an abolitionist, Mary Ritner herself was no insurrectionary, and she was deeply unhappy about her entanglement in Brown's conspiracy. She had barred her door to Hazlett, and she would later chase away Owen Brown, Charles Tidd, and Barclay Coppoc when they came begging for food. Virginia Cook had become at most an inconvenient (and nonpaying) guest, and Ritner was anxious to see her depart. Virginia would later say that she "had to leave Mrs. Ritner's," although she did not say whether she had been given a firm deadline by the innkeeper.

Unable to go home and without money or friends, Virginia desperately sought assistance from other boarders. Two of them, Franklin Keagy and Thomas Cochran, turned out to be very generous, immediately volunteering to provide sufficient funds for her to travel to the home of her brother- and sister-in-law, Robert and Fanny Crowley, in Brooklyn. Overwhelmed with shock and grief, and in "a flood of tears," Virginia and child departed Chambersburg the next day, according to Keagy, which would have been October 22 or 23, and several days before Cook was captured and incarcerated.[32] In one final irony, Robert Crowley himself passed through Chambersburg almost simultaneously, already on his way to Harper's Ferry in search of his wife's brother.

Cook was no doubt thinking of Virginia when he sat in the Chambersburg jail (which was less than a block away from the Ritner boardinghouse), and he may still have hoped to find her following his expected escape. He apparently never talked about his wife during his meetings with McClure on October 26—perhaps because he did not want to risk implicating her in his crimes—and he therefore had no way of knowing that she was already on her way to Brooklyn.

❀ ❀ ❀

Cook began to inform on his comrades as early as the wagon ride from Mont Alto to Chambersburg, when he attempted to ingratiate himself with his captors and negotiate for his release. He tried making "disclosures about himself to get free," and when that did not work he went further. He told Logan and Fitzhugh that there had been "three others with him on the mountain," confirming that one of them—no doubt Charles Tidd—was a man who had earlier been spotted in the woods with "a blue blanket over his shoulders, and carrying a Sharp's rifle and a double barreled gun." Based on Cook's information, search parties were dispatched the following day. The fugitives' abandoned supplies were found concealed in some bushes, including a rifle with Tidd's name engraved on the mounting. That was the first hard evidence of the Maine lumberman's escape as it was initially believed that he had been killed during the insurrection.[33]

At some point en route, Cook's captors were joined by a Virginia police detective named William Kelly, who conducted an intensive interrogation of the prisoner. Understandably in a state of shock, Cook was in no condition to put up much resistance to the grilling. He had endured over a week of near starvation, as well as the constant antagonism of Charles Tidd, before he was arrested as a consequence of his own recklessness. Then he had been assured of his eventual freedom in Chambersburg, only to be suddenly extradited in chains. Despite the bravado and determination he had shown in his conversations with Alexander McClure, he must have been disoriented and despondent when Kelly began questioning him.

It was reported in the proslavery press that Cook was in good spirits during the trip back to Virginia (which was no doubt false), but "when some allusion was made to his wife he shed tears" (which was likely true). In fact, he had probably been physically abused. According to one account, he had been kicked and beaten leaving "his face and head [with] great marks of violence." The authorities, as could be expected, vigorously denied roughing up their prisoner—claiming to have handled him "in the kindest manner"—but there were credible reports that Cook had been mistreated in custody. There is no question, for example, that he was taken in shackles onto a hotel balcony and cruelly exhibited to a jeering mob in Hagerstown, Maryland, during a stopover to change trains.[34] The stress of fear and intimidation—along with Cook's incurable volubility—surely explains what happened next.

From the outset of the journey, Cook "talked very freely of the insurrection and related many incidents connected with it," and in an apparent attempt to gain favor he also entertained his guard with stories of his exploits in Kansas. Although claiming to have been a dupe, he readily confessed his own role in the raid and admitted that he had "engaged in the murders and other crimes perpetrated by John Brown and others at Harper's Ferry." More shockingly, he informed Kelly that Barclay Coppoc had been with Cook "just before his arrest," adding that Coppoc had "fled from the State of Virginia, and is now in the State of Pennsylvania." He also revealed "that C. P. Tidd . . . and one of Brown's sons," as well as Francis Merriam, had been with him near Chambersburg.[35]

Perhaps even worse, Cook came close to betraying Alexander McClure, the man who had tried so sincerely to free him. He told his captors that a rescue had been planned from the Chambersburg jail, and that it "was to have been attempted had he been kept [there] twenty four hours longer." Although he did not mention McClure by name, the lawyer was obviously a likely suspect in the thwarted jailbreak, as he was the only outsider who had access to the prisoner.

What's more, Cook apparently confirmed that Merriam had been in Chambersburg "a short time previous to the outbreak at Harper's Ferry" and "had his will drawn up, by an Attorney . . . bequeathing his property for the emancipation of slaves." There were other antislavery lawyers in Chambersburg, but McClure was the most prominent among them and therefore the most vulnerable to Cook's disclosures.[36]

It was also on the train to Virginia that Cook began to implicate Frederick Douglass, claiming that Douglass had at the last minute broken his promise to lead a band of armed men in support of the raid. If Douglass had not "acted the coward," Cook asserted, the insurrection would have been successful. "I conveyed the arms there for him," he said, "and waited till nearly night, but the coward didn't come."[37] The story was untrue—Douglass had never agreed to participate in Brown's operation—but it is possible that Cook actually believed it. Brown had always insisted that the small Harper's Ferry band was only the vanguard, and that they would later be joined by hundreds, or even thousands, of enthusiastic abolitionists and fugitive slaves. Brown might well have mentioned Douglass as one of his silent supporters, or Cook might merely have assumed that Douglass would be at the head of the next wave. In either case, Cook's mere mention of Douglass was provocative and just the sort of information that Detective William Kelly had been hoping to obtain.

As Governor Wise's most reliable agent, Kelly undertook many other assignments for his boss. Two weeks after Cook's arrest, Kelly would return to Pennsylvania with a corrected requisition for the extradition to Virginia of Albert Hazlett, who was still imprisoned in Carlisle. Yet later, Wise entrusted Kelly with a warrant for the arrest of Frederick Douglass on charges of "murder, robbery, and inciting servile insurrection in the State of Virginia." Recognizing the need to be "very secretive in this matter," Wise requested that President Buchanan provide Kelly and another agent with "a permit and authority to act as detectives for the post-office department" as a necessary pretext for traveling through the North. Because of the delay in obtaining his "nominal authority" as a federal agent, however, Kelly was unable to serve the warrant. He arrived at Douglass's Rochester home only hours after the black abolitionist departed for safety in Canada. The detective also went on to Canada, but he could not track down his quarry.[38] Kelly showed the same doggedness in questioning Cook, reporting the successful interrogation back to Wise and alerting the governor that further pressure was likely to yield even more information about the conspirators in Harper's Ferry and beyond.

Cook would continue talking for weeks, providing the Virginia authorities with much additional information that could be used to pursue his comrades who were still at large, and also implicating several of Brown's allies and financial supporters in the North. The initial revelations about his fugitive comrades might have been unavoidable, given Cook's utter defenselessness at the time, but he did not stop there. According to one Chambersburg newspaper, "Cook, while here, informed some one that he intended making a full confession of the whole plot of the insurrection, with a disclosure of the names of all connected with it." That turned out to be much more than a rumor. By the time he arrived in Virginia, Cook had become even more communicative with his captors.[39] He would go on to make several extremely expansive confessions that were facilitated by his own lawyers, who adopted a proslavery strategy designed to accommodate the prosecution. Cook's Virginia defense attorneys could not have been more different from Alexander McClure—in both politics and tactics—but they did make a concerted and calculated effort to save their client's life.

By the early morning of October 28, 1859, Cook would be back in the Commonwealth of Virginia, where he would face trial on charges of murder and treason. It had been twelve days since he cut the telegraph wires to begin the Harper's Ferry raid and ten days since he began his failed escape. A great deal had happened in the meantime.

❀ SIX ❀

Charlestown

John Brown had been seriously wounded when he was captured on Tuesday morning, slashed and stabbed several times by Marine Lieutenant Israel Green. Fortunately for Brown, Green had forgetfully worn his lightweight, ceremonial sword that day, rather than his real saber. That mistake saved Brown's life. Green later explained that his dress sword was so dull that it could not do any lasting damage, although his saber was as sharp as a razor. Even so, Brown was bloodied and stunned from Green's beating, unable to stand on his own. There were four other survivors of the raid. Aaron Stevens—who had been shot five times in the head and breast—was thought to be near death. Two black men were uninjured: John Copeland, of Oberlin, and Shields Green, who had been introduced to Brown by Frederick Douglass. The other survivor was the Springdale Quaker Edwin Coppoc, Barclay Coppoc's older brother, who was also unharmed.

Brown and Stevens were brought into the paymaster's office of the armory, where they were placed next to each other on straw bedding. Both men were bleeding and caked with mud and sweat, and neither had eaten or slept for over two days. Brown was stoic and composed, but Stevens was nearly delirious with pain.

Although the insurrection had been completely crushed, that was not yet apparent to the victors. It seemed almost impossible that Brown had attempted such a daring raid with fewer than two dozen troops, and it was therefore believed that numerous reinforcements—probably under the command of Captain Cook—were still poised somewhere in the surrounding hills. That assumption was strongly bolstered when Brown's weapons caches—including hundreds of firearms and nearly a thousand fearsome pikes—were discovered at two locations in Maryland. It was therefore imperative to obtain as much information as quickly as possible, and that required immediately questioning Brown and Stevens. Brown was soon surrounded by a claque of soldiers, politicians, and journalists, including Virginia Governor Henry Wise and Senator James Mason, Ohio Congressman Clement Vallandingham (who happened to be en route from Washington, D.C., to his home district), reporters from Richmond and New York, and a crowd of others. Robert E. Lee warned the interlocutors not to harass his prisoner, but Brown was actually eager to explain himself. The first questions came from Virginia Congressman Alexander Boteler, whose greatest concern was the possibility of a renewed attack. How did Brown hope to take and hold Harper's Ferry with such a small force, he asked.

"I expected help," Brown replied.

"Where, whence, and from whom, Captain, did you expect it?"[1]

Brown was immediately wary and quite unwilling to provide a plain answer. "Here and from elsewhere," was all he would say.

Although more than willing to describe his plan to free the slaves, Brown would repeatedly draw the line at implicating others. Thus began an extended fencing match, in which the interrogators attempted to learn about Brown's comrades and supporters, while he steadily refused to name names.

Boteler turned the questioning over to Governor Henry Wise, who had rushed to Harper's Ferry as soon as news of the uprising reached Richmond. At age fifty-two, Governor Wise was unusually slender and remarkably intense. His features were severe, verging on gaunt—with high cheekbones, a long nose, and thin lips—and his unnaturally long arms and legs made him appear almost orthopteran. Wise had been outraged to learn that so few abolitionists had captured an entire town, and he was embarrassed that it had taken federal troops, rather than Virginia militia, to dislodge the invaders. His term as governor was going to expire at the end of the year, but he had presidential aspirations and he realized almost immediately that his handling of the rebellion would affect his ability to obtain the Democratic nomination in 1860. Wise had therefore taken control of the military operation as quickly as he could, and he would also closely supervise the investigation and prosecutions that followed.

Wise was keenly interested in the identities of Brown's backers. He was a lawyer, however, and he had two prominent local attorneys at his side, so he first made sure that Brown's statements could not later be challenged as coerced. Wise admonished the prisoner that "he did not desire to hear anything from him that he did not willingly . . . feel disposed to communicate," adding that the inevitable prosecution "would not in any degree, and could not, be affected by anything he told."[2]

Brown replied that "he had nothing, so far as he himself was concerned, to withhold," and that he was eager to explain the purpose behind the raid. Once again, Brown was attempting to deflect the interrogation, but the interrogators were not deterred.[3]

"Can you tell us who furnished money for your expedition?" asked Senator James Mason.

"I furnished most of it myself," said Brown, "I cannot implicate others."

Then in his thirteenth year as a senator, Mason was a grandson of George Mason, one of the drafters of the Bill of Rights. James Mason's own legislative accomplishments were less admirable than his ancestor's. He was the principal author of the Fugitive Slave Act of 1850, and he had been chosen to read aloud to the Senate the final address of the dying John C. Calhoun, threatening secession if southern demands for the protection of slavery were not met. Mason himself was not an especially imposing figure, with a receding hairline and a weak chin, but he was a bulldog when it came to confronting abolitionists.

"If you would tell us who sent you here," the senator pressed, "who provided the means?"

"I will answer anything I can with honor," Brown stubbornly replied, "but not about others."

Mason then tried another tack. "How many are there engaged with you in this movement?"

"I came to Virginia with eighteen men only, besides myself," Brown replied. That answer was true as far as it went. Owen Brown, Barclay Coppoc, and Francis Merriam had all been ordered to stay behind in Maryland and in fact had never entered Virginia. Brown believed them still to be at large, and he did not want to alert the authorities to their existence. (Brown did not yet know that Osborne Anderson and Albert Hazlett had slipped away, or that Cook and Tidd had been stranded on the other side of the Potomac; otherwise, he probably would have protected them by simply lying about the size of his army.)

The back and forth continued, as various questioners attempted to learn the identities of Brown's supporters.

Governor Wise was already certain that Brown had been financed by leading northern abolitionists, but he wanted specific proof. He would eventually settle upon Gerrit Smith, Samuel Howe, and of course Frederick Douglass as the prime suspects, especially when letters from those three, and several others, were discovered among Brown's possessions—along with copies of the Provisional Constitution and other incriminating documents. Wise had also received what was termed secret information that "Howe was in the plot with Brown," and he had dispatched detectives to Boston to gather intelligence.[4] The agents came back empty-handed, but Wise would later pressure John Cook for the production—or perhaps the creation—of evidence against Howe, Smith, and Douglass. For the time being, however, he could only try to pry the particulars out of Brown. He might just as well have saved himself the effort.

Brown remained remarkably self-possessed throughout the hours-long ordeal, responding only to the questions he chose to answer while taking every opportunity to condemn slavery. As prosecutor Andrew Hunter later put it, "whenever we touched upon any one that had not been captured he was 'mum.'"[5] Quite aware that there were journalists in the room, Brown informed his captors that he and his men had every right to attempt "to free those you willfully and wickedly hold in bondage."

But Aaron Stevens, who was far more seriously wounded, could not maintain the same discipline. When Brown denied freeing slaves against their will, Stevens interrupted. "In one case, I know the negro wanted to go back," he said.

Seizing an opportunity, Representative Vallandingham turned to Stevens, who had acknowledged passing through Ohio. "How far did you live from Jefferson?" he asked, hoping to ensnare the abolitionist congressman Joshua Giddings, who was from Jefferson, Ohio.

Brown realized that his comrade was in no condition to resist interrogation. "Be cautious, Stephens, about any answers that would commit any friend," he called out. "I would not answer that."

According to a reporter for the *New York Herald*, "Stephens turned partially over with a groan of pain, and was silent."

It was not reported in the press, but Stevens actually continued talking. Contrary to Brown's instructions, he told Governor Wise and Colonel Lee the names of eighteen of his comrades, omitting only Owen Brown, Barclay Coppoc, and Francis Merriam. Stevens added that Cook had escaped—which was already common knowledge—and he mistakenly included Charles Tidd and Albert Hazlett among the dead. Attorney Andrew Hunter took down the list of insurgents from Stevens, with the additional information that Cook was from "Connecticut formerly—here lately." In Stevens's defense, he no doubt believed that he had named only those who had been either killed or captured or previously identified. Still, the information was valuable to the authorities as it allowed them to start matching names to bodies and then to begin track-ing fugitives.[6]

Seriously injured and badly shaken, Brown fended off his interroga-tors and deprived them of the information they most badly wanted. He gave up no names at all, and he directly implicated none of his financial backers in the North. In little more than a week, however, that effort would be for naught, as John E. Cook would have few scruples about answering questions the Virginians put to him.

※ ❀ ※

While John Brown calmly faced his interrogators in the paymaster's office, the scene outside was chaotic. Hundreds of armed militiamen, many of them drunk, roamed the streets of Harper's Ferry and loudly demanded revenge. If not for the strong hand of Colonel Lee and a stern warning from Governor Wise, Brown and the other survivors might have been lynched on the spot. Fearing an outbreak of vigilante violence, Wise ordered Brown and the others to be transferred imme-diately to jail in Charlestown, the seat of Jefferson County, where they would soon face trial.

The prosecutors in the case were Charles Harding, the common-wealth attorney for Jefferson County, and Andrew Hunter, who had been specially appointed by Governor Wise. Harding inspired little confidence. He was "a bulky, bibulous man [with] several days' growth of scraggly beard on his receding chin."[7] A notorious alcoholic, Harding ate and smoked incessantly in court, sometimes dozing off with his feet propped up on the table. His clownish behavior might have been toler-able if Harding had been a talented advocate, but in fact he was given to poor preparation and rambling witness examinations that often evoked laughter as he sputtered before the bench. Although Harding was tech-nically in charge of the entire case by virtue of his elected local office, Governor Wise had scant faith in his ability to bring such a complicated and important matter to a favorable conclusion.

Wise therefore designated Andrew Hunter as his personal representative and Harding's nominal assistant. Hunter was everything that
Harding was not. He was trim and courtly, with a square jaw, wide eyes,
and wavy hair that swept away from his alert, intelligent face. Hunter
was perhaps the most capable and well-respected attorney in Jefferson
County, whose "distinguished bearing [and] vigorous Southern personality were well-matched to his vigorous, deliberate courtroom style."[8]
Hunter had accompanied Wise at Brown's initial interrogation, and he
therefore knew more about the case than anybody else in Charlestown.
In fact, he probably knew too much. He was related by marriage to
Fontaine Beckham, the murdered mayor of Harper's Ferry. More significantly, his son Henry had killed one of raiders—Brown's son-in-law
William Thompson—by shooting him at close range after he had surrendered. Even in the 1850s, connections of that sort would usually disqualify a prosecutor, but nobody objected to Hunter's participation, and
he had no inclination himself to cede the case to the ineffectual Charles
Harding. Hunter overshadowed Harding—whom he considered a "pes-
tiferous little prosecutor"—and the two men would barely speak to one
another as the case progressed. Their antipathy would matter little to
most of the defendants, but Harding would eventually assert himself in
a way that threatened serious consequences for John Cook.

Virginia's judicial system moved quickly. Brown and the others were
formally committed to the Charlestown jail on Thursday, October 20,
and a special examining court was convened five days later on Tuesday,
October 25. The examining court, comprising eight magistrates, was
unique to Virginia, and its sole function was to determine "whether the
charges are of sufficient importance to go before the grand jury."[9]

The presiding magistrate named two local lawyers, Charles Faulkner and Lawson Botts, to represent the defendants. Both men were slaveholders who were closely tied to the Jefferson County legal establish-
ment, and neither was eager to accept the job. Faulkner, in fact, objected
loudly. As a member of the Martinsburg militia, he had been among

the armed citizens who responded to news of the invasion. Moreover, Faulkner had been present during part of Brown's interrogation—advising Governor Wise and even volunteering a few of his own questions. Under those circumstances, Faulkner protested, it would be "improper and inexpedient for him to act as Brown's counsel."[10] The magistrate, however, was unmoved by Faulkner's objections and his appointment was allowed to stand.

Lawson Botts was the scion of a distinguished Virginia family. His grandfather had represented Aaron Burr in his treason trial, and his father was a military officer and prominent landowner.[11] Botts had also been "in the thick of events at Harper's Ferry," and he was related on his mother's side to Lewis Washington, the prosecution's most important witness.[12] Nonetheless, Botts evidently had no qualms about accepting the case. Perhaps he was less attuned than Faulkner to conflicts of interest, or perhaps he recognized that virtually every lawyer in Jefferson County was compromised when it came to representing John Brown. Whatever his reasoning, Botts informed the court that he was willing to undertake the case, either with or without Faulkner's assistance.

Brown equivocated when he was asked if he would accept the representation. He told the court that his friends in the North would soon dispatch lawyers for him. "I have applied for counsel of my own, and doubtless could have them, if I am not, as I said before, to be hurried to execution before they can reach me. But if that is the disposition that is to be made of me, all this trouble and expense can be saved."

It was not an unreasonable request for a man who faced the death penalty, but it was more than Charles Harding could bear. The boorish district attorney interrupted the defendant. "The question," he snapped, "is do you desire the aid of Messrs. Faulkner and Botts as your counsel. Please to answer yes or no."[13]

Brown half-relented. "If they had designed to assist me as counsel," he said, "I should have wanted an opportunity to consult them at my leisure." The court took that as acquiescence, and turned to the other four defendants. Stevens stated that he did not want to be represented by northern counsel, and was willing to take both Botts and Faulkner as his lawyers. Copeland, Green, and Coppoc also assented to the representation, recognizing that they had no real alternative.[14]

It took the examining court only a few hours to refer the case to a grand jury, which had already been impaneled for that purpose by Circuit Judge Richard Parker.

❊ ❀ ❊

Hon. Richard Parker had come to his position almost as a birthright. His father and great-grandfather had also been Virginia judges, and Parker had inherited from them both the respect of his community and a reverence for the law. He also inherited a stately stone mansion in the neighboring town of Winchester, which he managed with the help of ten slaves. Parker was far from charismatic—he was stoop-shouldered and heavyset, with a bulbous nose and tight, unsmiling lips—but his contemporaries considered him "an able, sound, and efficient judge." A deliberate man who was unimpressed by haste or bombast, Parker exercised complete control of his courtroom. Although he was "intensely pro-Southern in his views," Parker was committed to preserving the appearance of due process, at least insofar as it could be achieved expeditiously in the wake of the murderous invasion.[15] He would preside over Brown's trial—and later over Cook's—with a firm hand.

The grand jurors deliberated for several hours before adjourning on Tuesday afternoon and again for a while on Wednesday morning. It is obvious that they were not debating whether to indict Brown and company—that conclusion was never in doubt—so the overnight delay was probably because they were waiting for Andrew Hunter to finish drafting the indictment. And quite a document it was.

Approved unanimously by the grand jurors, Hunter's indictment consisted of four counts, each rendered in the baroque language of antebellum law. There were two counts of murder (both direct and "aiding and abetting") and another for conspiring to induce slaves "to make insurrection against their masters and owners, and against the government, and the constitution and laws of the Commonwealth of Virginia."

The heart of the indictment, however, was expressed in Count One, which charged that the five prisoners had committed treason against the Commonwealth of Virginia by conspiring "together with divers other evil minded and traitorous persons to the jurors unknown, not having the fear of God before their eyes, but being moved and seduced by the false and malignant counsels of other evil and traitorous persons, and the instigations of the Devil."

According to the indictment, Brown and his men had committed treason not only by plotting to "make rebellion and levy war" against the Commonwealth, but also by attempting to institute "a government separate from and hostile to the existing government" of Virginia and, in the language of the state treason statute, professing "allegiance and fidelity to said usurped government."[16]

The treason count provided no additional punishment—every one of the charges carried the death penalty—but it did complicate the case. Murder and incitement were straightforward crimes that would be relatively easy to prove, but treason required the prosecution to produce two witnesses to each overt act by each defendant. More significantly, treason, at its core, involved the betrayal of allegiance to one's sovereign, yet neither Brown nor any of the other prisoners had ever been a citizen, or even a resident, of Virginia. (Cook had lived in Virginia, but he was not included as a defendant in the initial indictment.) A further complication under Virginia law was that clemency for treason—unlike all other crimes—required the approval of the legislature and could not be granted by the governor alone.

In retrospect, it seems almost absurd to have charged that John Brown was "moved and seduced by the false and malignant counsels of other evil and traitorous persons." We know today that Brown was the ultimate free radical, attached to no one and stubbornly resistant to the advice of others. He kept the details of his plan secret from even his closest allies, and if he had received any counsel at all, it had been to abandon his scheme for invading Virginia. In the days immediately following the raid, however, it was still widely believed in the South that Brown had been in the vanguard of an invading army, and that other attacks were already percolating in the abolitionist strongholds of the North. Thus, the allegation that Brown had conspired with certain "evil minded and traitorous persons" was in fact the first step toward indicting other antislavery leaders who could not yet be identified but who were assumed to have played a sinister role in Brown's insurrection. Governor Wise already had his sights set on Frederick Douglass, Samuel Howe, and Gerrit Smith—and he would have been happy to include Wendell Phillips, William Lloyd Garrison, and many others. Andrew Hunter obliged his principal by drawing an indictment sufficiently flexible to later add anyone else who could be implicated by whatever means. Count One of the indictment would therefore assume an important role in the case against Brown (and an even greater role in the subsequent trial of John Cook).

※ ◉ ※

Charles Faulkner met privately with Parker during the grand jury deliberations, and he finally succeeded in persuading the judge to release him from the assignment. It is not clear whether Faulkner was truly motivated by a heightened sense of legal ethics, or whether he merely sought to avoid a distasteful duty. Most of the other lawyers in the Charlestown proceedings would eventually encounter one sort of conflict of interest or another—some of which were quite extreme—but Faulkner would be the only one to disqualify himself from the case.

With Faulkner's withdrawal, Lawson Botts balked at handling the defense alone. He implored Parker to appoint another attorney, and the court complied by naming Thomas Green, the mayor of Charlestown, as co-counsel. Green was a slaveholder and the cousin of Senator James Mason, but at least he had not been directly involved in capturing or interrogating Brown. He agreed to take the case, and Brown and the other defendants accepted the representation.

Judge Parker summoned a jury panel to appear on Wednesday, October 26—coincidentally, the same day that John Cook was brought before the court in Chambersburg. Jury selection was accomplished by the end of the session—with each side exercising its allotted eight strikes—and the court instructed the jurors to return the following morning to begin John Brown's trial.

The courtroom was packed when Commonwealth Attorney Harding presented the opening statement for the prosecution. Every seat was taken by local residents and reporters from around the country, and order was difficult to maintain. The room was so crowded that it was necessary "to erect rude scaffoldings of plank to shelter the officials [and] to enable them to perform their duties unencumbered." Some of the witnesses were unable to find seats and were therefore compelled to lie on the floor in front of the bench. Many of the spectators could not restrain themselves from shouting curses at the defendant, and others smoked and laughed out loud—frequently spitting chestnut shells onto the floor in a coarse manner that the eastern press found shocking. Several New York journalists reported that the shells were so deep that the lawyers' footsteps made a crackling sound like "trampling on glass."[17]

One important observer, however, stood out as an island of dignity in a loutish sea. Senator James Mason would attend the trial from beginning to end, always conducting himself with perfect manners, even toward the despised defendant. Mason was the very model of southern decorum, as he calmly settled into his seat to listen to the evidence against John Brown. Also present was Mary Ann Kennedy, the mother of Virginia Kennedy Cook, who sat through all of the proceedings in the hope of learning something about her son-in-law. It is not known whether Senator Mason recognized Mrs. Kennedy, but he would surely have treated her chivalrously had they met.

Reading aloud from the indictment, Harding opened his case by explaining precisely how Brown's crimes had violated the laws of Virginia. Harding also introduced a political theme that would be important throughout the proceedings that followed. Brown's war of liberation, Harding said, had been conducted against the will of the slaves themselves, all of whom "rushed back to their masters at the first opportunity." The absurd myth of the contented slave was essential to Virginians' sense of security, and the prosecutors therefore missed no opportunity to reinforce it. The same theme would be played out in Cook's later trial, although in a very different manner.[18]

❋　❋　❋

The trial's principal actors dispersed when court closed for the day. Botts and Green accompanied their client back to his cell, relying on the jailor John Avis to allow them to discuss the next day's strategy in relative privacy. Captain Avis also provided the three men with a lamp to facilitate their meeting, as well as an evening meal so that they could do their planning uninterrupted. Although he was ill disposed toward abolitionism—in fact, he was a part-time slave dealer—Avis was a compassionate man who did his best to make his prisoners as comfortable as possible. He had wispy blond hair and a long face, with narrow eyes and hollow cheeks that gave little hint of his generous nature. With Avis in charge of the jail, Brown and the others would have access to visitors, newspapers, and letters both to and from their friends and supporters, and they would be protected from angry citizens who attempted to insult or harm them. But even the accommodating Avis would have had to order lights out at some point, so Botts and Green no doubt returned to their homes after at most an hour or two.

Judge Parker may have taken his supper at one of Charlestown's several hotels, perhaps ordering one of the region's famous pies, which were said to "soothe all asperities, and overcome all crustiness but their own."[19] Or he might have gone straight home to his mansion, to be served a light meal by one of his waiting slaves before retiring to his bedchamber.

Andrew Hunter, however, could not go to bed early that evening. He first had to prepare for the next day's direct examinations—a task he shared with Charles Harding, whose hard drinking and late-night revels made cooperation difficult and unpleasant. But even then Hunter's work would not be finished for the night. He was obliged to meet the late train from Hagerstown, which was due to arrive after midnight carrying an important passenger.

John Cook had been ordered extradited from Pennsylvania on Thursday morning, October 27, just as Harding was giving his opening statement in Brown's trial. Hunter would have been notified quickly by telegraph that America's most wanted man would soon be on his way to Charlestown; perhaps he even received the message during the court's noon recess. Detective Kelly could be trusted to bring Cook safely to the jail, but Hunter would have wanted to learn the results of Kelly's interrogation and there would be little time to meet before court convened in the morning. It had already been rumored that Cook was planning to cooperate with the prosecutors, and Hunter definitely wanted to exert his influence over any eventual confession. Nor could Hunter exclude the possibility of a rescue attempt at the vulnerable moment when the prisoner was taken from the train. It would have been hard for him to sleep soundly until he confirmed that Cook had been safely escorted to the Charlestown jail.

Hunter's misgivings were reinforced when the other passengers debarked from the train. Among those arriving that night was a nervous young New Englander named George Hoyt, a neophyte lawyer from Boston—only twenty-one years old, though looking more like a teenager—who had been dispatched to Virginia by Brown's supporters. Hoyt was far from qualified to serve as defense counsel in such a serious case, and, in fact, his true assignment had been to act as an intermediary and scout. He had been told to learn "the location and defenses of the jail [and] the opportunities for a sudden attack and the means of retreat" in order to plan a possible rescue of Brown. The frail lawyer's nerves must have betrayed him, because Hunter immediately became suspicious of his mission. "A beardless boy came in last night," the prosecutor wrote to Governor Wise. "I think he is a spy."[20]

❈ ❋ ❈

Court did not open until 11:00 a.m. on Friday, although no reason was announced for the late start. It may have been a courtesy to Senator Mason, who was mysteriously delayed. Mason had spent the first few hours of the morning in John Cook's cell, where he began a successful interrogation that would have extraordinary consequences as the Virginia prosecutions continued. Mason's meeting with Cook soon became public knowledge—as did virtually everything in Charlestown—but the senator himself said little about it for the time being. The precise details of the questioning would remain shrouded until after the conclusion of John Brown's trial.

Judge Parker was well aware of Cook's arrival, which had been greeted with great rejoicing in Charlestown, but he knew nothing about George Hoyt until the young lawyer was introduced to the court by Lawson Botts. Hoyt requested temporary admission to the Virginia bar, although only for the purpose of observing the proceeding. Despite a half-hearted objection from Hunter, Judge Parker agreed. Hoyt was permitted to sit at counsel table, but with the understanding that he would not take an active part in the trial.

The prosecution case continued with testimony from Lewis Washington about his encounters with Cook and Brown, followed by Armistead Ball, the armory's master machinist who had been among the first of Brown's hostages, and then by John Allstadt, who recounted his kidnapping by Cook and the subsequent events in town. Andrew

Hunter also offered into evidence a copy of the Provisional Constitution as well as numerous letters—including several from Gerrit Smith and Frederick Douglass—that had been seized at the Maryland farm. There followed five more witnesses who testified about the shooting of Mayor Beckham, Private Quinn, and Brown's other victims. With that, Hunter rested for the prosecution.

Even though it was by then Friday afternoon, Judge Parker insisted that the defense begin its case. Brown had definite ideas about how his defense ought to be conducted, and he provided them to Botts and Green in the form of written directions. He wanted to show that "his desire to free the slaves was purely benevolent," and he expected to establish that with evidence that his "orders, from the first and throughout, were, that no unarmed person should be injured, under any circumstances whatever."[21] At Brown's insistence, Botts and Green had subpoenaed nine of Brown's hostages, of whom five were available to testify that afternoon.

The clerk called out the names of the four witnesses who had not answered to the defense subpoenas, but there were no responses. Brown became deeply agitated. He viewed the trial as a platform for his views, and he now sensed an opportunity to make a dramatic point. Rising to his feet, Brown addressed a statement to the court, although he was really speaking to the assembled reporters:

> I discover that, notwithstanding all the assurances I have received of a fair trial, nothing like a fair trial is to be given me. I gave the names . . . of the persons I wished to have called as witnesses, and was assured that they would be subpoenaed . . . but it appears that they have not been subpoenaed. . . . I have no counsel, as I have before stated, in whom I feel that I can rely.

Brown then requested a delay so that his own lawyers could represent him. "I ask, if I am to have anything at all deserving the name and shadow of a fair trial, that this proceeding be deferred until tomorrow morning."

That was too much for Lawson Botts and Thomas Green to take. They had done their very best to represent an unpopular and irascible defendant for no pay and few thanks. As Hoyt would later tell Thomas Wentworth Higginson, "Their management of the case was as good for Brown as the circumstances of their position permitted."[22] In fact, they had worked late into the night attempting to issue the requested subpoenas, only to be rebuked by their client. Green spoke for both lawyers when he asked to be relieved of the duty that had been imposed upon them: "Feeling confident that I have done my whole duty, so far as I have been able, after this statement of his, I should feel myself an intruder upon this case were I to act from this time forward."

Judge Parker agreed, releasing both attorneys from any further obligations to the defendant. That left only Hoyt to represent Brown, and the novice nervously asked the court to adjourn the case until the next morning. It "would be ridiculous," he said, for him to attempt to carry on that evening as he had no experience and "no knowledge of the criminal code of Virginia." And besides, he had recently received word that experienced lawyers would in fact arrive the next morning. For once, Judge Parker relented, hoping that the "foreign" lawyers would actually appear. If not, George Hoyt would have only one night to prepare for his very first trial.[23]

❧   ✳   ❧

Hoyt met with Brown in the jail on Friday night, no doubt explaining his dual role as attorney and spy. It is unknown whether Hoyt had by then given up plotting a rescue, which would have been as suicidal as Brown's raid on Harper's Ferry. But that did not matter because Brown himself had no interest in escaping, having already decided that he could advance his cause best as a martyr. "I am worth inconceivably more to hang than for any other purpose," he would later declare. Hoyt accepted his client's resignation and spent the evening working with Botts, who had generously volunteered to "sit up with him all night to put him in possession of all the law and fact in relation to this case."[24]

Fortunately, Hoyt's hastily acquired skills would not be tested. The much-hoped-for legal reinforcements arrived in Charlestown on the late night train, and two experienced northern lawyers—Hiram Griswold and Samuel Chilton—appeared on Brown's behalf when court opened on Saturday morning. Hiram Griswold, of Cleveland, was a prominent member of Ohio's extensive antislavery bar, and he was eager to defend Brown as a matter of principle. Samuel Chilton was a lawyer of an entirely different stripe. Born and raised in Virginia, he was closely tied to most of the prominent families of Jefferson County, although he now lived and practiced in Washington, D.C. Chilton disdained abolitionism, and he accepted the case only after Brown's supporters promised him the huge fee of $1,000.[25]

As capable as they were, neither Griswold nor Chilton had any useful information about Brown's case, and they quite reasonably requested a delay in the proceedings. Judge Parker granted them only an hour, which they spent meeting for the first time with their client. They were back in court by late morning, when Parker insisted that they begin calling witnesses. Remarkably, several of the previously missing witnesses were now available. The defense lawyers, however, had little success with their direct examinations, as all of the witnesses were deeply hostile to Brown. The best they could do was to elicit from the former hostages some grudging admiration of Brown's courage. With nothing more to offer in the way of evidence, the defense rested in the early afternoon.

Eager to get the trial finished, neither Hunter nor Harding had bothered to conduct any cross examinations. In fact, they proposed that the case be sent immediately to the jury, with both sides foregoing summations. Chilton, however, had a legal argument to make. He moved to dismiss the treason count of the indictment as technically defective on the ground that Brown owed no allegiance to Virginia. Hunter, of course, objected, and the court agreed. The jury would be instructed to decide the case on the indictment as drawn. In a rare concession to the defense, however, Judge Parker agreed to recess court until Monday morning, thus giving Brown's new attorneys a full day to prepare their final argument.

All three of Brown's attorneys met with him on Sunday morning, hoping to plan an appeal to the jury's sense of justice. There was no transcript to review, so Brown would have had to recount all of the testimony to his late-arriving counsel. They also discussed strategy, and Brown declared that he was well satisfied with his lawyers' plans.

At the same time and in the same jail, John Cook was meeting with several attorneys of his own, who were convincing him to adopt a dramatically different approach to his defense. There is no record of an encounter between Brown's lawyers and Cook's, but they could not have missed seeing each other in the corridors of the small jailhouse. Cook's lawyers were quite distinguished, and their arrival from the North had been duly reported in the press, so it is certain that Chilton and Griswold were aware that other notable legal minds were then working on the case. On Sunday, however, it appears that Brown's lawyers were concentrating on their own client's defense, giving little or no thought to any other prisoners or their counsel.

On Monday morning, Hiram Griswold delivered the first argument on Brown's behalf. Griswold asserted that Virginia lacked jurisdiction over crimes that had been committed on federal property, and that Brown could not be convicted of treason because he was not "a citizen of the State or government against which the treason so alleged had been committed." He commended Brown as a "man of indomitable will" whose only purpose had been to free the slaves.

Samuel Chilton followed Griswold, taking good advantage of his distinctive southern accent. "This prisoner is not a citizen of Virginia," Chilton argued, and therefore cannot be found guilty of treason against the Commonwealth. The murders, moreover, had all been committed by others, and there was no direct proof that Brown himself had killed anybody. Chilton attempted to shift some of the blame to the other four indicted prisoners—meaning Aaron Stevens, Shields Green, Edwin Coppoc, and John Copeland, none of whom he represented—while pointing out that Cook's kidnapping of Washington and Allstadt had been accomplished without violence and thus without legal malice.[26]

Judge Parker committed the case to the jury in the early afternoon, although the outcome was recognized by observers as "a mere matter of form."[27] The jurors deliberated only briefly before returning to court with their verdict: "Guilty of treason, and conspiring and advising with slaves and others to rebel, and murder in the first degree." Even though it was still relatively early in the day on Monday, the attorneys all appeared too exhausted to continue, and Judge Parker therefore set sentencing for Wednesday morning. Tuesday would be devoted to legal arguments and, almost incidentally, to the trial of Edwin Coppoc.

※　◉　※

Brown had been compelled to endure his own trial in near silence. Virginia adhered to the "interested party rule"—as did every state in 1859—which prohibited a criminal defendant from testifying in his own behalf. The rule was thought to be necessary to avoid the temptation to perjury, but it also prevented defendants such as Brown from appealing directly to the jury or to the public. That would change when Brown came before the court for sentencing.

Judge Parker ordered Brown to stand before the bench on Wednesday morning while the clerk read the obligatory question. Did the defendant have "anything to say why sentence should not be pronounced upon him?" Eloquently and defiantly, Brown seized the moment:

> In the first place, I deny everything but what I have all along admitted, of a design on my part to free slaves. . . .
>
> This Court acknowledges, too, as I suppose, the validity of the law of God . . . which teaches me that all things whatsoever I would that men should do to me, I should do even so to them. It teaches me further to remember them that are in bonds, as bound with them. I endeavored to act upon that instruction. . . .

I believe that to have interfered as I have done, as I have always freely admitted I have done, in behalf of His despised poor, I did no wrong, but right. Now, if it is deemed necessary that I should forfeit my life for the furtherance of the ends of justice, and mingle my blood further with the blood of my children and with the blood of millions in this slave country whose rights are disregarded by wicked, cruel and unjust enactments, I say let it be done.[28]

Needless to say, Brown's oratory had no effect on Judge Parker, who simply remarked "that no reasonable doubt could exist of the guilt of the prisoner." He sentenced Brown to be hanged in public on Friday, December 2, 1859.

❊　❂　❊

The Virginia authorities—Parker, Wise, Hunter—had good reason to be satisfied with their work. In the wake of Brown's unprecedented attack on their commonwealth, they had successfully asserted Virginia's jurisdiction over his crimes, thwarted the very real possibility of lynching, and brought the matter to a dignified conclusion in only two weeks. True, there had been criticism in the northern press that the case had proceeded with unseemly haste and with insufficient regard for Brown's choice of counsel. In the end, however, they had managed to observe all the "judicial decencies," although, in Hunter's words, they had done so in "double quick time."[29] In any event, Brown's guilt was beyond question, as had been proven by numerous witnesses and Brown's own admissions. In one sense, of course, the trial had been nothing more than a formality—a ritual preface to an inevitable execution. But proper procedural form was important in both law and politics (then as now). If Wise and company had any misgiving about the trial, it was only that it had failed to produce sufficient evidence implicating Brown's financial backers—a shortcoming they expected to remedy when Cook faced trial the following week.

However great the Virginians' victory at first appeared, it would quickly come undone—with events moving at the speed of telegraphy. Journalists in the courtroom transcribed Brown's remarkable speech, and it was soon published in newspapers across the country. Brown's eloquent condemnation of slavery struck a deep chord in the North, "unleashing powerful imagery that would vastly deepen the meanings of his puny act of physical rebellion." Even abolitionists who had initially criticized or condemned the Harper's Ferry raid soon found themselves praising Brown's courage and dedication while denouncing his captors. "John Brown has twice as much right to hang Governor Wise as Governor Wise has to hang him," said Wendell Phillips, and he was far from alone in his sentiment. The reaction was equal and opposite—or perhaps even amplified and antagonistic—in the South, where Brown's fortitude came to be seen as a sign of pure villainy. Worse yet in southern eyes, the lionization of Brown appeared to portend an irreparable breach with the free states. As one outraged Virginian put it, "This robber & murderer, & villain of unmitigated turpitude . . . is now the idol of the abolitionists, & perhaps of a majority of all the northern people." If the malevolent John Brown was a hero in the North, then what security could there be for slaveholding within the Union?[30]

To the eventual dismay of his southern prosecutors, it was Brown who had seized control of the courtroom by reversing their roles and placing slavery itself on trial. In less than half an hour, he had transformed himself from a murderer to a martyr who would, in Ralph Waldo Emerson's words, "make the gallows glorious as the cross."[31]

※　⊛　※

Nearly every account of Brown's historic speech has ended with his stirring commitment to mingle his blood with the blood of slaves. But in fact he continued speaking for some minutes more, departing from soaring rhetoric to express something much closer to a petulant complaint. Brown concluded with an unexpected rebuke of "some of those who were connected with me." He denied that he had induced any of the others to join him, and he deplored the weakness of the prisoner who had apparently made that claim.[32] Although Brown did not name names, he surely had John Cook in mind, and he might even have been looking directly at him. Cook had been in the courtroom for his own arraignment earlier that afternoon, and it is not known whether he was returned to the jail before or after Brown's sentencing. In either case, word had spread for several days of Cook's intended cooperation with the prosecutors, and Brown was so deeply distressed by the impending defection that he could not ignore it, even in his finest hour.

✳ SEVEN ✳

Confession

John Cook's sisters rushed into action as soon as they learned the alarming news that their brother had been implicated in the terrible events at Harper's Ferry. Although John had been out of touch with his relatives for well over a year—leaving them worried that he had been killed in Kansas—the Cook sisters still loved their baby brother deeply, and they were determined to come to his assistance. Robert Crowley, the wealthy merchant who was married to Fanny Cook, departed for Harper's Ferry even before Cook had been captured, dispatched by his wife in the hope of locating her wayward brother. Another of John's sisters had an even more influential husband. Caroline Cook, one of the twins with whom John had practiced his handwriting, was married to Ashbel Willard, who was then the governor of Indiana. Caroline urged her husband to head to Charlestown as soon as it became known that John would face trial in Virginia. Neither Crowley nor Willard was an abolitionist, and both had good reasons to avoid any possible association with John Brown. Willard was a proslavery Democrat with a promising political career to consider, and Crowley did considerable business in Virginia. Many men in like circumstances would have balked at jumping so quickly to the aid of a troublesome brother-in-law, even if their wives were in tears. But the Cook sisters were strong women who had been raised to dominate their households. Fanny and Caroline seemed to have no trouble convincing their uxorious husbands to drop everything for young John's sake.

Governor Willard was the first family member to meet with Cook, visiting him in the Charlestown jail on Friday morning. Cook had always liked his brother-in-law—although he once confided in a friend that he "abhorred his politics"—and he must have been overjoyed when Willard unexpectedly walked into his cell. Willard was accompanied by his friend and fellow Democrat Senator James Mason, whom Willard hoped to influence in Cook's favor. After only a few minutes, Mason politely offered to leave the cell so that Willard and Cook could meet privately. After all, Mason pointed out, he would "feel bound to testify" to anything Cook might say. That was good advice, but Willard did not take it. Although he was himself a member of the Indiana bar, Willard was much more a politician than a lawyer. He saw little point in attempting to develop a legal defense for Cook, and he was much more interested in currying favor with Mason and other members of Virginia's aristocracy. Thus, Willard declared that "he himself would be a witness in court to any facts communicated," and he insisted that Mason remain at the meeting. Willard warned Cook that he had little hope of exoneration and urged him to "to make a full confession of all he knew connected with the affair at Harper's Ferry."[1]

As of yet, Willard had no idea how deeply involved Cook had been in Brown's scheme or how much damaging information a full confession would include. He had lost sight of his brother-in-law for several years and had not even suspected his whereabouts until he saw Cook's name in the newspapers following the insurrection. Willard knew virtually nothing of Cook's adventures in Kansas, his participation in the Chatham conference, or his life as a spy in Harper's Ferry. He certainly did not know that Cook had fired several rounds at the Virginia militia from his hilltop perch and therefore might be held directly responsible for the death of George Turner. Nonetheless, Willard pressed Cook to "exonerate those who were innocent" and implicate those who were guilty, "as the only atonement he could now make."[2]

Willard sincerely had Cook's interests at heart, not to mention concern for Caroline's great distress at her brother's dire situation. But Willard also had other considerations in mind. He had been elected governor of Indiana in 1856 at the age of only thirty-six, making him the youngest chief executive in the state's history. A handsome man with wide blue eyes, a florid complexion, and a Roman nose, Willard was an energetic campaigner who was largely responsible for his party's successes at the polls. He was also a classic doughface—pro-southern, proslavery, and strongly in favor of enforcing the Fugitive Slave Act. He had been an ardent supporter of the Kansas-Nebraska Act, and he afterward sided with President Buchanan in the controversy over the fraudulent Lecompton Constitution that had been foisted on Kansas by the illegitimate votes of Missouri's border ruffians. He applauded Chief Justice Roger Taney's opinion in the *Dred Scott* case because "any other decision would have liberated every slave in the southern states." Willard appeared to have a bright political future, perhaps as a United States senator, an ambassador, or a cabinet member, but much depended upon his zealous opposition to the rising tide of "Black Republicanism." Even the slightest connection to John Brown could thus prove disastrous to his prospects for higher office, and his political enemies had wasted no time circulating rumors that Willard's brother-in-law had somehow inveigled the governor into Brown's conspiracy. Political discretion would have dictated that Willard stay back home in Indiana, and perhaps even denounce his radical brother-in-law. But family ties—and Caroline's sorrowful pleading—proved stronger than politics. He had to do something to help his unlucky relative, but he could still try to avoid destroying his career in the process.[3]

Cooperation with the prosecution promised to be the perfect solution to Willard's dilemma. He could offer Cook's confession as proof of remorse and use it to seek a pardon or reprieve from his friend Governor Wise. At the same time, he could avoid the appearance of giving even a shred of sympathy to the radical abolitionists, especially if Cook could be persuaded to renounce John Brown and everything he stood for. Willard therefore sharply pressed Cook, telling him that a confession was in the best interest of his family, but it is unknown how much more of his thinking he shared during their first meeting. Willard probably believed that the strategy was too obvious to require explanation, given Cook's limited options. In any case, Cook was in no position to argue with his older and more worldly brother-in-law. His ordeal—of running, hiding, starving, capture, and extradition—had now lasted nearly two weeks. All of his own resources had failed him and he was desperate for any glimmer of hope. Without taking much time to think, Cook agreed to make a written confession, although he could not yet have realized what that would require of him. Either Mason or Willard soon told a reporter of Cook's willingness to confess, and the news quickly spread—first throughout Charlestown and then across the country. The infamous Captain Cook was going to betray his friends.

Willard's plan might have been obvious or even inexorable, but that did not mean it would be easy to effect. The first step was to open communications with Governor Wise, which Willard could certainly handle on his own. But Cook would still need a lawyer—meaning a real trial lawyer and not simply a politician—to represent him in the proceedings to come. It would also be necessary to begin talking with the prosecution, so that Cook's proposed cooperation might yield something in return. There was no telling where those negotiations might lead, but they obviously had to be started as quickly as possible. Brown's trial was already winding down, and Cook's first court appearance would occur no later than the following week. Fortunately, Willard had access to some excellent attorneys, and he was willing to call in favors to get them on the job.

Even before he left Indianapolis, Willard got in touch with two of Indiana's foremost lawyers, Attorney General Joseph McDonald and United States Attorney Daniel Voorhees. Both lawyers were politically ambitious and therefore closely tied to Willard and the Buchanan wing of the Indiana Democratic Party, and both quickly agreed to come to Cook's assistance without demanding a fee. Voorhees, in fact, had been in the midst of presenting a case "in a distant county" when he received the message from Governor Willard, but he broke off the argument and rushed immediately to Charlestown.[4] McDonald would later play only a small role in the proceedings, but Voorhees would take over Cook's defense and use it to gain national renown for himself en route to a brilliant career.

Having secured first-rate counsel for his brother-in-law, Willard turned his attention to Governor Wise. Explaining that Cook had always been "a wild, erratic boy," Willard wrote to Wise for assistance. Reminding Wise that he was a fellow Democratic governor, Willard hoped for at least some hint of a possible pardon: "I wish most heartily that I could in this, to me a most trying hour, have the advantage of your counsel and advice. The crime is a great one, and the law appears to me clear. If you can suggest to me anything which I could do, I should be most thankful."

Willard was not thinking only of Cook. He also needed political cover for himself, so he concluded by asking Wise to confirm "that my acquaintance with you and my reputation would shield me against any misconstruction of my conduct."[5]

By the time he arrived in Charlestown, Willard would have had some idea about the anger of Virginians over the abolitionist invasion of their state, but he probably did not realize how deeply Cook was despised for having deceived the citizens of Harper's Ferry. Brown's courage and principles had won some grudging admiration among Virginians, but Cook—who had been a spy and seemed about to become a turncoat—was viewed almost entirely with contempt. Wise regarded Cook as "the worst of all these villains," so it is unsurprising that his response to Willard was decidedly cool. "I regret that my position will not allow me to tender to you any counsel or advice," he wrote.[6]

But Wise also had his own agenda—which was to implicate additional abolitionist figures in the North—and he quickly saw an opportunity to use Cook to his advantage. Careful to avoid making any commitments, Wise went on to suggest that Willard explore a bargain with Andrew

Hunter. "Cook's part in this tragedy is peculiar, and his trial may fully develop the whole plot with all parties in other States implicated, and to that end much will depend upon his temper and disposition at trial. . . . [I] hope you will confer candidly with the Assistant Com'lth's Attorney, Mr. Hunter." A true Virginian, Wise also made a point of offering "to aid in any way in assuaging your grief," as well as offering "the hospitalities of my house without reserve." He closed by assuring Willard that "your course in looking after this prosecution is natural and humane, and can give rise to no imputation."[7]

❊　◉　❊

Attorney Daniel Voorhees did not need to be convinced that Cook's best hope was in an arrangement with the prosecution. He began negotiations with Andrew Hunter the moment he arrived in Charlestown, and he would eventually spare no effort to provide the prosecutor with everything he requested.

Voorhees was a big man with broad shoulders, standing over six feet tall and weighing more than two hundred pounds. Along with a lean face, strong features, bushy eyebrows, and a jutting chin, he had a shock of "titian-bronze" hair that he brushed straight upward—thus making him seem even taller—and he sported a long, wavy Vandyke of the same color. "The way his hair stood out in a porcupinish style like the fibers of a sycamore ball, together with his height, earned for him the title of 'The Tall Sycamore of the Wabash.'" Voorhees was born in 1827 to a Dutch-Irish farming family that was originally from New Jersey. His paternal grandfather had fought in the Revolutionary War, joining Daniel Boone in Kentucky for the disastrous Battle of Blue Licks. After the peace, the Voorheeses moved first to Ohio, where Daniel was born, and then to western Indiana, settling on a farm close to the Illinois border. Daniel had a strong distaste for farm labor, and his parents recognized that his future would be better served by studying than by following a plow. They managed to send him to the newly chartered Asbury College (now DePauw University) in Greencastle, where he won second prize in the senior declamation contest of 1849. That was only a hint of things to come. In later years, Voorhees would be acclaimed as one of the greatest orators of his era (no doubt to the chagrin of the college declamation contest's winner, of whom no record survives). Voorhees was admitted to the Indiana bar shortly after graduation, and he quickly made a name for himself as a rising young attorney, specializing in jury persuasion. Voorhees's practice spanned the state line, and in 1851 he was recommended for temporary admission to the bar of Vermillion County, Illinois, by none other than Abraham Lincoln.[8]

Lincoln's professional courtesy notwithstanding, Voorhees's political allegiance was always to the Democrats. Just like Senator Mason and Governor Wise, he was an ideological descendant of Andrew Jackson, believing devoutly in localism, agrarian virtue, and white supremacy. Although born and raised in the North, he was a staunch defender of slavery and a diehard racist, whose "fear and dislike of the negro was only equaled by his hatred of the abolitionist." He opposed "the bestowal of social and political rights on the negro," even in the free states, warning that equality would inevitably "destroy our Anglo-Saxon civilization, and the supremacy of the white man, the purity of our social structure, [and] would make America the home of mongrel breeds and decadent morals." Years before the *Dred Scott* decision, Voorhees declared, "Property in slaves is not to be distinguished from other kinds which are protected by the same Constitution." Voorhees would later be one of Lincoln's most outspoken opponents during the Civil War, comparing the Republican administration to the rule of "Attila, Genghis Khan, Tamerlane, and Hyder Ali." In opposition to Lincoln, Voorhees denounced the Emancipation Proclamation, and he argued vehemently against adoption of the Thirteenth Amendment, which he called "the bloody, dripping sword of irresponsible power."[9]

Voorhees supported the Kansas-Nebraska Act in 1854, and he ran for Congress in 1856 on a platform that supported the expansion of slavery. He campaigned fiercely, accusing the Republicans of deception and fanaticism and labeling his opponent a "woolly head."[10] Voorhees narrowly lost that election, but he planned to run again. He sided with President Buchanan in the struggle over Kansas's Lecompton Constitution, and he was rewarded for his loyalty in 1858, at the age of only thirty-one, with an appointment as United States attorney for Indiana. In fact, Buchanan fired the incumbent United States attorney— who had sided with the more moderate Senator Stephen Douglas of Illinois—in order to give Voorhees the plum position. Not that Voorhees was unqualified for the job. He had already proven himself to be one of the best trial lawyers in the state, and he was also one of Indiana's smoothest politicians.

If there was ever a doubt that John Cook would cooperate obediently with the Charlestown prosecution, it vanished the moment Daniel Voorhees entered his cell. Any of Cook's remaining principles and loyalties were completely overwhelmed by Voorhees's commanding personality. While most of Cook's earlier admissions had been physically coerced, there would be no need for any such intimidation with Voorhees in control. Instead, Cook would do as he was told, providing a stream of information—not all of it wholly truthful—for the convenience of Andrew Hunter and Governor Wise.

Cook's first assignment was to further betray his fellow escapees. He had already provided four names to Detective Kelly, so the prosecutors knew that Owen Brown, Francis Merriam, Barclay Coppoc, and Charles Tidd were still at large and probably in Pennsylvania. But names alone were not much help in tracking down antebellum fugitives. Andrew Hunter needed physical descriptions of the wanted men, and Voorhees and Willard made certain that Cook obliged. As the prosecution records show, Cook provided the following detailed descriptions:

Owen Brown is 33 or 34 years of age, about 6 feet in height, with fair complexion though somewhat freckled. He has red hair and very heavy whiskers of the same color. He is a spare man with regular features, and has deep blue eyes.

Barclay Coppoc is about 20 years old, is about 5 ft. 7 ½ inches in height, with hazel eyes and brown hair, wears a light mustache, and has a consumptive look.

Francis J. Merriam is about 25 years of age, is about 5 feet 8 ½ inches in height, has black hair and eyes and brown mustache. He has lost one eye, sometimes wears a glass eye. His face is somewhat blotched from the effects of Syphilis. Complexion dark.

Charles P. Tidd stands about 5 feet 11 inches, has broad shoulders and looks like a very muscular and active man. Has light hair, blue eyes, Grecian nose, and heavy brown whiskers. Looks like a fighting man, and his looks in this respect are in no way deceptive.[11]

On the basis of Cook's descriptions Governor Wise issued a proclamation for the arrest of the four men, "offering a reward of Five Hundred dollars in each case." Most historians have glossed over Cook's central role in Wise's proclamation, frequently conflating it with the much earlier $1,000 reward that was offered for Cook alone.[12] The reality, however, was that Cook's descriptions—including his sharply opinionated characterization of Charles Tidd—put his former colleagues in significant additional peril of capture.

Voorhees realized—much sooner than Willard, who was unduly optimistic—that it was going to be extraordinarily difficult to obtain leniency for John Cook and that he would need some help to make it happen. Willard had known Cook as a teenager—John had attended the 1847 wedding of Ashbel and Caroline—and the governor was naturally somewhat blinded by his wife's attachment to her brother, as well as by his own sense of self-importance. Voorhees, in contrast, brought a trial lawyer's cold-eyed objectivity to the situation. He understood that most Virginians saw Cook not as a misguided youth, but as a murderous, dangerous, treacherous invader. And he thus understood that Governor Wise was going to be influenced far more by public opinion than by any warm feelings toward Ashbel Willard, no matter how close their friendship or political alliance. The case would have to be made much more broadly because Wise would grant a reprieve only if he could be assured of some measure of public support.

Local lawyers would therefore be necessary, not so much to try the case—Voorhees could easily handle that by himself—but rather to influence local opinion and generate as much sympathy for Cook as possible. Voorhees quickly located two lawyers who were both well connected and willing to help. They were also extremely familiar with the case, perhaps even too familiar. Cook's local counsel would be Lawson Botts and Thomas Green.

The retention of Botts and Green was a smart maneuver on Voorhees's part. Both men were highly regarded in Jefferson County; Green was the mayor of Charlestown and Botts served on the town council. Their stature had if anything improved following their dismissal by Brown, as their fellow citizens recognized that Botts and Green had done their best, only to be spurned by their ungrateful client. In modern terms, of course, Botts and Green had an irresolvable conflict of interest. Cook's defense was going to be highly antagonistic toward Brown, their former client. Under the ethics principles of the time, however, the lawyers' duties toward Brown ended the moment he discharged them, and they were free to take on a new client even if that meant attacking Brown's character and credibility (while also undermining his slight chance of a successful appeal).

It is quite possible that Green had already been informally engaged in the case when, in his capacity as a part-time justice of the peace, he obtained an affidavit from Cook that further jeopardized the four known Harper's Ferry fugitives. Cook's statement averred that the four others "were banded as conspirators with said John Brown in the attack made at Harper's Ferry [and] that they were active co-conspirators with said Brown in making preparations for said attack, and were actively aiding and abetting the same." To support a potential treason charge, Cook added that his four comrades "were bound by an oath to carry out and sustain the purposes set forth in [Brown's] 'Provisional Constitution.'" And he wrapped things up by stating his belief that the four others were at large "either in the State of Pennsylvania, New York, or some other of the Free States of the Union where the institution of slavery does not exist."[13]

Cook's statement to Thomas Green might be called the third stage of his eventual "full confession" (following his statements to his captors in Chambersburg and Detective Kelly). The detailed information was used to issue arrest warrants for the four hunted men, and Thomas Green made certain that Cook's official cooperation became widely known. Within days, the Indiana press reported it to be "almost certain that Cook will plead guilty, first submitting a written confession or statement of his connection with Brown." Another newspaper claimed to have gotten the scoop directly from Governor Willard, who was said to have "nothing to say to [Cook] privately which he wishes withheld from the public eye. He advises Cook to make a frank confession of his connection with the Harper's Ferry affair, and to divulge its objects and those who aided or abetted it."[14]

※ ◉ ※

John Cook's first court appearance in Virginia was on Wednesday, November 2. The calendar was crowded that morning—with both John Brown and Edwin Coppoc scheduled to appear—and Cook had to wait through parts of other proceedings before his own case came up.

The opening order of business was the completion of Edwin Coppoc's trial, which had started the previous day. Twenty-four-year-old Edwin had a large head, a round face, tiny eyes, and a sharply sloping forehead that had the unfortunate effect of giving him a rather "stupid look" (although his friends said he was quite intelligent). He was strongly built, with an athletic physique that suggested no trace of the consumption that so badly impeded his brother Barclay during his escape. At first, Edwin appeared to show stoic determination, calmly facing his accusers without any obvious display of emotion. He told one interviewer that he was "prepared to bear his fate like a man." At second glance, however, Edwin could be seen to bite "his under-lip . . . as if striving to repress his quivering."[15]

Compared to Brown's trial, the prosecution of Coppoc was conducted quickly and efficiently, with many of the same witnesses who had testified against Brown. Botts and Green had initially been appointed to represent the young Iowa Quaker, but they evidently regarded their dismissal by Brown as a release from the other defendants' cases as well. Instead, Coppoc was represented by Hiram Griswold, who remained in Charlestown awaiting Brown's sentencing. The evidence for the prosecution included two witnesses who "swore positively that it was Coppoc who shot and killed Mayor Beckham."[16] Griswold put up a spirited fight—presenting legal and jurisdictional motions—but Judge Parker denied every defense objection, leaving the outcome in no doubt.

Cook's case was called during what was understood to be a short recess for the deliberation of Coppoc's jury and the predictable guilty verdict. Voorhees and McDonald (but not Willard) requested temporary admission to the Jefferson County bar, which was granted by the court on the condition that they "honestly demean themselves in the practice of law." Cook was entitled, as Brown had been, to a preliminary hearing before a magistrates' examining court. Voorhees, however, waived the proceeding and, along with it, the opportunity to learn the extent of the evidence against the defendant. That was a clear signal to the court that Cook did not intend to raise a factual defense. Of course, Andrew Hunter already knew that, having been in frequent contact with Voorhees about Cook's confession in progress. The press, too, picked up the cue. One reporter expected Cook to "make a clean breast of it" in the hope of saving his own life, and another astutely predicted that Cook would soon "be brought to confess pretty much what was wanted" by the prosecution.[17]

Cook's brief appearance before the bench was followed by John Brown's sentencing. The jail stood across the street from the courthouse, separated by several barrooms and lawyers' offices. During business hours, the entryways to both public buildings were constantly thronged with visitors, and the streets were filled with "earnest orators" who hurled invectives at Brown and his men. Given the logistics of moving prisoners back and forth through the hostile crowd—which required an armed escort with fixed bayonets—it is possible that Brown and Cook were brought over to the courthouse together. And in any case, it is probable that they were in the courtroom at the same time, even if only in passing and perhaps for much longer.[18] That would explain the incongruous coda to Brown's impassioned condemnation of slavery.

Brown would have been taken aback to see Cook in the courtroom, especially if he had noticed accommodating smiles pass between Hunter and Voorhees as the latter waived Cook's preliminary examination. Brown later explained that he had not expected to address the court that afternoon, and that his speech had therefore been entirely extemporaneous and not precisely what he had intended to say.[19] With more forethought, Brown would have omitted scolding the other prisoners—so that he could end on a more elevated and inspirational note—but such restraint was evidently impossible with the traitorous Cook in view. That turned out not to matter to Brown's northern friends and followers, who concentrated on his acceptance of martyrdom in the name of freedom. But John Cook would have realized that he had irredeemably crossed a line. Brown's contempt for Cook would increase as the date for his execution drew closer, but it was already palpable when Brown was sentenced on Wednesday afternoon.

Not that Cook had been anything other than wholly committed to the strategy of confession and cooperation. He had been "busily engaged writing" his confession ever since his initial meeting with Voorhees, filling sheet after sheet of oversized foolscap with an elegantly handwritten history of his service to John Brown. Voorhees had great hopes for

Cook's confession, but he was not otherwise optimistic about his client's chances. He wrote to a friend in Terre Haute that he saw little hope "of saving him from being condemned and executed." Voorhees felt a little better with the completion of Cook's confession on Friday, November 4, although he still "could not tell what will be the result of Cook's trial."[20]

By Friday evening, the draft of Cook's confession had been submitted to Hunter for his approval, hand delivered by Governor Willard. The prosecutor, however, did not like what he saw. Although the confession was twenty-two pages long, it did "not refer to any of the conspirators outside of the immediate band." Such a confession would not come close to satisfying Governor Wise, who was insistent on obtaining evidence against Douglass, Smith, and others whom he accused of inciting the insurrection. Hunter therefore promised Governor Wise that he would get more out of Cook before any agreement could be confirmed.[21] With his life at stake, and the die already cast, Cook had no choice but to comply. He would soon expand his confession in exactly the direction that Wise and Hunter demanded.

Wise and Hunter had more in mind than simply excoriating abolitionists and Republicans. They had conceived of a plan that would allow them to prosecute northern abolitionists in Virginia. They could, of course, use the Commonwealth courts to indict anybody they chose, but indictment and effective prosecution were two different things. Virginia's ability to serve its own subpoenas ended at the state line, and it was unlikely that they would get much help from state authorities in the North. For the better part of two decades, northern state courts had frequently resisted rendition requests for fugitive slaves, so it seemed doubtful to Hunter and Wise that any greater cooperation could be obtained in the production of prominent journalists, congressmen, and clergymen. It is true that Pennsylvania quickly extradited Cook and Hazlett, but that was done in the immediate aftermath of the raid in which the two disreputable men had been direct participants. A conspiracy case against upright citizens, none of whom had left their homes, was bound to meet with something close to outright defiance in the courts of Massachusetts, New York, and Ohio. As had been the case with fugitive slaves, the answer to the southern dilemma was to obtain the assistance of the federal government.

It therefore occurred to Governor Wise that it could be useful to bring at least one prosecution in the Federal District Court for the Western District of Virginia, which would sit in Staunton, 120 miles from Charlestown. Despite his posturing—he had earlier offered to give the national government only the corpses of the invaders—Wise realized that there could be significant procedural advantages to a federal prosecution. Federal warrants and subpoenas could be served throughout the nation, which meant that witnesses could be compelled to travel to Virginia from any northern state. The trial of one conspirator could thus be used to amass evidence against others, who could then be indicted in the same court. Even more important, all of the writs, subpoenas, and warrants would be served by federal marshals who were political appointees of President Buchanan. As steadfast Democrats, the federal marshals would not owe any loyalty to the more liberal political establishments in their home states, and they could be backed up by federal troops if necessary. And though any eventual trial would be held in a federal courtroom under federal jurisdiction, the judge and the jurors would nonetheless be Virginians.

The prospect of federal prosecution was also advantageous to Cook. Although a conviction would still be all but certain—carrying the death penalty for either treason or murder—the trial could not be held for several months, thus allowing tempers to cool somewhat. More significantly, the pardon power following a conviction would be in the hands of President Buchanan rather than Governor Wise. As president, Buchanan was eager for support in every region of the country, and he would thus be less susceptible to parochial political pressure from Virginia and more likely to heed clemency pleas originating in the northern states. It could not hurt that Voorhees and Willard were key Buchanan allies in a state that was a Democratic stronghold.

In his first communication with Ashbel Willard, Henry Wise raised the possibility of transferring Cook to the federal jurisdiction. "One suggestion I may venture," he wrote, is "that it may be policy to have one of the prisoners, at least, tried in the U.S. District Court in order that *process may reach out of this State to bring witnesses from other states.*"[22] Wise emphasized the need to reach beyond Virginia's border as a sharp reminder to Willard that the price of the federal transfer would be cooperation in naming northern abolitionists. Choosing his words carefully, Wise also pointed out that perhaps only one of the prisoners—and not necessarily Cook—might be turned over to the federal authorities, and that the relatively lucky defendant would be chosen on the basis of his assistance to the prosecution.

Willard and Voorhees probably thought that they had a deal, especially after Cook provided so much useful information to Hunter. But Cook's betrayal of his comrades in arms did nothing to advance Wise's ultimate goal, so the Virginia governor felt justified in withholding the ultimate prize. He continued to correspond with Hunter about whether "to turn Cook or another one of the villains to the U.S. tribunals," but he did not reveal his intentions, or his doubts, to any of the defense lawyers.[23] Voorhees would just have to keep the information flowing while hoping for the best.

At some time on Friday night or Saturday morning, Voorhees delivered the dispiriting news to Cook. His twenty-two-page confession was not good enough. More names were needed if he hoped to avoid the noose.

❈ ❂ ❈

Cook was not due back in court until Monday, which gave him plenty of time to improve his confession. On Sunday, November 6, he also took the time to write a long and revealing letter to his wife. Although there is no mistaking the prose as anyone's other than Cook's, it is obvious that some of the letter's contents were intended for readers besides Virginia Cook. All of the jail's outgoing mail was reviewed by Andrew

Hunter, and Daniel Voorhees was too good a lawyer to pass up an opportunity to send a covert message to the prosecutor (and by extension,
to the governor's mansion). Cook's letter began with words of profound
love for his wife. "A dungeon bar confines me; a prisoner's cell is mine.
Yet there are *no bars* to confine the immortal mind, and *no cell* that can
shut up the gushing fountain of undying love." Cook made no mention
of Virginia's traumatic exile from her home or the panic she must have
endured, but he assured her that nothing could "sever the golden links
of that eternal chain which binds my throbbing heart to *my life's partner and my child.*"

Cook's vivid expressions of affection were no doubt sincere—he
included a reference to Banquo's ghost, which would have reminded
Virginia of the times he had read aloud to her from Shakespeare—but
he turned soon enough to his other purpose. Most of Cook's letter was
devoted to an elaborate justification of his actions at Harper's Ferry. "I
was actuated only by the tenderest feelings of sympathy and humanity," he wrote. "I had been led to believe, as had my comrades, that it
was the daily prayer and life wish of the masses of slaves for freedom."
Cook then explained that he now regretted following Brown, who had
misled him badly. "I gave my heart and hand to a work which I deemed
a noble and holy cause. The result has proved that we were deceived;
that the masses of the slaves did not wish for freedom." Finally, Cook
insisted that he did not share Brown's guilt for the murders of Mayor
Beckham and others. "The wrong I have done has not been one of intention. In this work no man's blood rests upon my hands. I had no part in
the death of those who were killed at the Ferry."[24]

In the meantime, Shields Green and John Copeland, the two black
prisoners, would face trial. Green's case was the first to be called. He
was represented by George Sennott, another young lawyer who had
hastened from Boston at the instance of Brown's friends. Sennott was
a Rabelaisian figure, whose large waistline, extravagant personality,
and prodigious appetites caused much spiteful laughter in Charles-

town. The local newspapers could not find enough insulting things to say about the Boston lawyer. "George Sennott has come to us upon a mission of great bigness, and his size, so far as latitude is concerned, shows him fully up to the immortal standard of envoys extraordinary," said one reporter. "When he is out of Boston," cackled another journalist, "we presume lager beer has an opportunity to accumulate." In fact Sennott was an excellent attorney. He was an abolitionist Democrat—a combination unusual in the North and unheard of in the South—and the contrast between his moral convictions and his political affiliation might have contributed to the derision he had to endure. One observer called him "the celebrated Damphool," although that was before anyone saw him in action.[25]

Unlike the apologetic Samuel Chilton, Sennott did not hesitate to speak up for his clients. He boldly said that it was his honor to defend Green and Copeland, and he declared in court that "the system of Slavery is illogical and absurd." Needless to say, that did not endear him to the public in Charlestown, where he was accused of "making an Abolition harangue" in court. Eventually, however, he earned grudging admiration for his legal skills. One Charlestown newspaper reported with surprise that Sennott was "doing his damndest" for Shields Green—who was condescendingly described as "a regular out-and-out tar-colored darkey"—and that there was actually a chance at an acquittal.[26]

The evidence against Green, however, was overwhelming. Lewis Washington testified that Green had been in charge of guarding the hostages and that he had been armed with a rifle, a revolver, and a butcher knife. Washington had seen Green firing at the surrounding militia, but that was not his worst offense. Far more heinous, in Washington's eyes, was Green's "impudent manner." Although he had been born in slavery, Green had a self-confident bearing that led his friends to affectionately call him "Emperor." Washington, in contrast, was accustomed to enforced deference from black men, and he therefore saw only effrontery where others recognized dignity. He was especially offended that Green had dared to give orders to a white man.

Washington also considered Green a coward. When the final attack was made on the engine house, according to Washington, Green threw away his weapons and attempted to act as though he was one of the local slaves. There was nothing really cowardly about trying to live to fight another day, and in fact, Green showed considerable courage after he was captured. Despite what must have been intense pressure, Green refused to provide any useful information to the prosecution. Thus, his relationship to Frederick Douglass was never revealed at the trial for the simple reason that it remained unknown to the authorities. Just like the "old man" whom he had followed—and unlike Stevens and Cook—the Emperor was noble enough to protect his friends.

George Sennott first showed off his flashy legal skills in defense of Green. "His struggle with the prosecution was a sort of guerrilla warfare [in which] he attacked the indictment on all points." Most effective was his motion to dismiss the treason charge "on the strength of the Dred Scott decision, which deprives negroes of citizenship, and consequently of their treasonable capabilities." Sennott's argument was both ironic and incisive, and he used it to point out the hypocrisy of slavery itself. The spectators gaped in "amazement at the utterance of 'Abolition sentiments' in a Virginia Court of justice," but Judge Parker realized that he had been backed into a corner. A treason conviction had to rest on a betrayal of allegiance, but Chief Justice Taney had ruled that black men could not be citizens of a state, which negated any duty of loyalty to Virginia. Andrew Hunter objected to the motion, but the logic of Sennott's position was undeniable and the treason count was dismissed by the court.[27] Sennott's other arguments did not fare well. He sought the dismissal of the other counts on various technical grounds—including a farsighted challenge to the composition of the jury that was over a century ahead of its time—but Parker denied every motion. Then, after only the briefest deliberation, the jury returned verdicts of guilty on the charges of murder and conspiracy.

John Copeland's trial followed immediately after Green's, with Sennott again appearing for the defendant. Next to Brown and Cook, Copeland was the most notorious of the prisoners. Described in the press as a "bright mulatto," Copeland had been born free in North Carolina and raised in Oberlin, Ohio. He had been a highly visible leader of the Oberlin fugitive slave rescue, which led to his indictment in early 1859. Copeland evaded arrest, and he was already a fugitive when he fled Ohio to join John Brown. His capture at Harper's Ferry therefore attracted the immediate attention of United States Marshal Mathew Johnson in Cleveland. Within days of his arrival in Charlestown, Copeland was interrogated in his cell by Marshal Johnson, who was accompanied by Marshal Jefferson Martin of Virginia and a local sheriff's deputy named Andrew Kennedy.

Marshal Johnson was a staunchly partisan, proslavery Democrat who had been responsible for rigging the juries in the trials of the Oberlin rescuers. Having been frustrated by Copeland's escape from Ohio, Johnson jumped at the opportunity to get his hands on the fugitive, intending "to ferret out testimony implicating the other parties" to Brown's raid. Like his political ally Clement Vallandingham, Johnson was especially interested in gathering evidence against Republican Congressman Joshua Giddings, who was the bête noir of Ohio Democrats. The marshal's questioning was relentless, and Copeland eventually buckled under the pressure. Johnson proudly informed the press that he had successfully extracted a full confession from the prisoner.[28]

In reality, Copeland provided only limited information, none of which could be especially helpful in the prosecution of Giddings or others. He admitted that he had been recruited by Brown (who had already been convicted) and Kagi (who was dead), while insisting that his only intention had been "running off slaves" as Brown had done in Missouri. He told Johnson that two prominent Oberlin Republicans, the brothers

Ralph and Samuel Plumb, had given him $15 for expenses and added cryptically that other unnamed persons in Cleveland had also given him "money to join John Brown."[29] Notably missing from the confession, however, was any mention of Boston abolitionists, and even the Plumbs' involvement appeared to be slight and indirect. Ohio's Marshal Johnson might have gotten something he wanted out of Copeland, but Virginia's Governor Wise was disappointed to say the least. Unlike Cook, however, Copeland had no influential relative to negotiate with the prosecution. No efforts were made to improve his confession in the hope of leniency, and it was therefore submitted to the court in its original form.

Sennott opened Copeland's defense by again moving for the dismissal of the treason count. This time the prosecution agreed to abandon the charge, while insisting that Copeland's confession was sufficient to find him guilty of both murder and inciting a servile rebellion. Sennott argued that the confession was inadmissible, as "it had been made under influence as well as threats." While Sennott's factual assertion was undoubtedly true, Judge Parker overruled the objection on legal grounds. Nineteenth-century Virginia law did not presume that black prisoners were entitled to remain silent when questioned by white authorities. The imaginative Sennott, however, had another argument up his sleeve. In that case, he contended, Copeland's confession had to be taken as a whole. The defendant had admitted only to attempting to "run off slaves," which amounted to the crime of slave stealing, as opposed to murder, conspiracy, and rebellion. Slave stealing, however, had not been charged in the indictment, and the prosecution "could not be allowed now to contradict their own story."

For the first time in four trials, Parker appeared to be moved by a highly technical legal argument. The judge complimented Sennott for his persuasiveness and visibly hesitated before ruling on the defense motion. Realizing that his entire case was in trouble, Hunter sputtered that the prosecution had proved a common purpose among the raiders that Sennott's "ingenious pleading" could not evade. But still Parker hesitated, creating a palpable stir among the spectators. Finally the court ruled that mere "evidence of a conspiracy to run off slaves did not and would not support" the indictment, but that the jury could decide whether there had been sufficient proof of a "common design [of rebellion] chargeable upon all the conspirators."[30] With that instruction, the jury retired and, for the first time in any of the proceedings, a spirited discussion could be heard in the jury room. Sennott's argument had given the jurors some pause, but they eventually returned a verdict of guilty on every count save treason.

There had now been four trials and four convictions. Brown had been condemned to hang, and there was no doubt that Coppoc, Green, and Copeland would also receive the death penalty when they faced sentencing the following week. Nonetheless, Governor Wise's greater objective had not been achieved. Although he could now execute the four prisoners at hand, he had obtained no evidence against Frederick Douglass, Samuel Howe, or any of the others whom he wanted to ensnare. That made the forthcoming trials of John Cook and Aaron Stevens even more important. Which case could be manipulated to provide the most useful evidence? Should one or the other be transferred to the federal court in Staunton? And could Cook in particular be persuaded to expand his confession in the necessary direction?

EIGHT
Intrigues

Following the convictions of Green and Copeland, Judge Parker ordered a recess until 10:00 a.m. on Monday, November 7. When court opened that morning, Cook's case was immediately referred to a grand jury, which spent the next two hours hearing evidence from twelve witnesses—including the kidnap victims Lewis Washington and John Allstadt—before returning a five-count indictment on the usual charges of treason, murder, and conspiracy.[1] By then, Cook had been working on his confession for over a week, on the assumption that a deal was in the works for a transfer to the federal court (as the first step toward an eventual reprieve). Although the formal indictment was a significant step toward prosecuting the case in a Virginia state court, the defense team was not alarmed. Cook's handwritten confession had already been delivered to Andrew Hunter, and Voorhees expected his client to be delivered to the custody of the United States marshal when court reconvened after lunch.

Cook's attorneys were not the only ones who assumed that his confession was the key to obtaining a federal trial. A correspondent for the *New York Tribune* had already reported that "Gov. Wise is supposed to have granted to Cook the permission to be tried in the United States court . . . with some hope, how much is uncertain, of lenient treatment." The object of the transfer, according to the *Tribune*, was "to enable the prosecution to summon as witnesses the persons who are named in Cook's confession." The reporter did not identify his sources, but they appeared to include Daniel Voorhees.[2] As things turned out, however, the *Tribune*'s well-informed power of prediction fell somewhat short.

At the opening of the afternoon session, John Cook and Aaron Stevens were brought from the jail together. Stevens was still suffering from severe wounds to his head and chest. Swathed in bandages, he appeared weak and disoriented, and he had to be provided with a cot rather than a chair. One reporter speculated that Stevens was groggy due to "the abstinence from food and the large quantity of medication taken by him."[3] He had not been in court since his arraignment, nearly two weeks earlier, when he had briefly agreed to representation by Botts and Green. Now he had a new lawyer, George Sennott, whom he hardly knew. It would soon become evident that Sennott had barely been able to meet with his client or to plan a defense.

Cook, in contrast, arrived with an entourage. He was accompanied on either side by his brothers-in-law, the influential Ashbel Willard and the wealthy Robert Crowley. Also with him were his four high-powered lawyers, who surrounded their client as he made his way down the crowded aisle. The effect of this circle of supporters—which was no doubt intended—was to make the diminutive Cook look even smaller and therefore unthreatening. Just as Daniel Voorhees had planned, the fearsome Captain Cook of Harper's Ferry fame had been replaced by a slight and slouching, and if anything somewhat effeminate, young man. "Were it not for the fact that he is quite round-shouldered," noted one observer, he "would be considered handsome."[4]

Judge Parker was in his accustomed place at the rear of the room, presiding from an elevated platform that allowed him to see over the crowd of spectators. Parker sat "amid a chaos of law-books, papers and inkstands, and holding upon his knees a volume bigger than all the rest," while he wondered how to begin the proceedings.[5] Neither the judge nor the defense lawyers knew quite what to expect as Andrew Hunter had not yet made clear his intentions for the day.

The confusion was not Hunter's fault. He had received a series of contradictory directives from Governor Wise about which defendant he should next bring to trial. Wise had instructed Hunter to refer at least one of the prisoners to the U.S. District Court, but he could not decide whether to deliver Cook or Stevens—or perhaps even Albert Hazlett, who had yet to be conclusively identified—to the federal authorities. Hunter had argued in favor of transferring Cook, not only as an accommodation to Governor Willard but chiefly because Cook's cooperation could be used to ensnare future defendants. The wounded Stevens seemed likely to die before a federal trial could be held, and Hazlett had thus far followed the advice of his attorney to remain completely silent. From a strictly tactical perspective, therefore, Cook was the most logical of the three defendants for removal to federal court.

Wise, however, had been under heavy pressure to do otherwise. The widespread rumors of Cook's impending transfer to federal court had resulted in a deluge of letters and telegrams from Virginians, all demanding that Cook be tried and hanged by the commonwealth. Typical was a letter from Alfred Barbour of Harper's Ferry, which went on for three pages describing Cook as "the greatest villain" and "a sworn spy." The local community had "been most brutally betrayed by him, and he should suffer death right here among this people." Barbour warned Wise that the citizens of Jefferson County "would die before they would suffer Cook to be removed to the Federal jurisdiction."[6] As late as Monday morning, Wise was still undecided about how to proceed and Hunter was completely in the dark.

Surprisingly, the first prosecutor to speak that day was Commonwealth Attorney Charles Harding, who had played only a minor, and mostly somnolent, role in the four earlier trials. Harding informed the court that several witnesses were present who had nothing to say about Stevens, and he therefore proposed to proceed with Cook's case first. That development was not what Cook's attorneys had anticipated, as it appeared to cut off the possibility of further negotiations with Wise and Hunter. Someone whispered to Harding that "Cook might possibly be taken to another place for trial," but the district attorney was unmoved. "No, Sir," he hissed, "If the United States want him they . . .

must wait till we get through with him. We caught him, and we mean to have the first chance at hanging him."[7] If Cook had not been frightened by the prospect of hanging, he might have smiled at Harding's pompous boast. In fact, Cook and his comrades had escaped rather easily from Virginia's inept militia, and he had been caught almost accidentally by two freelance Pennsylvanians. Hazlett had likewise been arrested by Pennsylvania bounty hunters, and the other prisoners had been captured by federal troops. Virginia had the upper hand in the current prosecution but not as the result of any martial prowess.

Shocked at the turn of events, neither Voorhees nor Willard knew what to say in response. Turning to Hunter for an explanation, they would have seen him seated tensely at counsel table, perhaps clenching his fists while doing his best to appear expressionless. Fortunately for the defense, Thomas Green jumped to his feet. Exploiting his familiarity with local practice and with local practitioners, Green insisted on professional courtesy from his fellow Virginians. "He was unable to proceed with the case," said Green, because he had not yet had time to read the indictment or to decide what plea his client should enter to the charges. On behalf of his colleagues, Green demanded "that the Commonwealth . . . proceed with the case of Stephens, which would allow them time to prepare the case of Cook."[8]

Harding huffed a bit, but he ultimately acceded to Green's request. They were friends and neighbors, after all, and the indictment had been issued only that morning. Through all of the discussion, Hunter still remained uncharacteristically silent.

Now it was George Sennott's turn to feel betrayed. His badly wounded client had to be carried into court on a stretcher, and he appeared to be in no condition for an immediate trial. Sennott moved for a delay or, failing that, a transfer to another county. Sennott's demand was eminently reasonable. He had just recently concluded the cases of Shields Green and John Copeland, while Cook's lawyers had enjoyed over a week's worth of preparation. It was simply unfair to rush the seriously injured Stevens to trial ahead of Cook. Nonetheless, Judge Parker deferred to Cook's well-connected counsel and ruled that the case against Stevens would have to proceed that day. The jury panel was called into the courtroom, and "a considerable number of jurymen" were quickly selected for Stevens's case.

Only then did Andrew Hunter finally speak up, to the consternation of almost everybody in the courtroom. There had evidently been "an accidental delay in communications" from Richmond, and Hunter announced that he had just "at that moment received a telegraphic dispatch from Governor Wise" that would necessarily "interfere with further proceedings." Hunter read the telegram out loud: "I think you had better try Cook, and hand Stephens over to the federal authorities."[9] The bargain with Cook had been rescinded.

Hunter was evidently embarrassed by his own sudden volte-face, or perhaps he felt that he had to apologize for misleading Willard and Voorhees. For whatever reason, Hunter went on to explain that he had "for some time been in communication with Governor Wise upon this subject, and it had partly been determined to give up Cook to the United States Court." In fact, that had been Hunter's initial recommendation, based on "a number of facts important to the development of this case, which were unknown to the public and would for the present remain so." The governor, however, had just that day decided otherwise, based on other undisclosed facts that made Stevens's case the most likely vehicle for "bringing before the Federal bar a number of prominent Abolition fanatics of the North." Hunter dutifully added that he now fully supported Wise's decision. "What we aim at is not only the destruction of these men whom we have in confinement; we now strike at higher and wickeder game."[10]

It appears, however, that nobody had bothered to alert Charles Harding to the discussions between Hunter and Wise. Once he realized what was going on, Harding objected forcefully to the transfer of either defendant to another jurisdiction, thus setting off an unseemly quarrel between the two prosecutors. The chaos on Judge Parker's desk was nothing compared to what now descended on the courtroom, as Harding loudly denounced everyone connected with the nefarious plot to supersede his own authority. "Hunter has honeyfugled me long enough," he declared, "and now I'm going to take the bit in my teeth." The bellicose commonwealth attorney protested that he "was not in league with Governor Wise," but it soon became apparent that he was more concerned about his own pocketbook than about political alliances or lines of authority. Unlike Hunter, who was on Wise's payroll and who would be paid no matter where the proceedings were held, Harding's fee depended on keeping the matters in Jefferson County. He was paid $50 for every case he tried, and he would not receive even the "small pittance allowed" by the county for any prosecution that was transferred to federal court. Once roused from his habitual torpor, Harding was prepared to fight vociferously—"with all the intensity of inebriation"—for the preservation of his income.[11] He did not owe his office to Wise, and the governor's grander strategies could be damned.

Seeing the division on the prosecution team, George Sennott decided to jump into the fray. He announced that he would not consent to his client being transferred to the jurisdiction of the United States government. Sennott's reflexive response had been to protect northern abolitionists from federal subpoenas, and he assumed that Stevens would feel the same way. Why should they cooperate at all with the prosecution in the hunt for its higher and wickeder game? But Hunter called Sennott's bluff, announcing that he would be just as happy to bring Albert Hazlett to trial in federal court and to go forward that day with Stevens's case.

Sennott finally realized that his client—faced with the prospect of hanging—might very well prefer to delay his trial, no matter what the reason. He asked for a moment to consult with Stevens and announced that they would after all "accept the offer of the State to hand him over to the Federal authorities."

Stevens was then delivered to the custody of United States Marshal Martin and returned to jail. Harding was outraged to see half of his remaining fee virtually walking (or rather, being carried) out of the courtroom door. He demanded that the clerk "enter his earnest protest against the whole proceedings as wrong" and insisted that it be shown on the docket. Judge Parker, however, had run out of patience for Harding's cupidity. "Do no such thing," he ordered the clerk, adding, "I wish no such protest on the docket of this Court." Harding reluctantly took his seat, "muttering vengeance as he withdrew."[12]

When the dust finally settled, John Cook was the only defendant left in the courtroom, the victim of an exquisite double cross. His confession was in the hands of the prosecutor, completed and embellished exactly as he had been instructed, but the promised bargain had not been kept. Voorhees attempted to reassure his client, but there was little he could do about the distressing turn of events. At least he would be able think about things overnight. The entire day had already been spent in jurisdictional wrangling, so Judge Parker recessed court and directed that a new jury be assembled the following morning. John Cook's trial was about to begin in earnest.

※　◉　※

The prosecution had no difficulty preparing the case against Cook. Oblivious to all intrigues, Harding had already summoned over a dozen witnesses in the expectation of beginning the trial on Monday afternoon, and he simply had to re-subpoena them for return to court on Tuesday. No subpoena was really necessary, however, for the main witness against Cook. Lewis Washington had already testified numerous times—at the four earlier trials and related preliminary proceedings— and he was ever ready to take the stand against the man who had deceived and kidnapped him.[13]

Washington was not the only person eager to get into the courtroom on Tuesday. Interest in the trials had waned in the aftermath of

Brown's conviction and sentencing, but it quickly returned when it became known that Cook was about to face justice. Although the streets had been relatively quiet over the preceding weekend, they were now once more in an "explosive state" as armed patrols again took to the streets with muskets and Sharps rifles. The trials of Coppoc, Green, and Copeland had been relatively anticlimactic—notwithstanding George Sennott's heroic exertions—because the defendants were seen as minor participants and the outcome of the cases had never been in doubt. Cook's case was different. As one observer noted, the locals expressed more hostility toward Cook than to all of the other prisoners combined. It was widely thought that Cook, in addition to his other crimes, had "heartlessly married [a] young girl only for the purpose of establishing himself more fully in the confidence of the community, with a direct view to the preparations for the outbreak."[14]

It was therefore unsurprising when a rowdy crowd gathered in front of the courthouse by 7:00 on Tuesday morning, hurling denunciations and making threats that required the intervention of the sheriff to keep the peace. Otherwise respectable citizens unabashedly debated the merits of lynching. The situation was not helped when Charles Harding arrived looking as though he had not slept all night. Harding noisily complained about Governor Wise's manipulation of the case—cornering anyone who would listen to his long-winded arguments—which further infuriated the knotted crowd.

The courtroom remained locked despite the clamor, with only the participants and journalists allowed to enter. Then a bell rang at exactly 9:30, and the crowd was allowed to pour in through the doors. As they scrambled to find seats, the spectators might have noticed that John Cook and his lawyers were already seated at counsel table. Neatly dressed and looking even smaller than before, Cook's pale complexion and stooped shoulders "detract[ed] from the manliness of his presence," and his darting eyes betrayed "an irresolution of purpose" that distinguished him from the earlier defendants.[15] While Brown, Coppoc, Green, and Copeland—and even the badly wounded Stevens—had done their best to appear steadfast in public, Cook was unable to conceal his fear of the prosecutors and perhaps his doubts about the plans of his own lawyers. The man who had once boldly defied the Kickapoo Rangers was nowhere to be seen in court that morning.

Soon the distinctive sound of cracking chestnut shells could be heard throughout the room. It was understandable that the spectators were hungry. Many had been waiting on the street for nearly three hours, and quite a few had traveled for hours before that, either by wagon or on foot, as they swarmed into Charlestown from outlying villages. They were no doubt even more avid for entertainment than they were for food, but they would have to wait awhile longer to hear the evidence against Cook.

Judge Parker first ordered Cook to stand for the reading of the indictment. The prisoner arose, hands rigidly at his side, while his attorneys whispered encouragement to him. Lawson Botts, in particular, sat coiled in his chair, as though he was watching for opportunities that he could turn to his client's advantage. When the clerk at last finished reading the three long counts, it was time for Botts to spring upon the prosecution. The indictment was defective, he argued, because the treason count was inconsistent with the requirements of the common law. Botts moved to quash the crucial treason charge, which was the only one that threatened to place Cook beyond Governor Wise's power to grant a reprieve.

Andrew Hunter, who had drawn the indictment, was not amused. "With a power of resistance that show[ed] him to be altogether the ablest of the Charlestown lawyers," he vigorously refuted Botts's argument point by point. But Hunter would not have the last word. Under Virginia practice, the moving party was allowed a rebuttal argument, and that assignment fell to the formidable Thomas Green.[16]

Green was an ungainly man, "long, angular, uncouth and wild in gesture" who at first seemed "deficient in all rhetorical graces." He spoke in mangled sentences that sometimes appeared only half formed. His rustic pronunciation—"in which 'thar' and 'whar' were the least of his offenses"—was nearly unbearable to northern listeners. But Green had no interest in the aesthetic prejudices of urban journalists. As the mayor of Charlestown, he was well aware of his audience, and his presentation was precisely suited to the circumstances. In his own hometown, Green demonstrated powers of persuasion "so decided that, while he is upon his legs, he carries everything with him."[17]

Had the motion been determined solely on the quality of the advocacy, Green might well have won the day for his client. Judge Parker, however, recognized the centrality of the treason count, and he naturally proved unwilling to cripple the prosecution case. Perhaps the count was defective under the traditional common law, he ruled, but it was nonetheless valid under Virginia's criminal code. The defense attorneys were clearly disappointed, but they could not have been surprised. It would have taken courage beyond belief for any Virginia judge to eviscerate Cook's indictment on the basis of a pleading defect. Nonetheless, the gauntlet had been thrown down. Cook's case would be defended where it mattered most. With no real chance of exoneration, the lawyers would still try to save their client's life.

But first a jury had to be seated. The court ordered the sheriff to summon a panel of "twenty four freeholders of your county, residing remote from the place where the felony was committed." Even with the precaution of excluding residents of Harper's Ferry, it might have seemed that impartial jurors would be hard to find in Jefferson County. But the court nonetheless "had but little difficulty" in the selection. Judge Parker cared only if a prospective juror "had expressed an opinion which would prevent [him from] giving the prisoner a fair and impartial trial," and he was willing to rephrase his questions until he got the right answer. One exchange was typical:

JUDGE: Have you heard the evidence in the other cases?
JUROR: (Eagerly) Yes, sir.

JUDGE: I mean, if you have heard the evidence, and are likely to
be influenced by it, you are disqualified here. Have you heard
much of the evidence?

JUROR: No, sir.[18]

Parker did employ more searching questions to ensure that no juror
held any "conscientious scruples" against imposing the death penalty,
and twelve such men were quickly found, most of whom were farmers. Nine of the jurors were slaveholders, having owned at least thirty
slaves among them. The southern press proudly reported that Cook's
jury was "possessed of a fair share of intelligence."[19]

Once the jury was sworn, Judge Parker ordered Cook to stand for a
second reading of the indictment. This time, the court demanded that
the defendant enter a plea. In a "firm and dignified" voice, Cook declared that he was not guilty of treason.

Then, to the surprise of the gallery, Cook pled guilty to the second
and third counts of the indictment, which charged murder and incitement of a slave rebellion. Thomas Green quickly elaborated on his client's unexpected plea. Cook was willing to admit "the fact of conspiring
with slaves to rebel, which was punishable with death or imprisonment
for life," but he denied the more serious charge of treason, which carried a mandatory death penalty that could not be commuted by the governor.[20] It was an unorthodox tactic, but the reasons for Cook's guilty
plea would be revealed within moments.

❊　❀　❊

Andrew Hunter took the floor and announced that "he held in his
hand a confession written by John E. Cook." The existence of Cook's
confession had been rumored all week, but the document turned out
to be longer than expected. "There were twenty-five foolscap pages of
it."[21] With the court's permission, Hunter began to read the confession
to the jury, and the reason for Cook's guilty plea immediately became
apparent. Cook had admitted his extensive participation in Brown's

invasion, from its beginning in Canada to the night of the raid. He spared no detail about his own involvement, including his deceitful reconnaissance in Harper's Ferry, the treacherous kidnapping of Colonel Washington, and even the pot shots he had taken at the militia from a Maryland hilltop. Standing alone, the confession provided more than enough evidence to convict Cook of murder and conspiracy—and its admissibility could not be challenged—so there was absolutely nothing to be gained by a plea of not guilty. Governor Willard had irrevocably eliminated that option as soon as he delivered the first draft of Cook's confession to Andrew Hunter.

It took Hunter over half an hour to read the entire confession, which very nearly amounted to the story of Cook's life, beginning with his departure for Kansas and concluding with his escape into Pennsylvania. The jury and spectators learned about Cook's first meeting with Brown in Kansas, their brief stay in Iowa, and all of the events that brought them to Virginia. The confession included only a few references to Cook's year in Harper's Ferry, and it understandably minimized the extent of his spying exploits. In Cook's account, he had been ordered to Harper's Ferry over his own objection, and he had afterward attempted to discourage Brown from carrying out the attack. Other information included a description of life at Brown's Maryland headquarters and an account of the doomed army's nighttime march across the Potomac and into Harper's Ferry. It was not possible for Cook to deny his role in kidnapping Colonel Washington and John Allstadt, which he therefore explained in some detail.

Hunter had once harbored doubts about proving the murder charge against Cook, but they were resolved by Cook's incriminating admission that he had fired several shots at the Virginia militia.[22] Although Cook characterized his actions as nothing more than "an attempt to draw their fire upon myself," Hunter was later able to argue that Cook was responsible for killing George Turner, one of the three Virginians who died in the raid. That damning fact would never have been revealed if Governor Willard had not prompted Cook's confession, and Hunter therefore savored the moment when he read it aloud.

The greatest interest in Cook's confession, however, did not concern the defendant himself. There had been much public anticipation that Cook would implicate others, preferably including Boston abolitionists as well as his immediate comrades in arms. The speculation had been fueled by the implicit promises of Hunter and Wise, supported by the secret assurances that Voorhees and Willard had given to the press. The courtroom therefore fell especially silent whenever it seemed that Hunter was about to announce new names. Cook had done his best to satisfy the prosecution. He included the names of most of Brown's raiders, although they had already been identified by Stevens and, in any case, the majority of them were dead. He also mentioned his four fellow fugitives—Charles Tidd, Francis Merriam, Barclay Coppoc, and Owen Brown—all of whom were by then well beyond Virginia's reach. More helpfully, Cook named Aaron Stevens as the leader of the kidnapping sortie, and he added that Stevens read aloud Brown's constitution and had helped administer an oath to the recruits on the evening of the raid. That information could be useful at Stevens's forthcoming trial, to refute any defense based on purported ignorance of Brown's plan.

But what about the "higher and wickeder game" against whom Hunter had inveighed the previous day? Had Cook implicated, as promised, the fiendish abolitionists who had inspired the raid from the safety of northern pulpits and meeting halls? He certainly named them. Cook's confession disclosed for the first time that Frederick Douglass and Gerrit Smith had received Brown's invitations to the Chatham conference. He added that Smith, Samuel Howe, Thaddeus Hyatt, and Franklin Sanborn might have been Brown's "aiders or abettors," but he did not know precisely how they were "connected with his plan." He recalled that Brown had sent a letter to Boston announcing the readiness of his "machines" and his intention to "start them in a few days." The recipient might have been Howe, who had already given Brown "a breach-loading carbine [and] a pair of muzzle-loading pistols." Howe's weaponry notwithstanding, that was not the smoking gun Hunter had hoped to produce. Although more than enough to convict Cook, the confession provided only modest support for future subpoenas or warrants.

※ ◉ ※

Once Hunter finished reading, it was expected that he would offer the confession itself into evidence. That would have been routine and unobjectionable. But rather than introduce the written confession, Hunter explained that it would be withheld from the court and published as a pamphlet by a local printer. Hunter's ostensible purpose was altruistic. The printer had agreed to sell copies of the pamphlet and donate the proceeds to Samuel Young, a citizen of Harper's Ferry who had been severely wounded by Brown's men. If entered into the court record, the confession would have become publicly available, which would have diminished the value of the printed edition. Thus secrecy was essential to the success of the venture.

Hunter had also obtained the agreement of local newspapers to publish only a summary of the confession rather than a full transcription. Several southern reporters were briefly shown some pages of the confession and were able to verify that it was "written in a smooth style," as well as its length, but the full text was withheld for the time being. Northern reporters, however, were not allowed even a glimpse of the confession, leading the *New York Tribune* to complain that the document had been too jealously guarded by the prosecution. "It is quite a Virginia notion," reported the *Tribune*, "this turning of a public paper into private uses." The reporter's protests did not help. "The paper is kept secret, and will not be permitted to be published at present."[23]

The sale and circulation of Cook's confession was not wholly charitable, however, and not exclusively for the relief of the injured Samuel Young. Cook himself was desperately in need of public sympathy, and he obviously hoped to benefit from a show of compassion toward a vic-

tim of the raid. In fact, the publication arrangement had been negoti-
ated by Botts and Green who, acting as Cook's attorneys, certified the
accuracy of "the original manuscript, for the purpose of making a ver-
batim copy."

The pamphlet was rushed into print and appeared for distribution the
next day, leaving no doubt that it was meant to demonstrate Cook's remorse. Samuel Young was described on the cover as "a non-slaveholder,
who is permanently disabled by a wound received in defence of southern institutions." The reference to Young as a "non-slaveholder," was
of course intended to contradict Brown's claim that he had acted nobly
to free the slaves, and the reference to Young's "defence of southern
institutions" was intended to show the solidarity of Virginia's citizens
in repudiating abolition. Both points were repeated and emphasized in
the pamphlet's preface:

> Mr. Young is a non-slaveholder and a poor man, but who neverthe-
> less showed an allegiance to the institutions of the South in peril-
> ing his life in defence of her rights, which is worthy of the highest
> commendation, and which should be rewarded in some public and
> substantial manner.[24]

The preface also included an endorsement by Botts and Green, who
had evidently brokered a partial repudiation of abolitionism on Cook's
behalf.

Andrew Hunter sincerely wanted to assist Samuel Young, and he
was therefore willing to allow Cook to make a pitch for sympathy, but
the prosecutor also appears to have had an ulterior reason for withholding the original document from the official record. The first version of Cook's confession—which had been given to Hunter on Friday,
November 4—was only twenty-two pages long, and Hunter rejected it
because it did "not refer to any of the conspirators outside of the immediate band." The prosecutor had promised the governor to get more
out of Cook, and by Tuesday he had made good on his pledge.[25]

By the time it was read in court on Tuesday morning, the confession had been expanded to twenty-five pages, and it now included specific references to Frederick Douglass, Samuel Howe, Gerrit Smith, Thaddeus Hyatt, and Franklin Sanborn—most of whom had earlier been singled out by Governor Wise as targeted abolitionists. Wise had inveighed against Smith, Howe, and Douglass from the day he arrived in Harper's Ferry following the raid, and his interrogation of Brown had repeatedly raised their names as potential conspirators. At least one reporter had been tipped in advance that Smith and Howe would be "implicated by Cook's confession."[26]

It is evident that Cook had been induced to add the five damnable names over the weekend in the hope of cementing his deal with Wise and Hunter. Because the multiple references to the northerners were scattered throughout the confession, it is quite possible that Cook accomplished the emendation by inserting pages, or partial pages, and with strikeovers or interlineations. If so, it is understandable the Hunter would not have wanted the public or the court to examine what was clearly an altered manuscript. For evidentiary purposes, it was sufficient to read the confession aloud. For authentication purposes, it was sufficient to allow a few favored journalists to take a look at Cook's handwriting.[27]

Cook's own attorneys, of course, would have been happy to collude with Hunter in suppressing the messier version of the written confession since they hoped to curry public favor through publication of the pamphlet. The necessity for cooperation further explains Botts's and Green's addition to the pamphlet's preface, in which they vouched for its fidelity to the original. Ongoing negotiation over the form and content of the confession would also explain Hunter's visible discomfort on Monday while anticipating Wise's decision about whether to transfer Cook to federal court. It seems certain that Hunter had already informed Wise of the additions and improvements he had obtained from Cook, and he was waiting to see if he could fulfill his tentative bargain with the defense. If the deal had gone through as planned, thus shipping Cook off to Staunton for a later trial, there would have been no need ever to produce the confession in Charlestown and consequently no reason to care about the appearance of extra pages and other last-minute changes.

It turned out that Hunter did need the confession for Cook's trial, but there was insufficient time to have it completely rewritten by the next day. Hunter was thus left holding an inconveniently discontinuous set of pages in his hand when he stood up in court on Tuesday morning, causing him to temporize. This account is necessarily speculative, given that the handwritten confession has not survived, but it closely fits all of the known facts, including Cook's eleventh-hour revisions, Wise's sudden change of heart, and Hunter's subsequent unwillingness to produce the confession in public. In any case, we know that Governor Wise's dissatisfaction caused him to insist on an immediate trial in Jefferson County, to Cook's dismay and perhaps Hunter's regret. An intrigue was thus set in motion, in which the printer received the written confession and the court did not.

❊ NINE ❊

Defense

Cook's confession was sufficient to convict him of murder and con-spiracy, but it did not resolve the charge of treason or settle the question of punishment. There would still have to be a trial on those issues, meaning that witnesses would have to testify. It was after dark, how-ever, by the time Hunter finished reading the confession, so the court adjourned until the next day.

Despite the usual uproar from the gallery, Cook appeared to be in unusually good spirits as he took his seat between Governor Willard and Robert Crowley on Wednesday morning, leading one reporter to speculate that he was "evidently buoyed up with the hope of a favorable result from the verdict of the jury." Nothing encouraging had happened yet in court, but perhaps Daniel Voorhees had whispered something optimistic to his client. Then again, Cook could have been putting on a show of bravado for the sake of his mother-in-law. Mary Ann Kennedy was present in the courtroom, and she appeared to be "in great distress of mind and [she] wept considerably" as the judge called the case to order.[1] Mary Ann was accompanied by her teenaged son James, who unsuccessfully attempted to comfort her, and Cook's forced smile might have been intended for his benefit as well.

There was no reason for Cook to keep smiling once Colonel Wash-ington took the stand. The well-practiced witness delivered devastat-ing testimony that closely tied Cook to the events at Harper's Ferry. Under prosecution questioning, Washington detailed his first meeting with Cook, explaining that the abolitionist spy had gained his confidence through a show of false friendship. Washington described his capture at his plantation in the middle of the night and his delivery into Brown's hands as a hostage. As could have been expected of a witness after four earlier trials, there were several inconsistencies with Washington's previous testimony, but they were generally unimportant. Voorhees did not bring them up, if he noticed them at all. Instead, the cross examination established Cook's contrition. Voorhees had evidently arranged a jailhouse meeting between Cook and Washington, at which Cook apologized for the kidnapping and expressed regret for his deeds.

The Byrne brothers, Terrence and James, also testified about their seizure by Cook. Terrence refuted Cook's claim to be a reluctant kidnapper. As the witness put it, Cook told him "that he was his prisoner and must go with him." When Terrence balked, "Cook said that he did not want any parlaying in the matter; he must go or run the risk of being shot." James backed up his brother's story, but he was also compelled to admit that Cook had not been entirely hard-hearted. "Upon pleading sickness . . . he was permitted to stay at home" and was not taken to the armory along with the other hostages.[2]

The fourth occurrence witness was Lind Currie, the principal of the school where Cook had stashed Brown's rifles. Cook had actually been rather courteous to Currie, allowing the schoolmaster to take home a child who was frightened by the commotion. But that did not prevent Currie from embellishing his testimony to Cook's disadvantage. Currie claimed that Cook had responded to the sound of distant gunfire by telling a slave, "There, that's another one of your oppressors gone." It is remotely possible that Cook actually said something of that sort, but Currie was not finished putting words in his mouth. According to Currie, Cook had volunteered that several leading abolitionists were involved in the insurrection: "Gerrit Smith and Fred Douglass he mentioned. He said they were interested in it and knew of it." That implausible testimony was obviously prompted by the prosecution in an attempt to achieve the goals of Governor Wise. Voorhees, however, did not object. The implication of Smith and Douglass was consistent with the defense that he planned to raise, so he allowed Currie's obviously contrived testimony to stand unchallenged.

By far the most questionable, if not fraudulent, witness of the day was a man who claimed to be Cook's father-in-law. Identified only as "Mr. Kennedy," he had virtually nothing to say about the events surrounding the insurrection, but appearing as sort of an anti-character witness, he claimed that "Cook had ordered him from his own house shortly after having married his daughter." In an inspired bit of understatement, the *Baltimore American* reported that "the witness did not speak in a very flattering manner of Cook, and intimated pretty strongly that he would not object to seeing him hung."

However deep or justified was his animus, the witness was not in fact Cook's father-in-law. Virginia Kennedy's real father had died at least a decade earlier. The witness's true identity is unknown, but evidently he did have some connection to the Kennedy family. Mary Ann Kennedy was in the gallery that day, and she did not raise any objection to the faux Mr. Kennedy's testimony. Moreover, Mary Ann Kennedy and Charles Harding were cousins, and even a drunken prosecutor would have known better than to put an outright imposter on the stand. The most likely answer to the mystery is that the witness had been living with Mary Ann Kennedy but had never married her. Anne Brown later speculated as much, and that would explain why Mary Ann Kennedy herself did not protest his testimony. It therefore seems that "Mr. Kennedy" was telling the truth about everything other than his name: he did have a confrontation with Cook, he had been thrown out of the boardinghouse, and he definitely wanted to see the defendant hang. Daniel Voorhees wisely allowed the witness to leave the stand without any further opportunity to vent his spleen.[3]

The prosecution called several more witnesses who testified to the violence of the insurrection, although none of them had anything specific to say about Cook. Continuing its tradition of understatement, the

Baltimore American noted that witnesses "did not throw any additional light on the case." By then it was time for the midday break, and the prosecutors rested their case.

❊ ◉ ❊

It had been obvious from the beginning of the trial that Voorhees was going to make a plea for mercy based on Cook's relative youth and naïveté. It was going to be a hard case to make. The defendant was thirty years old, and his sixteen months as a spy in Harper's Ferry had given him ample time to realize the error of his ways. If nothing else, Cook's calculated betrayal of Colonel Washington's friendship had been the deliberate act of a dedicated conspirator rather than an impulsive mistake by a misguided youngster. Whatever illusions Governor Willard might once have harbored, it was apparent by Wednesday after noon that Cook was the most despised man in Jefferson County. If the jurors were to be persuaded to spare Cook's life, something had to be done to change their impression of him. Throughout the earlier proceedings, Voorhees and company had "been moving heaven and earth . . . to get up a feeling in favor of Cook," and now they were entering the last stage.[4] The defendant badly needed character witnesses, and they were going to have to do a remarkable job.

As either seducer or friend, Cook had spent his entire life seeking the favor of women, so it was almost inevitable that two prim southern ladies were called upon to speak up for him. The first was Elmira L. Steptoe. Although the elderly Mrs. Steptoe lived in Jefferson County, she testified by way of affidavit, perhaps because she was fearful of appearing in court and facing the wrath of her neighbors. (Mrs. Steptoe visited Cook in jail, so it is evident that she was in town during the trial.) By the sheerest coincidence, she was well acquainted with Cook. Six years earlier, Mrs. Steptoe had spent the winter in Philadelphia, at the same time that Cook was working there as Robert Crowley's sales representative. As it happened, they both lodged at the Union

Hotel, where they spent much of their free time together. Based on that experience, Mrs. Steptoe regarded Cook "as a good hearted young man [who was] always remarkably polite and attentive." Cook had been especially generous to children, frequently playing with them and providing them with gifts of baked goods and candy. Needless to say, Cook had "endeared himself to her and the remainder of the lady boarders" at the hotel.[5]

Lucy Thompson, who had been one of the children at the Union Hotel, also submitted an affidavit on Cook's behalf. A granddaughter of Mrs. Steptoe, Lucy was about sixteen at the time of the trial, which may be one reason that she did not testify in person. Like her grandmother, Lucy had been captivated by Cook, who had shown her much courtesy and consideration. Once, when she expressed a desire to have her own calling card, Cook had gone out of his way to find an engraver to create one for her. All of the children, she said, "were very fond of him, and he was a general favorite."[6]

Though the jury might have been impressed by Cook's kindness toward old women and children, neither Elmira Steptoe nor Lucy Thompson had provided any persuasive justification for mercy. Even the most thoughtful and polite individual could be held accountable for his later crimes, unless there was some intervening excuse for his actions. Voorhees attempted to provide such a link by offering the affidavit of John Stearns, who had been Cook's employer in Brooklyn. Even before Cook was captured, Stearns had published a letter in the *New York Times* in which he provided a general defense of Cook's character. Now the Brooklyn lawyer submitted a copy of the letter, with an attached affidavit attesting to its accuracy.

Harding objected to the double hearsay, shouting at "the top of his voice" that it was inadmissible and pausing only when "a large and valuable deposit of tobacco . . . unfortunately dropped out of his mouth." For once, Harding had made a coherent point, but Judge Parker was more interested in Hunter's position. With a wave of his hand, Hunter signaled to the court that he had no objection to the evidence, and the affidavit and article were therefore received. At the time it seemed that Hunter was merely being gracious by allowing the defense some latitude in a losing cause.

Stearns did not exactly provide a ringing defense of Cook. Rather than "justify and excuse the rash . . . and criminal proceedings of the Harper's Ferry riot," it was his intention only "to note some facts and antecedents in [Cook's] life which show him to be rather the subject of fanaticism in this matter than the monster of crime which the fears of the Virginians have painted him." Cook was, according to Stearns, an impressionable dreamer with a loose grasp on reality. Despite his skill as a marksman, Cook would never harm a soul of his own volition. The young man had never displayed any interest in radical abolitionism, and if he had been driven to violence it must have been a reaction to his encounters with border ruffians in Kansas. Stearns did not mention John Brown, but he made clear that he condemned "the foolhardy fanaticism evinced . . . in the late Virginia riots." His only goal was to "facilitate a fair and impartial trial, that shall separate his acts from the *fear* of the people, and lead to a charitable judgment of the conditions of mind that has induced these transactions." The southern reaction to Stearns's statement was mixed. One writer mocked the attempt to characterize Cook as "a meek and inoffensive man, or a mere moonstruck poet." But another journalist was receptive to the explanation that "Cook did not contemplate anything like treason, and that his conduct was rather the impulse of the moment than a deep laid scheme of outlawry."[7]

The interested party rule prohibited Cook from testifying in his own behalf, which might have been a curse or a blessing. Cook's ability as a storyteller might have helped him convince the jurors that he deeply regretted his involvement in the conspiracy, but it may also have backfired. Many modern defendants have been undone by overconfidence in their own persuasiveness, and there is no way to know whether Cook would have charmed or alienated the Charlestown jurors. Of course, they were all men, which would have worked to Cook's disadvantage.

As it was, Governor Ashbel Willard would be the only live witness for the defense. He began with a brief history of Cook's life, from his childhood in Haddam, to his working life in Brooklyn and Philadelphia, and finally to his disappearance into Kansas. Willard described his brother-in-law as kindhearted and generous, but the true purpose of his testimony was to outline the circumstances surrounding Cook's confession. After describing his arrival in Cook's cell with Senator Mason, and Mason's caution against saying anything incriminating, Willard recounted his own advice to Cook "that he had better make a confession stating all he knew about the matter." In Willard's words, "Cook coincided with him, and hence the confession." That was not much, but at least it showed that Cook had voluntarily cooperated with the prosecution. Willard's testimony was received very favorably in Indiana, but the reaction in Virginia was yet to be seen.[8]

The defense case had lasted less than an hour. The final arguments of counsel—ultimately pitting Hunter against Voorhees—would take much longer.

❈ ❀ ❈

Jury argument was essential to a trial lawyer's success in the 1850s, even more so than today. At a time when interested parties could not testify, the practice of rigorous cross examination—using only leading questions—had not yet emerged. Direct examinations were conducted without the benefit of pretrial discovery, and they, too, were rudimentary by contemporary standards. Final argument, however, had already developed into a fine art. In an era when popular entertainment consisted largely of lectures and sermons, attorneys also adopted techniques that originated on pulpits and in revival tents.

Daniel Voorhees was a master of jury argument, although his other legal skills were no better than fair. "His knowledge of the law was neither broad, nor deep, nor even accurate," but he could speak eloquently in support of virtually any cause. "Others gathered the evidence and planned the fight; he made the speech." And what a speech it could be. Voorhees had a magnetic presence that amplified his "clear and penetrating insight into human nature." In later years, Voorhees would be renowned as one of the greatest courtroom advocates of his age, specializing in the defense of crimes of passion. He would have such great success in obtaining acquittals that Indiana's rules of criminal procedure would be changed to minimize the impact of his jury arguments.[9] The defense of John Cook was his first great challenge on a national stage.

Andrew Hunter was more than two decades older than Voorhees, and he was revered as one of the finest advocates in the commonwealth. His patrician bearing gave him nearly total command of the courtroom, and his unrivaled knowledge of Virginia law allowed him to sweep aside legal points raised by the defense. Voorhees greatly respected Hunter for both his talent and temperament, and he later remarked admiringly that the prosecutor had never shown "a single note of malevolence or exasperation."[10] Hunter could afford to be courteous. He had already obtained the defendant's confession, which made his case nearly uncontestable, and he was operating on his own home ground.

The eagerly awaited duel between Voorhees and Hunter could not begin immediately. First, Charles Harding would have to be given his due. The district attorney's disjointed arguments had not yet bored or baffled anyone to death, but that afternoon he would come close. "For two mortal hours [Harding] poured out a stream of his peculiar eloquence," to the great annoyance of all in attendance. Harding's antics made the spectators laugh out loud, but Judge Parker virtually ignored him, using the time "to read his newspaper and examine his order book." Voorhees and Hunter paid only slightly more attention as they "collected their authorities and arranged their points." That was just as well, given that Harding's "sneering allusion to the foreign counsel for the defence" would have angered Voorhees while offending Hunter's sense of honor.[11]

Harding seemed oblivious to his wearisome effect on the court and jury. He stopped speaking only when he "exhausted his tobacco-box" and the nearby spectators mercifully refused to provide him with an additional plug. Harding's clichéd final words were *fiat justitia ruat caelum*, although at that point it was far more likely that the heavens would have collapsed in exasperation than fallen for the sake of justice.[12]

At last it was time for Voorhees to speak, and he proceeded to deliver an appeal that would be counted among "the most powerful ever made in the Circuit Court of this county."

❋ ✿ ❋

Daniel Voorhees well understood that outsiders were often under intense suspicion in outlying towns and that the fresh trauma of Brown's invasion had rendered Charlestown especially unwelcoming. Although he had been received with superficial courtesy, it could not have escaped his notice that most other strangers were "hemmed in by vulgar scrutiny, and forced to undergo continual inspection." Voorhees therefore began his argument by attempting to establish a bond of familiarity between himself and the jurors. "I come from the sun-set side of your western mountains," he told the jury, "not as an alien to a foreign land, but rather as one who returns to the home of his ancestors, and to the household from which he sprang."[13] Voorhees's ancestors, in fact, were mostly from New Jersey, a detail that he conveniently neglected while reminding the jurors that Indiana had been part of Virginia in the days before the Northwest Territory was ceded to the national government. It is unlikely that any of the jurors felt the remotest connection to Indiana, which had been detached from Virginia for over seventy years, but Voorhees had a more important point to make about his home state. Virginia's "laws there once prevailed, and all her institutions were there established as they are here," he claimed.

By "institutions," of course, Voorhees meant slavery. And his shaky claim of Virginian heritage was the beginning of an attempt to establish himself—and by extension his client—as friends of slavery and enemies of abolition.

Never one to be constrained by facts, Voorhees did not point out that the Northwest Ordinance of 1787 had prohibited slavery in the territory that later became Indiana. Nor would he be constrained by law. "I am not here . . . to talk to you about technicalities of law born of laborious analysis by the light of the midnight lamp," he admitted. Rather, his plea on behalf of this "pale-faced, fair-haired wanderer" would be based "on the common call which the wretched make for sympathy."

Pure sympathy was Voorhees's métier, and he would provide three compelling reasons for the jury to show mercy to Cook. First, was the character of the defendant himself. John Cook was the child of a fine family. His grandfather had fought in the Revolution, as his father did in the War of 1812. His brother-in-law was the esteemed (and proslavery) governor of Indiana. Yes, Cook had participated in a great crime, but he was at heart "a poor deluded boy," a "wayward misled child" who was "young and new to the rough ways of life." He had a kind heart and "a cheerful, obliging, though visionary mind." The jurors needed only to look at Cook to see that he had been nothing more than an innocent naïf. "Never did I plead for a face that I was more willing to show," said Voorhees. "If evil is there, I have not seen it [because] it is a face for a mother to love."

Next, Voorhees explained that Cook had fallen prey to the malign influence of John Brown and other sinful abolitionists. He was an innocent youth who had been "thrown into contact with the pirate and robber of civil warfare." Dreamer that he was, Cook had not recognized that "grim-visaged war, civil commotion, pillage and death, disunion and universal desolation thronged through the mind of John Brown." Indeed, Brown was a "despotic leader and John E. Cook was an ill-fated follower of an enterprise whose horror he now realizes and deplores."

There was a vast moral distance between Brown and Cook, claimed Voorhees, and they should not be punished alike. "Can it be that a jury of Christian men will find no discrimination should be made between them? Are the tempter and tempted the same in your eyes? Is the beguiled youth to die the same as the old offender who has pondered his crimes for thirty years?"

Although he played loose with facts and ignored the law, Voorhees's argument had an undeniable logic of its own. Punishment had to be calibrated, with the ultimate penalty reserved for the very worst offenders. Yet there were others even guiltier than Brown—and immeasurably guiltier than Cook—who would regrettably go free. The very indictment, Voorhees pointed out, alleged that Cook had been "seduced by the false and malignant counsels of other traitorous persons." And so it was. The doctrine of abolitionism had been advanced by zealous criminals for twenty years, and yet none of the "sages of abolitionism," the preachers of "wicked and unholy doctrines," stood to face punishment along with Cook. Voorhees named the perpetrators: Henry Ward Beecher, Wendell Phillips, William Seward, Joshua Giddings, Theodore Parker, Charles Sumner, and William Lloyd Garrison. Until they were on the scaffold, mercy was due John Cook.

In the biblical cadence of a preacher and with the fervent passion of a tragedian, Voorhees "uncorked the vials of his wrath and poured their contents upon the devoted heads of the abolitionists."[14] The true murderers, he said, were "older and wiser" than his client:

Midnight gloom is not more somber in contrast with the blazing light of the meridian sun than is the guilt of such men in comparison with that which overwhelms the prisoner. They put in motion the maelstrom which has engulfed him. They started the torrent which has borne him over the precipice. They called forth from the caverns the tempest which wrecked him on a sunken reef. Before God, and in the light of eternal truth, the disaster at Harper's Ferry is their act, and not his. May the ghost of each victim of their doctrines of disunion and abomination sit heavy on their guilty souls!

Belatedly, to be sure, Cook had seen his great error and sought to atone. He had confessed and told the truth about Brown's conspiracy. From the time of his "first interview in his prison with Governor Willard, in the presence of your senator, Colonel Mason . . . the influence of good, and not of evil, once more controlled him." Voorhees conceded that Cook, "in the early morning of his life [had come] under the baneful influence of a school of philosophy which he once thought sincere and right." But that was then. Having seen the light, "he now, here, once and forever, to you, and before the world, renounces [it] as false, pernicious, and pestilential."

Then Voorhees turned to an outright defense of slavery itself. Because of Brown's raid, he said, "the institution of domestic slavery today stands before the world more fully justified than ever before in the history of this or, indeed, perhaps, of any other country." To Voorhees, it was obvious that slavery was beneficial to both master and slave: "The bondsman refuses to be free; drops the implements of war from his hands; is deaf to the call of freedom; turns against his liberators; and, by instinct, obeys the injunction of Paul by returning to his master." Slavery, thus, was the black man's fate, "assigned to him . . . by the law of his being, by the law which governs his relation to a white man wherever the contact exists."

In closing, Voorhees asked the jury to acquit Cook of treason, arguing that he lacked a "motive of disloyalty" to the government of Virginia. "Not a syllable of proof warrants such a conclusion." There had been plenty of proof of murder and conspiracy, however, so Voorhees returned to the themes of mercy and comparative guilt. "Leave the door to clemency open; do not shut it by a wholesale conviction. God spare this boy, and those who love him."

Cook "wept bitterly" throughout his lawyer's paean to slavery, but were they tears of sorrow, fear, or shame? We cannot know how much

Cook nodded in agreement or grimaced in anguish while his lawyer spoke, but the general reaction to Voorhees was almost adulatory. "The picture of mercy as drawn by the eloquent gentleman was both truthful and beautiful," said one observer. "Few eyes were left dry" in the courtroom, as Voorhees's description of the "gloom of the affair . . . produced a profound silence." Some proslavery northern newspapers were even more admiring. The *Indiana State Sentinel* commended the speech to its readers, "not merely because of its great merit as a forensic effort of unusual brilliancy, but [also] for the scathing denunciation which it contains of those who planned, and those who instigated and encouraged the insurrection at Harper's Ferry." The *Chicago Herald* called it "the great plea of one of the most gifted minds of the West" and "a truthful exposition of the infernal spirit in which the insurrection originated." Even the abolitionist-minded *Philadelphia Press*, while disagreeing with the approval of slavery in Voorhees's address, conceded that "no one can fail to admire the forensic skill and ability it displays, and the touching eloquence with which it pleads for a merciful verdict." The *New York Tribune* was more judgmental, curtly noting that Voorhees was "throwing the blame on the Republican party and the Abolitionists, and beseeching mercy, or at least a recommendation for mercy."[15]

The most important audience, of course, was in the jury box, and it appeared that Voorhees's plea had made a noticeable impact there. Most of the jurors were seen to be in tears, and even the "sternest had their hearts so opened that they wept like women." One southern newspaper observed that "men who had gone into the court-room strongly prejudiced against Cook, now favored commutation of the prisoner."[16] That augured well for the defendant, as he waited to hear what Andrew Hunter would have to say.

❈ ◉ ❈

The prosecution of John Cook had taken many strange turns over the course of three days, but none had been more startling than the announcement made by Andrew Hunter before he began his final argument. As he rose from counsel table, the prosecutor informed Judge Parker that because "the Commonwealth had failed to establish the charge of treason, he would abandon . . . the first count in the indictment."

That was good news for Cook, but it must have come as a great shock to the court (and to Charles Harding who, as usual, had not been consulted). Barely a week earlier, and in the very same courtroom, Hunter had vigorously and successfully resisted John Brown's efforts to have a virtually identical treason charged dismissed. Edwin Coppoc had also been convicted of treason although, like Brown, he had never actually lived in Virginia. John Cook, in contrast, had spent well over a year living and working, and of course marrying, in Virginia. Cook surely owed greater allegiance to the commonwealth than Brown or Coppoc ever did, and the treason charge against Cook was consequently far stronger as a matter of both fact and law.

Why did Hunter change course so dramatically? Surely he had not been persuaded by Voorhees's argument that proof of treason was lacking, which leaves only two alternatives. First, the prosecutor may have been acting under orders from Governor Wise. There was much speculation at the time that an "arrangement undoubtedly was [made] to get rid of the count for treason, which Governor Wise could not overset, and to take a conviction for conspiracy and murder, which it is thought he can and will pardon." One newspaper further opined that dismissal of the treason charge had been intended to allow "Willard to put in a political lever and pry" out a reprieve.[17] There is, however, no record of any instruction to that effect from Wise, even though most of his correspondence has been preserved. Therefore, a more intriguing possibility is that Hunter acted on his own, either out of compassion for the defendant or, more likely, out of a sense of obligation to Voorhees and Willard. Only two days earlier, Hunter had backed out of a deal with defense counsel, in what must have seemed to them a cynical double cross. Now the honorable Virginian had an opportunity to make amends, and perhaps he took it. Although only to a point.

Hunter pursued the remaining four counts with his usual vigor and force. A cagey and experienced advocate, the prosecutor understood that he could not compete with Voorhees's sheer eloquence. Therefore, rather than confront the defense argument, he neatly sidestepped it by expressing his sympathy with the distress of Cook's loyal family, while allowing that he himself "admired the effort of counsel for the defence." Hunter, in other words, would not attempt to refute or belittle any of Voorhees's highly emotional claims. Instead, he quietly explained that "his duty, as prosecutor in this case, rendered it necessary that he should deal with the prisoner at bar without anything like sympathy." Conceding the natural inclination toward mercy, he called upon the jurors to do their own duty, and to render a verdict "not influenced by outside considerations."[18]

In what might have seemed like a magnanimous gesture—but was equally a stratagem—the prosecutor cautioned the jurors that they were obliged to acquit Cook if they had any reasonable doubt as to his guilt. Following Cook's written confession and admission in open court, there was absolutely no possibility of an acquittal, and Hunter was actually admonishing the jurors against considering any sort of merciful compromise. In effect, Hunter was reminding the jurors that they had to decide between mutually exclusive verdicts: Cook was either guilty or not guilty, and a recommendation of mercy was not among the available choices.

Hunter spoke for under an hour, but his dispassionate appeal to law enforcement was the perfect counterweight to Voorhees's overheated ardor. In a case that had incited so much anger, and even hatred, Hunter had wisely chosen to assert a calming influence, trusting that a jury dominated by slaveholders could not be swayed for long by Voorhees's ornate plea for lenience.

Judge Parker then instructed the jury. Regarding the crucial murder charges, Parker told the jurors that "if the prisoner at the bar was present at the murders charged . . . then he is alike guilty with the parties who directly committed such murders." The court added that "presence" did not require that Cook was actually "standing by" during the murders, but only that he was within sight and close enough "to aid and assist the actual perpetrators."[19] The instruction strengthened the prosecution case. Cook had been nowhere near the armory during any of the killings, but he had taken shots at the militia from his hilltop perch on Monday afternoon—a fact that had become known only because it was disclosed in his confession. Thus Cook's responsibility for the murders had been greater than Voorhees admitted. Cook was not merely Brown's lackey, wagon driver, and misguided errand boy; rather, he had voluntarily participated in a shooting at a time when he just as easily could have escaped.

The case was committed to the jurors at 8:00 p.m., and they retired to deliberate in an adjacent room. Under antebellum Virginia law, the jury was the ultimate decider of both law and fact, and it was therefore necessary—even in light of Cook's guilty plea and Hunter's abandonment of the treason charge—to enter a formal verdict on every count. The real question, of course, was whether the jury would go further. As the deliberations extended for close to an hour, some observers speculated that Cook would indeed "be recommended to mercy." Others thought that the absence of the treason charge made that unlikely because the "the Governor could commute the sentence to imprisonment for a number of years without the recommendation."[20]

Finally, at 9:00 p.m., the jurors reported that they had reached a verdict. "A most breathless silence now prevailed," while the jury filed back into the courtroom. The clerk then called out, "Gentlemen of the jury, look upon the prisoner: Is he guilty of the offences with which he is charged, or is he not?" The foreman, Charles T. Butler, the owner of six slaves, read out the prepared verdict in a clear voice:

> We the jury find the prisoner at the bar, John E. Cooke, not guilty of Treason as charged in the first count of the indictment—and we find him guilty of advising and conspiring with slaves to rebel and

make insurrection, as charged in the second count of the indictment; and we further [find] him guilty of advising and conspiring
with certain persons to induce slaves to rebel and make insurrection as charged in the third count of the indictment; and we
further find him guilty of murder in the first degree as charged in
the fourth and fifth counts of said indictment.[21]

It had taken no more than a minute to read the verdict, but it must
have seemed like much longer. As the foreman ticked off each count,
everyone in the courtroom waited to see if there would be a recommendation of mercy in addition to the foregone findings of guilt. There was not.

Judge Parker set Cook's sentencing for the following morning, when
the court would also sentence Edwin Coppoc, Shields Green, and John
Copeland.

❈ TEN ❈

Repentance

Despite the best efforts of Daniel Voorhees, little had gone favorably for John Cook in Charlestown. For all of his cooperation with the prosecution, Cook had obtained neither a transfer to federal court nor a favorable recommendation from his jury. As matters stood on Thursday morning, Cook was legally not much better off than Shields Green, John Copeland, or Edwin Coppoc, none of whom had confessed.

Cook's one advantage had been the quality of his lawyers, who had argued persuasively that their client could be convicted of murder and yet spared execution. To a slight extent, that seemed to have worked. Although the jurors had not urged lenience, neither had they specifically called for the death penalty. And the treason acquittal meant that it was still within Judge Parker's discretion to recommend an executive commutation of Cook's sentence. Perhaps Parker had been impressed by Voorhees's moving address (and Cook's lofty connections) even if the jury had not. Parker had already condemned Brown to hang, and the cursed abolitionist leaders—Frederick Douglass, Samuel Howe, Henry Ward Beecher, Wendell Phillips, William Seward, Joshua Giddings, Theodore Parker, Charles Sumner, and William Lloyd Garrison—were all beyond the reach of the court. It was not out of the question that Parker would accept Voorhees's argument that lesser guilt required a lesser sentence. The southern press reported "a strong feeling of sympathy had been enlisted in [Cook's] behalf during the last few days," so perhaps Parker would favor incarceration rather than execution. With Voorhees at his side, Cook had reason to hope.[1]

Parker waited until noon to convene court for sentencing, presumably to allow the defendants sufficient time to gather their thoughts and compose their remarks. The four convicted conspirators were led into the courtroom together and seated in a row of chairs facing the judge. Copeland, Coppoc, and Green appeared to be alone. Cook was accompanied, as he had been throughout his trial, by Willard and Crowley, both of whom "seemed bending beneath the weight of sorrow" as they took seats beside their brother-in-law. Voorhees was present in court as well, although he did not sit next to his client.[2]

The clerk directed the prisoners to stand and then read out the crimes of which each man had been convicted. In language required by the Virginia statutes, he then asked if any of them "had anything to say why sentence according to the terms of the verdict, should not now be passed."

Coppoc spoke first, "with much composure and in a clear and distinct voice." He denied "any intent to commit treason, murder, or robbery" and declared that his "whole purpose . . . was to liberate slaves, whom he believed were "anxious to escape from bondage." Coppoc insisted that he had been completely unaware of Brown's true intentions until just before the raid. Even still, "he had shot no one, and had done no man any injury, but he knew he had violated the laws of the state." He accepted responsibility for his acts, and understood "that he should be punished for his foolhardy attempt, but he thought it should have been lighter than had been adjudged." Looking around the courtroom, Coppoc sensed little sympathy. "If those who desired his life sought it, he had nothing more to say."[3]

Judge Parker next turned to the two black men, Shields Green and John Copeland, and asked whether either man wished to speak before sentencing. Both "declined saying anything," out of either fear or hopelessness.

Then it was Cook's turn to stand. For a moment, he seemed to shrink in fear. One observer remarked that "though apparently a youth of some 26 years," Cook was "of feminine rather than masculine appearance." As he began to speak, however, it became obvious that the defendant was well prepared for the moment. In a confident and forthright tone, Cook addressed the court.[4]

Almost nobody in the courtroom actually knew much about John Cook; even his brothers-in-law had not seen or spoken with him for many years. A few fatal hours of Cook's life had been described by Lewis Washington and other witnesses, and the confession—which had been written in collaboration with Voorhees and Hunter—had been read aloud, but the real person remained a mystery. His years in Kansas had been reduced to a few paragraphs in his confession, and his outspoken devotion to abolitionism was omitted entirely. None of Cook's passion, daring, and commitment had been related to the court, as that would have undermined Voorhees's portrait of an ingenuous man-child who had been seduced by the wily Old Brown.

Only the other three prisoners had any sense of Cook's life and character before his capture and interrogation. Shields Green and John Copeland had been at the Maryland farm before the raid, and they knew that Cook had been one of Brown's strongest supporters. They were probably aware of the role that Cook played in persuading Tidd and others to remain in Brown's army, and they definitely knew that Cook had argued strenuously in favor of the attack on Harper's Ferry. Edwin Coppoc, too, had lived at the Maryland farm, and he had wintered with Cook in Iowa, at a time when Cook was writing fervent letters and poems about his hatred of slavery. Even more than Copeland and Green, Coppoc must have wondered how deeply his cellmate embraced Voorhees's ringing encomium to the slave system.

At the sentencing hearing, Cook at last had an opportunity to express—or continue to hide—his true feelings toward Brown, toward abolitionism, and toward the Commonwealth of Virginia. He could simply plead for mercy, invoking his prominent family and saying nothing at all about broader issues. Or he could, like Coppoc, plead ignorance of Brown's actual plans while admitting his hope to free the slaves. Or he might wholeheartedly embrace Voorhees's unconditional approval of slavery. As Cook rose to address the court, Voorhees was unsure whether his client would adopt or reject the defense he had so carefully crafted. Until he started speaking, Cook himself may not have known how thoroughly he would repudiate his friends.

"If it may please the court," Cook began, in the formal language of the law, "some of your citizens have testified against me wrongfully, though without intention." Obviously referring to Lewis Washington and Lind Currie, Cook wanted the court to believe that the witnesses had somehow either misunderstood his actions or misinterpreted his words. "I deny ever having come into your community as a spy; I had no such intention or design." Rather, he continued, "having met with John Brown in Kansas some two years or more ago, I was induced through him to locate here" solely for the purpose of learning whether Hugh Forbes had betrayed Brown's plans and "ulterior objects." Brushing quickly past that apparent contradiction, Cook added that "he had never attempted or coerced any slave to leave his or her master," which had the virtue of being more or less true.

Taking another cue from Voorhees, Cook continued to blame John Brown for his troubles. Brown had "deceived [him] as to the desire of the slaves for freedom," which Cook now realized to be untrue. Cook claimed that he had been "almost a pro-slavery man" until meeting Brown, who had misled him into believing "that the slaves of Maryland and Virginia were eager and anxious for liberation."[5] In reality, it had been Cook who misled Brown into thinking that a slave rebellion was already brewing in Virginia, but that fact had been neatly elided from Cook's confession.

Desperate to save his own life, Cook continued to reinvent the past. "As for the relics that had been taken from Col. Washington's," that had been done "at the express orders of Captain Brown" and not on Cook's own initiative. He regretted taking Washington hostage, but that had

not been his own idea. In fact, Cook said that he had "neither committed or connived at any violation of law" other than "for the good of
humanity and the best ends of the government."[6]

❈ ❂ ❈

Cook's claims were almost entirely false, but they had been stated
with all the art of a practiced storyteller. Voorhees was no doubt proud
of his client's performance, while Copeland and Green, and especially
Coppoc, must have been sadly disappointed at what they heard. Brown
was furious when he later learned of Cook's duplicity. The only opinion
that would matter that day, however, belonged to the court.

Judge Parker was "obviously laboring under much feeling" when he
commanded the four prisoners to rise. Coppoc's stoicism had made a
good impression on the spectators, and Cook's plea for mercy had also
drawn sympathy, as the two men stood resolutely still. No observer
thought to comment on the appearance of the two black prisoners,
whose silence had been taken for resignation and who, in any case,
could never expect to receive any quarter from the Commonwealth of
Virginia. Only the fate of the white men held the gallery's rapt attention. For once, even the sound of cracking chestnut shells faded away,
with "the silence of death almost pervading the Court-hall."[7]

The court addressed all four prisoners at once. "These crimes have
all grown out of a mad inroad upon the State, made with the predeter-
mined purpose to raise ... the standard of a servile insurrection," Parker
began. "In your efforts to push your bold and unholy doctrine," he continued, "you have taken human life in no fewer than five instances."
The reference to an "unholy doctrine" was a two-edged sword for Cook.
He alone among the defendants had renounced abolitionism, blaming
the sway of "wicked and unholy doctrines" for his own fall from grace.
If the court believed that the "influence of evil" had truly controlled
Cook, then perhaps he might be spared. But there was little hope if
Parker instead attributed the sinful dogma to Cook himself.

Then Parker repeated a fiction that was essential to the self-regard of a slave-holding commonwealth:

> Happily for the peace of our whole land, you obtained no support from that quarter whence you so confidently expected it. Not a slave united himself to your party, but, so soon as he could get without the range of your rifles, or as night gave him opportunity, made his escape from men who had come to give him freedom, and hurried to place himself once more beneath the care and protection of his owner.[8]

The court's observation was inaccurate. A good many slaves had taken up Brown's arms in Harper's Ferry, and Charlestown slaves continued to show veiled support for Brown and his men even during the trials. "People say what they please of the indifference of the negroes to the passing events, but it is not true," reported the *New York Tribune*. "They burn with anxiety to learn every particular, but they fear to show it." One hotel servant quietly told the reporter that it would be a pity to hang John Brown. The journalist replied that sparing Brown would put white Virginians in danger. "Pity they wasn't," said the porter, "shuffling away very much discomposed."[9] Nonetheless, the supposed docility of slaves provided great comfort to frightened Virginians, and Parker's embrace of the fiction held out hope for John Cook. Voorhees had raised the very same point in Cook's defense, arguing that the failure of Brown's raid had actually strengthened the institution of slavery.

"In spite of your offences against our laws,' Parker said, "I cannot but feel deeply for you, and sincerely, most sincerely, do I sympathize with those friends and relations whose lives are bound up in yours." At that moment, the court appeared to be speaking directly to John Cook. Judge Parker knew nothing of the other prisoners' friends or relations, but Cook had been surrounded by relatives and supporters from the moment he first arrived in court. If Parker would not spare Cook for his own sake, it appeared that he might do so for the sake of Willard and Crowley and their wives, whose hearts, as the court recognized, would be "wrung with grief." But then he realized the implications of his words, which he hastened to explain.

"For them we all do sorrow," Parker continued, "while a due regard for our safety may not permit us to forgive the offences of which you have been guilty, I hope that they will turn for consolation, and you for pardon, to that good Being, who in his wrath remembereth mercy." That was as close to a clemency recommendation as Parker was willing to get. And while nobody would have confused Governor Henry Wise with a benevolent capital-B Being, Parker's suggestion was nonetheless unmistakable. Mercy would have to come from a higher power than the Circuit Court of Jefferson County.

"To conclude this sad duty," said Parker, "I now announce that the sentence of law is that you, and each one of you. . . . be hanged by the neck until you be dead." The court set the execution date for Friday, December 16. The sheriff was ordered to hang the two black men "between the hours of eight in the forenoon and twelve noon," with the two white men to follow "in the afternoon of [the] same day."[10] Even in death, Virginia demanded strict segregation of the races.

Almost before the ink was dry on the death warrant, Willard, Voorhees, and Crowley departed for Richmond, where they intended to meet with Governor Wise. Although they had failed to obtain their ultimate objective in court, they had reason to hope for greater success petitioning for executive clemency. At least one southern newspaper liked Cook's chances, opining that "the feeling here now in favor of Cook is very great, and a commutation of punishment to imprisonment would give great satisfaction to a large majority of the thinking portion of the community."[11] Perhaps.

※　◉　※

Despite its equivocations, Cook's confession had provided the first testimonial evidence against Brown's friends and financial supporters.

It therefore evoked strong emotions across the country, although reactions varied greatly from region to region. There was anger and resentment throughout the South, relief in parts of the North, and stark fear in certain salons of Boston and New York. It had been an open secret for over a week that Cook intended to confess, and his cooperation was thought by many to be part of "a scheme on the part of the government [to establish] the complicity of those northern gentlemen whom the people of Virginia are so eager to get within their grasp."[12] As early as November 2 it had been reported in the antislavery press that Cook would make an expansive confession—saying "pretty much what was wanted"—in order to advance Willard's and Wise's political goals. The Republican *Indianapolis Journal* noted that prisoners facing death "usually care more for their necks than their characters" and predicted the fabrication of some "astounding revelations about Governor Chase, Mr. Seward and Mr. Lincoln." Two days later, the same newspaper predicted that Cook would claim, on the advice of Willard and Voorhees, "that the Republican party is responsible for the insurrection."[13]

That was the cynical northern perspective. Proslavery newspapers, both North and South, also thought that Cook would implicate abolitionist leaders, although they did not indulge the suspicion of Willard's and Voorhees's ulterior political motives. The *Indiana State Sentinel*, for example, was proud that Willard had advised Cook to "confess the whole plot and reveal the transactions from first to last." Cook's case was already hopeless, according to the *Sentinel*, so it could not be hurt by a confession, while the ends of justice would be served by exposing the damaging influence of the Republicans.[14] And in every quarter there was intense speculation about which names would be revealed. Would they include Frederick Douglass, Joshua Giddings, Samuel Howe, Gerrit Smith, William Lloyd Garrison, William Seward, or others?

Given all of the anticipation, Cook's actual confession had been deeply frustrating. Thanks to the intervention of Andrew Hunter, Cook had indeed named five leading abolitionists—Gerrit Smith, Frederick Douglass, Thaddeus Hyatt, Franklin Sanborn, and Samuel Howe—but he had not accused them of direct involvement in the Harper's Ferry plot. Virtually every southern observer expressed disappointment at the absence of "a complete revelation," with Hunter himself complaining that the confession had not lived up to his expectations. In Jefferson County, the *Shepherdstown Register* complained that Cook did "not disclose any new fact of importance," and worse, that "in regard to the most prominent citizens at the North, he disclaims all knowledge that could implicate them." The *Richmond Enquirer* likewise dismissed the confession as adding "nothing new."[15]

It was widely supposed that Cook was "keeping back part of his story," and it was assumed that Judge Parker and Governor Wise felt the same way. "It is thought by the Court," opined the *New York Tribune,* "that Cook has played a double game in preparing it—that he has pretended to reveal to the authorities in good faith, all that he is able to, and at the same time attempted to preserve his fidelity to his old master." The *Baltimore American* believed that reaction to the confession "was of the most unfavorable character" because its few references to Douglass and Howe were "not in a way to deeply implicate them."[16]

Southerners disparaged the value of Cook's confession because they believed it did not go far enough. Many northerners belittled it as well, but for a much different reason. There had been great fear that Cook would implicate prominent Republicans and abolitionists, leading to their arrest and prosecution whether they were guilty or not. Thus there was correspondingly great relief when it turned out that Cook said almost nothing specific about any individual. It was reported eagerly that Cook's "confession tells all he knew, and that, in fact, there is nothing to tell." While the confession "cast the odium upon Brown," there was nothing more than "pretended implication of [other] parties at the North." In the words of the American Anti-Slavery Society,

Cook's confession did not include "a full revelation of the supposed complicity of distinguished northern citizens . . . for the very cogent reason that there was nothing . . . to be revealed."[17]

Not everybody discounted the potential impact of Cook's confession, however, and certainly not the people who had been named as possible aiders and abettors. For all of Cook's frustrating evasiveness, there was no avoiding "the fact that he implicates Fred. Douglass and Dr. Howe with the affair," connecting them to Brown—along with Hyatt, Smith, and Sanborn—by the "presentation of pistols, money, etc."[18] All but Hyatt were indeed among Brown's key supporters and confidants, as was also suggested by certain correspondence recovered from Brown's Maryland headquarters. Although the extent of their involvement was still unknown, Howe, Sanborn, and Smith were members of the clandestine committee—the Secret Six, as they called themselves—who had conspired to finance Brown's southern invasion, and Douglass had met with Brown in Chambersburg on the eve of the insurrection. That participation alone, if discovered by the authorities, might have been enough to warrant hanging in Virginia. Everyone connected with Brown was therefore panicked at the prospect of exposure, and Cook's confession, even as vague as it was, promised to make things worse for the men he singled out. Feeling themselves in great jeopardy, Hyatt, Howe, and Douglass could not risk ignoring Cook's allegations.

Frederick Douglass acted first, responding directly to Cook's initial charges against him. Unlike the others, Douglass had been privy to Brown's actual plan, and as a black man he could expect less protection from the northern courts. Douglass therefore fled to Canada as soon as the news broke of the Harper's Ferry fiasco, and that is where he first learned that Cook had accused him of joining the conspiracy, only to have "acted the coward" by failing to appear with the agreed-upon reinforcements. From Canada, Douglass wrote a letter to the *Rochester Democrat* refuting Cook's charge that he had "promised to be present in person at the Harper's Ferry insurrection." Douglass declared that he had never once met Cook, while sarcastically allowing that "Cook may be perfectly right in denouncing me as a coward." "I am most miserably deficient in courage," he continued acerbically, "even more so than Cook, when he deserted his brave old Captain and fled to the mountains." Although he had nothing but contempt for Cook—whom he called "wholly, grievously and unaccountably wrong"—Douglass was deeply shaken by the accusations. He repeated six times that he had not ever promised to join Brown at Harper's Ferry, while emphasizing that his "field of labor for the abolition of Slavery has not extended to an attack upon the United States Arsenal."

Ever the militant, Douglass also made it clear that he did not disapprove of the raid. From his safe haven in the British Empire—he would soon depart for London—Douglass wrote that "it can never be wrong for the imbruted and whip-scarred slaves, or their friends, to hunt, harass, and even strike down the traffickers in human flesh." He praised Brown as "the noble old hero whose . . . ghost will haunt the bedchambers of all the born and unborn slaveholders of Virginia through all their generations." Douglass declared his readiness to be tried before an impartial New York jury, but mindful of Cook's continuing betrayal, he was unwilling to be exposed to Virginia's courts. "I have quite insuperable objections to be . . . 'bagged' by Gov. Wise."[19]

Samuel Howe also published an exculpatory letter in Boston and New York, in which he denied "all knowledge of Cook, Brown's lieutenant, who, in his confession, hinted at Dr. Howe's direct complicity with Brown." Howe was the scion of a prominent New England family, a leading antislavery activist (his wife, Julia Ward Howe, would later write the lyrics to "Battle Hymn of the Republic"), and an enthusiastic member of the Secret Six. His name had surfaced very early in the investigation of the raid, but his first impulse was to ignore what he called the "mingled" rumors.

Following Cook's trial, however, in which his "complicity [was] distinctly charged by one of the parties engaged," Howe felt that he had no choice but to make a statement: "As regards Mr. Cook, to the best of my knowledge and belief, I never saw him; never corresponded with him; never even heard of him until since the outbreak at Harper's Ferry," an event that "was unforeseen and unexpected by me." Howe admitted that he knew Brown and vouched for Brown's "characteristic prudence, and his reluctance to shed blood, or excite servile insurrection." Those statements were half-truths at best, as Howe surely knew the details of the Missouri slave rescue, in which a slave owner had been killed, and he must also have heard the stories of the Pottawatomie Massacre. Howe had knowingly contributed substantial funds to finance a slave rescue in the South, and he could not have expected it to be accomplished without some risk of violence. Nonetheless, he condemned Virginia's judicial proceedings as "false and revengeful," and he fled to Quebec rather than risk answering to Cook's uncomfortably accurate accusations.[20]

Thaddeus Hyatt was a wealthy New York industrialist and an antislavery activist. Although he had only a slight connection to John Brown, Hyatt had been a supporter of the Kansas free-state movement, which is probably how Cook learned his name. Cook's allegation against Hyatt was oblique, to say the least, claiming only that Hyatt had conveyed some erroneous information to Brown about Colonel Hugh Forbes. Even if it had happened, the alleged communication was not very incriminating, but Hyatt still felt endangered, and he therefore published an indignant response. "It is scarcely necessary to say," wrote Hyatt, "that this poor young man Cooke is in error. No such nonsense was ever uttered by me . . . and lest it should be supposed, from the mentioning of my name in Cooke's narrative, that I was privy to the plans of John Brown, I take this occasion to say that . . . I neither knew nor suspected the Harper's Ferry raid." Like the others, Hyatt took the opportunity to defend Brown and condemn the "encroachments of the Slave Power," and he predicted that Brown's theory of liberation would one day pass "from the realm of insane vagary into the hard region of historic fact."[21]

Franklin Sanborn and Gerrit Smith did not publish replies to Cook's confession, the latter no doubt because he committed himself to a "lunatic asylum" upon hearing that he had been implicated by letters found at Brown's Maryland headquarters. Time would tell whether discreet silence or public denial was the wiser response, but there was clearly good reason for all of Brown's associates to be alarmed by John Cook's revelations and for them to fear that there might be more yet to come.[22]

⁜ ✲ ⁜

As they sped by rail toward Richmond, Willard and Voorhees understood that it would be no easy task to convince Governor Wise to spare Cook's life. Voorhees had exhausted his considerable forensic talents in attempts to persuade either the judge or jury in Charlestown, but his arguments had failed to obtain a recommendation of mercy. The teary-eyed jurors had deferred the decision to Judge Parker, who proved to be unmovable. Parker later explained that, contrary to Voorhees's characterization, he considered the defendant to be highly culpable. Far from a dupe, Cook was "an active member of [Brown's] band, and a quick-witted, intelligent man" who had willingly helped prepare for the invasion. Worse, Cook had, in Parker's view, "aided his party by firing from the high ground opposite to Harper's Ferry" and was thus responsible for the death of George Turner. After sentencing, Parker had informed Voorhees that Cook was, in his estimation, "the least entitled to mercy of any of the prisoners."[23] The defense attorneys had to assume that Parker had conveyed the same sentiment to Governor Wise.

Political considerations made Wise's position even more difficult to predict. His term as governor would end on December 31, and his successor would come from a bitterly competing faction of the Virginia Democrats. Wise's well-known presidential ambitions depended on overcoming the rivalry within the Virginia party, and his plans might therefore be either advanced or derailed by his decisions in the Harper's Ferry cases.[24] With the 1860 election still almost a year away, the Democrats' nominee was far from certain. The national party was badly divided between northern and southern blocs, and there was a good possibility that a compromise candidate might be chosen who could appeal to both regions. Ashbel Willard's backing could therefore be crucial to Wise's chances for the 1860 Democratic nomination, but only if it could be obtained without some corresponding political cost in his home state. As Willard surely recognized, that would be the rub for Henry Wise.

Wise had already been besieged by thousands of letters seeking clemency for John Brown. Some of the petitioners argued that a display of mercy would show that Virginia could be "magnanimous to a fanatic in its power," and not the barbarous slave-pen caricatured by abolitionists. Others maintained that execution would make Brown a martyr, thus strengthening the abolitionists. Former president John Tyler—a native Virginian who would later side with the Confederacy—urged Governor Wise to put anger and retribution aside in favor of "a political policy as cold as marble." Although Brown deserved "to die a thousand deaths upon the rack, to end in fire and termination in Hell," wrote Tyler, hanging him would only inspire further acts of martyrdom and violence. Taking a third tack, attorneys Griswold and Chilton, acting without the consent of their client, explored the possibility of a pardon based on Brown's alleged insanity.[25]

None of the entreaties, however, had the desired effect. Brown's treason conviction meant that the governor could not pardon him without the consent of the legislature, and Wise was not disposed to open the issue for widespread political debate. Wise wrote privately to Andrew Hunter that he did not intend to pardon Brown, and he leaked word to the *Richmond Enquirer* that Brown's fate "may be considered as sealed."[26]

Willard and Voorhees were aware of the nature of the petitions on Brown's behalf, if not the enormous volume of letters that had poured into the executive mansion. As an advocate, Voorhees realized that none of the arguments raised for Brown were likely to work for Cook. It would have been wholly implausible to claim that Cook, having betrayed the cause, would ever become an abolitionist martyr, and a belated plea of insanity would only undermine the value of his confession. The best argument for Cook, therefore, was to tout him as an exemplary anti-abolitionist, the victim of the "Kansas freedom-shriekers and other Black Republicans." It would not be far-fetched to maintain that Cook had been lured into the net of abolitionism, only to be abandoned by the true villains in Boston who now petitioned for Brown's reprieve while leaving his innocent subordinate to his fate. Willard's political organ, the *Indiana State Sentinel*, had already made that precise claim. "Where now," asked the *Sentinel*, "are those creatures who were ever ready to use the dauntless courage, the untiring energy, and the generous qualities of young Cook when they wished a dangerous duty performed?"[27] The same compelling question was certain to be raised with Henry Wise.

Thanks to Hunter's abandonment of the treason charge—and Cook's subsequent acquittal—Wise had sole authority to commute Cook's sentence to a term of imprisonment or even to grant him a full pardon. There would be no need to debate the issue in the legislature, but that did not mean the governor would be free from public scrutiny or constituent pressure.

※ ◉ ※

Voorhees and Willard might have been momentarily buoyed by the speculation of the *Baltimore American*—that the "thinking" population favored Cook's pardon—but only as long as they avoided reading other newspapers or speaking to actual Virginians. In fact, the general attitude toward Cook had always been extremely hostile, and it did not soften following the trial. In one typical, if exaggerated, comment, a Harper's Ferry schoolteacher accused Cook of "freeloveism, Socialism, Spiritualism & every other ism that was ever thought of by man or Devil."[28]

Mindful that Wise would be meeting with Willard and Voorhees, the

Jefferson County press vehemently opposed Cook's pardon. The *Virginia Free Press* published a lengthy editorial that amounted to a comprehensive brief against clemency. "For the life of us, we cannot see anything in this case . . . that affords just ground for executive interference," it began, given that Cook "was even more criminal that any of his confederates." Neither Cook's confession nor his "connection with eminent and high toned gentlemen" should allow him to "escape the just penalty of his crimes." As for Governor Willard's intervention, the *Free Press* issued a stern warning: "It cannot be that party politics is to operate upon the mind of our chief magistrate—such an idea is too contemptible to be considered." A week later, the *Free Press* took special care to refute the sympathetic observation of the *Baltimore American*. The "thinking portion" of the population, wrote the *Free Press*, in fact regarded Cook as "one of the deepest dyed villains that ever planted foot upon the soil of our state." There could be "no valid reason—not even the slightest pretext—upon which Executive clemency can be leveled for this man, and we cannot believe that Governor Wise is to be swayed by the appeals which are to be made to him." Returning to the subject in its next issue, the *Free Press* fumed that there were not "ten men in the County of Jefferson who would [stand for] a commutation of punishment to imprisonment."[29]

Other Virginia newspapers took the same stand, including the *Richmond Enquirer* which observed that "the commutation of [Cook's] sentence, so far from giving satisfaction to a majority, would not be endured at all." While expressing pity for Governor Willard and his family, the *Enquirer* noted that "it would be most unnatural that [Cook] should receive any sympathy from a community whose hospitality he has basely violated." Also arguing against any "leniency," the *Independent Democrat* branded Cook the worst of Brown's "hellish miscreants" because he had visited "the houses of the citizens of this and neighboring counties, for the purpose of prying out information" to prepare for the insurrection.[30]

Against that torrent of acrimony, Willard and Voorhees had but few resources of their own to marshal. An exceptionally creative article in the *Indiana State Sentinel* argued that Republicans were actually hoping for Cook's execution, with a "feverish anxiety," on the theory that it would increase northern mistrust of Virginians. "The day on which Cook dies," claimed the *Sentinel,* "will be one of feasting to party hatred and prejudice. No greater disappointment could be given [the Republicans] than the escape of young Cook from the death penalty which now awaits him."[31] The *Sentinel's* disingenuous ploy was transparent even in an age when the art of jiujitsu had not yet reached the West.

More likely to succeed, and less rhetorically devious, were the personal appeals from Cook's friends and family. As they always had before, Cook's sisters did their best to save him. Caroline Cook Willard implored Wise to commute the death sentence, writing that "if circumstances were changed and it were your wife thus afflicted I think my husband would not hesitate to grant her wish and I would use my influence in her favor." Caroline's twin, Kate, added that "for one who is young, who has up to this time borne a good character, and who has been deceived and led astray by bad men, it seems an awful fate" to be hanged. "It would bring sorrow, and disgrace lasting as life on those whom you cannot but respect." Fanny Cook Crowley enlisted further support from New York, obtaining a short character reference from a prominent law professor. Caroline mustered "the ladies of Indianapolis" to send a joint letter to Governor Wise. "We petition you," the good ladies wrote, "not with law or logic, but with beseeching tears to exercise your prerogative of pardon." While holding no "womanly sympathy for the criminal or his crime," the ladies begged the governor to "shield his innocent and suffering relatives." If nothing else, mercy was due Mrs. Willard, who herself had often played the role of "interceding angel, ever ready to plead for executive clemency with importunate words, and eloquent tears, in behalf of the misguided, the penitent guilty, and the unfortunate" condemned prisoners of Indiana.[32]

But for every letter Wise received on Cook's behalf, there were many more that called for his execution. Lewis Washington alerted the governor to the rampant rumors that Cook was about to be pardoned in exchange for the revelations in his confession. "I took it upon myself," wrote Washington, "to deny the charge in your name and hope I shall meet with your sanction in doing it." A committee of citizens from Charlestown petitioned the governor "Not to Spare Cook's Life" and called the defendant "the same black hearted villain he was before his sentence." Acknowledging the general sympathy for Cook's relatives, the signatories expressed their hope that Wise was "made of sterner stuff than to yield to interposition on his behalf." Many Virginians appealed to Wise even more urgently, fearing that furtive abolitionists and runaway slaves were still lurking in Jefferson County. Regarding a series of seemingly mysterious barn and hayloft fires, one constituent wrote to Wise that it was "Cooks instruction to our negroes or to some secret emissaries . . . who wish to distract the community from the prisoners . . . while a rescue may be effected." Consequently, "interposition in any way in favour of Cook would meet with universal execration" and perhaps more. "We are congratulating ourselves that we have a Governor who has nerve to carry out the law & had we not that confidence Lynch would" already have hanged Cook and the others.[33]

Governor Wise was indeed committed to carry out the law, but the law included his authority to issue pardons and reprieves. He therefore graciously received Willard and Voorhees in the executive mansion, and he listened politely to their entreaties. Willard stressed the great torment suffered by his wife and her family, and Voorhees emphasized Cook's repentance and cooperation. Wise made no commitment, assuring his guests only that he would give their petition serious consideration.

Upon their return to Indiana, Willard and Voorhees were quite mindful that they might yet influence Wise's decision. They were therefore full of praise for Virginians and Virginia justice. Voorhees told the press that "from the time of their arrival to their departure, they had every attention and kindness shown them" and had enjoyed "the old fashioned Virginia hospitality." He complimented Judge Parker's conduct of the trial and commended the prosecutors for allowing the defense every latitude in presenting Cook's case. Continuing the theme of his final argument in Charlestown, Voorhees allowed that Cook could offer "no justification for this wicked attempt to incite a servile insurrection," but he again pointed out "the moral responsibility of those who hold and teach the 'irrepressible conflict' doctrine for the acts of these misguided men." Willard added his own thanks to the "leading Democrats" of Virginia, who had shown "every proper token of sympathy [and] unbounded hospitality and kind attentions to him."[34]

The *Indiana State Sentinel*, which often spoke for Willard, offered its own appraisal of the situation, noting that "Governor Wise has a reputation for courage and magnanimity, and generosity, which is beyond question." While disavowing any intention "to intermeddle with the domestic affairs of a sister State," the *Sentinel* observed that it would be beneficial to the entire country if Virginia were "to mitigate the punishment from the death penalty to imprisonment." Recognizing that commutation might currently be unacceptable due to "the present irritated state of the public mind, increased by the taunts of the Northern Abolition press," the *Sentinel* proposed that Governor Wise at least grant a temporary stay of execution so that the public might have time to realize that life imprisonment would be "a greater punishment than the gallows."[35]

Cook also did his best to influence Wise's decision. He wrote letters and poetry from his jail cell—quite aware that his correspondence was monitored and reported to the governor—in hopes of portraying himself as a repentant Christian. His letters were full of religious imagery and professions of deep remorse, but they included not one critical word about slavery. Reading the letters in isolation, one would know only that Cook considered himself to be a "straying, erring child," and it would not be possible even to guess that he had once been a stalwart abolitionist. To his parents—and indirectly to Wise—Cook wrote: "The voice of prayer is rising for us to the Throne of God. We, too, add our humble supplications to him, for mercy and for pardon." And in case that had been too subtle, Cook added, "Should 'Executive' clemency be granted, I shall hasten to your extended arms, and remembering all the past, live for the future to cheer and bless *you, as you* near the shadowy vale." To his wife, Cook wrote, "to *you* my thoughts are turning . . . and in the future [I shall] live for thee and heaven." Again, Cook spoke also to Governor Wise: "I still have hopes that we again may meet; that through Executive clemency I may again . . . see our *child* and clasp its mother to my yearning heart." Cook being Cook, he concluded with some expressive poetry:

> If upon the earth we're parted,
> Never more to meet below,
> Meet me, Oh, thou broken-hearted,
> In that world to which I go.
>
> Where the Saviour's flocks are resting,
> By that River bright and fair,
> And immortal glory cresting,
> Every heart that enters there.[36]

Governor Wise remained sphinx-like, saying nothing about whether he would pardon Cook or allow him to hang. He attended a military parade in Charlestown on Monday, November 21, and there was speculation that he intended to meet with Cook at the jail. Instead, Wise visited only Brown, telling him to prepare for death. Brown replied that he was ready, leaving Cook to wonder about his own fate as Wise returned to Richmond.

Then, on Friday, November 25, the *Richmond Enquirer* carried a front-page editorial titled "The Pardon of Cook." Edited by Wise's son, the *Enquirer* often spoke for the governor. Those who understand the "character of Henry A. Wise," it began, realize that he cannot "be *bought* by political favor or extorted by personal threats." If "Cook deserved a pardon it would be extended to him," but that was out of the question because *"he is the most guilty of all the Charlestown prisoners."*

The editorial continued all the way down the front page, expanding on Cook's guilt and unworthiness. Not only had Cook encouraged Brown's plan, but he had then betrayed his own comrades by giving "descriptions of the persons of those who fled." Worse, the cowardly Cook himself had been the first to run away, thus "leaving his deluded friends to meet the fate his deceptions had brought upon them." And worst of all, Cook had "married in Virginia for the purpose of better concealing his designs, and not arousing suspicions; he is doubly criminal, for he sought the destruction of those near and dear to his wife."

"Does such a criminal deserve a pardon?" asked the *Enquirer.* "We do not believe any unbiased mind can, in the face of such facts, desire the pardon of this man." And then, as a final explanation, very nearly in the first person, the editorial concluded:

> The fact of his connection to Gov. Willard, while it will, doubtless, increase the regret which an Executive always feels in withholding pardon, will have no influence in the present case. When men have connections in high positions, it should be a restraint upon their conduct, and if such connection does not thus influence the vicious, it should never be permitted to become an incentive to crime, by the precedent of pardon.[37]

Voorhees's advocacy had failed, and Willard's plea had fallen on politically deaf ears. The governor of Virginia would show no mercy to John Cook.

❊ ELEVEN ❊
Eternity

As his implicit pardon message made painfully clear, Governor Wise held Cook in absolute contempt, and not only because he was a criminal. In Wise's view, Cook was a dishonorable man who had first abandoned and then informed on John Brown. Cook was also a scoundrel who had exploited the friendship of Lewis Washington, and who had probably taken callous advantage of an innocent young girl and her unsuspecting family. Or at least it seemed that way in Richmond. Cook's fellow prisoners knew him better. They recognized, at least, that Cook had not run away from the fight, and that his romantic relationship with Virginia Kennedy had not been part of any underhanded scheme. The others must also have realized that Cook had been under intense pressure to confess, if only for the sake of his family. (Apart from Brown, Cook was the only prisoner with a wife and child.) It would not have been unthinkable for Cook to expect some small measure of understanding from his jailed friends.

Brown himself was beyond the reach of reconciliation. The old man was inflexible in his beliefs, which had no place for accommodations with turncoats or with those who flinched when called to duty. Now Brown had resolved for himself that he could not "better serve the cause I love so much than to die for it," and he saw no reason why his fellow prisoners should hesitate to reach the same conclusion. Although he did not lack compassion, Brown had little tolerance for fear or weakness among his men. During the final siege at Harper's Ferry, he could not find it in himself to comfort his son Oliver, who was crying in agony from a mortal wound. "If you must die," said John Brown, "die like a man."[1] A manly death was his own objective, and he expected no less from those who followed him.

The rumor of Cook's impending defection had made Brown angry enough to lash out at his own sentencing hearing, and news of the actual confession sent him into a rage. For at least a decade, he had exhorted his followers to "make no confession," and instead to "stand by one another, and by your friends, while a drop of blood remains; and be hanged, if you must, but tell no tales out of school." Brown was not averse to revealing the details of the insurrection—as he had during his own interrogation—but he had done his best to protect the identities of his northern backers, whose names Cook had inexcusably spilled onto the trial record. That infidelity was more than Brown could tolerate— no matter how much Cook might apologize—and for weeks afterward he would growl his disapproval of Cook to everyone in the jail.[2] Brown also vented his suspicion that Cook had contrived with Hunter in an attempt to anger him into making additional admissions that he "would not *think* of doing under other circumstances." The other prisoners revered Brown, and they sought the approval of their commander by echoing his condemnation of Cook and assuring him "it was not they who confessed."[3]

Outside of Brown's presence, however, the men were more forgiving. With the exceptions of Stevens (who remained stalwart) and Hazlett (who continued to say nothing), the others all felt they had been misled by Brown. That made them receptive to Cook's apologies and excuses, none more so than twenty-four-year-old Edwin Coppoc. Born in Winona, Ohio, Coppoc had been left fatherless as a child and raised for a time by his uncle Joshua, and then by a neighbor named John Butler. As a teenager, he moved with his mother to the Quaker settlement at Springdale, Iowa, where he participated in local antislavery activities. Edwin and his brother Barclay met Brown during the training-camp winter of 1857–58, and again in early 1859 when Brown passed through Springdale with the slaves he had liberated in Missouri. Although both

Coppoc brothers remained in Iowa when Brown departed on his long trip through the free states to Canada, they evidently agreed to join him later. The call came in midsummer 1859. Believing that they had been recruited on another mission "to run off slaves into a free state," the Coppoc boys informed their mother only that they were about to embark on an expedition to Ohio. She was not fooled. "I believe you are going with old Brown," said Mrs. Coppoc. "When you get the halters round your necks will you think of me?"[4]

Barclay Coppoc managed to escape from the Harper's Ferry debacle, but Edwin indeed faced the prospect of a halter around his neck as he shared a cell with Cook in the Charlestown jail. Whatever Edwin first thought of Cook's confession, the two men eventually became friends. Coming from a community of simple pacifists, the young Quaker must have been fascinated by the stories of Cook's armed exploits in Kansas, and he would also have been impressed by Cook's amorous adventures among the young ladies of Springdale. Naïve and not well educated, Coppoc eventually came to depend on Cook for encouragement and advice in ways that would not end well for him.

In the weeks following the trials, all of the prisoners received visits from journalists, friends, supporters, and other interlocutors. Brown had launched an effective campaign of public justification, making his case to the nation through letters and jailhouse interviews, but the other men were not as forthcoming or expansive. They tended to spend their days either in prayer or writing letters to friends and family; none of them made public pronouncements or granted extended interviews to the press. Unlike Brown, none of the others spoke out in bold defense of the Harper's Ferry raid, although a few expressed their sentiments quietly. John Copeland wrote to his parents from his jail cell, urging them not to despair and reminding them that he was giving his life in a holy cause. "I die in trying to liberate a few of my poor & oppressed people from a condition of servitude against which God in his word has hurled his most bitter denunciations." Shields Green, on the other hand, lamented his decision to leave the safety of Pennsylvania.[5]

Although Brown was the main attraction, Cook received his share of visitors, especially females. As Edwin Coppoc recounted in a letter to his Iowa family, "Among those who called to-day were three young ladies from Harper's Ferry, friends and acquaintances of Cook." The women, who may have been either friends or rivals of Virginia's, stood at Cook's cell door and paused "for a moment with deep earnestness." Then they burst into tears. One of them assured Cook that they had all "formed the highest opinion of him," although of course she "regretted he should have gone into such a scheme."[6]

A number of reporters also met with Cook, and they were uniformly impressed by his calm demeanor and general good spirits. Cook was often found writing poetry, but he willingly put it aside to welcome visitors. He was constantly asked for his autograph, which he always provided in a "singularly clear and elegant" hand. (Brown's autographs were much more highly prized, but the old man had a "great repugnance to parting with any of his handwriting" and he refused all requests.) Cook eagerly "spoke with great emotion of his wife," and he denied that their marriage had been part of a subterfuge.[7]

From the very outset of his imprisonment, Cook had been visited by Rev. N. Green North of the Charlestown Presbyterian Church, who had been contacted by Governor Willard. Following Willard's departure, Governor Wise continued to facilitate Rev. North's visits, which seemed to bring Cook much comfort, and the intensity of Cook's prayers conspicuously increased as the weeks passed.

At least some of Cook's prayers appeared to be answered when he received word that his wife, accompanied by his sister Fanny Crowley, would be coming to visit him in Charlestown. Governor Wise ordered that the two ladies "be received with all the kindness and courtesy ever due to women," but the news of their impending arrival turned out to be mistaken. Cook waited anxiously for two days before giving up hope. A southern newspaper noted that Cook "was much disappointed at the non-arrival of his wife and sister, but otherwise he is much more cheerful than he was a few days ago."[8] The report of Cook's disappointment was surely accurate, but any renewed cheerfulness turned out to be part of an elaborate ruse.

Cook's despair over the missed visit was somewhat alleviated when his mother-in-law came to see him. Mary Ann Kennedy had always cared for John, welcoming him into her family even though it meant evicting her own common-law partner. She had seemed to accept the hasty departure of her daughter and grandson in early October, and she understood that it had something to do with Cook's connection to John Brown. When the fighting broke out at the armory, Mary Ann had rushed into Harper's Ferry in search of John, but she did not learn his whereabouts until much later. Their jailhouse reunion had evidently been orchestrated for the benefit of a reporter for the *Baltimore Sun*, but the scene was poignant nonetheless.

"Had I only known your business at Harper's Ferry," said Mary Ann, "you would not have been here, John."

"I know that very well," he replied. "*You* knew nothing of it." That was not quite true, but an obvious purpose of the interview had been to allow Cook to exonerate his in-laws, who were still at some risk of reprisal in Jefferson County. Another purpose had been to praise his defense counsel, of whom he "spoke in terms of eulogy," saying "they had done their whole duty." Finally, Cook acknowledged that the evidence at trial had been "positive and direct against him."

Upon saying good-bye to her son-in-law, Mary Ann "exhorted him to keep nothing back, and said, 'tell all you know.'"

In another set piece, Cook replied, "I have nothing further to tell; I have told all I know of it."[9]

※　◉　※

Serious pardon efforts were also made on behalf of the other condemned prisoners. Most affecting was a letter sent to Governor Wise by a "committee of colored persons" in Philadelphia seeking reprieves for Green and Copeland. "We plead," they wrote, for "the intervention of your executive influence in behalf of these poor, miserably misguided men." Walking a delicate line, the Philadelphians acknowledged the guilt of Copeland and Green, while pointing out the mitigating circumstance of race:

> Whatever may have been the impulse that moved them to this desperate act of self destruction, it must be remembered that they are of an identity of interest, complexion, and of *national proscription* with the men whose liberty they sought to secure.
>
> All these things may have operated on their minds as an incentive, driving them into the ranks of Capt. Brown, [so] do they not present strong arguments in the extenuation of their guilt, and may they not justly claim the interposition of Executive clemency in their behalf?

No Virginian, much less Governor Wise, could ever admit that black men had any valid reason to rebel, no matter how strong their "identity of interest" with unliberated slaves. Recognizing the hopelessness of their appeal for mercy, the Philadelphians thus made a much more modest request as well:

> We therefore humbly ask that you will grant to us, in the event of their being hung, the bodies of Shields Green and John Copeland, to be transmitted to us for a respectable interment.[10]

For black men in Virginia, even the decency of burial evidently required the intervention of executive authority. Decades later, both Judge Parker and Andrew Hunter wrote that they had favored a commutation of Copeland's death sentence—believing him to be the most "manly" and respectable of the prisoners—but that executive clemency was precluded by the treason conviction. In fact, Copeland had been cleared of treason by virtue of his status under the *Dred Scott* decision, and a clemency recommendation from either the judge or prosecutor could have been entertained by Governor Wise. Perhaps Parker and

Hunter belatedly wished they had spoken up on Copeland's behalf, but in any case their protestations of sympathy were untrue.[11]

The efforts on behalf of Edwin Coppoc were more promising. As a Quaker, Coppoc was able to draw upon the support of his coreligionists around the country, many of whom wrote to Governor Wise seeking mercy. Coppoc himself wrote an apologetic letter—ostensibly to his mother but clearly intended for other eyes as well—in which he acknowledged the folly of the raid but blamed it on others. He had been "led into it by those who ought to have known better," and he was "sorry, very sorry" that he had ever "raised a weapon against my fellow-man."[12]

As pacifists, Coppoc's fellow Quakers could not be accused of complicity with Brown's plans, and they received a very sympathetic hearing from Governor Wise, who decided at one point that Coppoc's life ought to be spared. Coppoc, unfortunately, had been convicted of treason, which tied the governor's hands. Wise, however, went so far as to recommend a pardon to a legislative committee, where a surprisingly large number of members were apparently ready to accept the proposal.

But before the full legislature could act, an improvident letter from Coppoc to John Brown's wife appeared in the national press. Coppoc expressed sympathy with Mrs. Brown's "sad bereavement" over the loss of her sons and the impending execution of her husband, assuring her that Watson and Oliver "fought bravely" in the insurrection. The letter then foolishly referred to Virginians as "the enemy," which was sufficient to evoke outrage in the commonwealth.[13] Seeing no reason to grant clemency to a still-avowed enemy, the full legislature refused to accept Wise's recommendation, and the pardon was denied.

Coppoc insisted to visitors and relatives that the fatal letter had in fact been written by Cook and that he had not even read it. The young Quaker's explanation was accepted by many Virginians, some of whom assumed that Cook had acted purposely "to bind Coppock's destiny to his own." That supposition was unwarranted—the literate and imaginative Cook would have used far more inflammatory language if he had really been trying to subvert Coppoc's pardon petition—although it well demonstrates the depth of hatred that Cook continued to evoke in Virginia. But with or without ill motive, Cook is known to have attached Coppoc's name to at least one other letter, and he seems to have served regularly as his cellmate's creative amanuensis. Coppoc's letters to his family are filled with the ornate prose that was Cook's hallmark, and such flowery language was rather unlikely to have originated from a plainspoken Quaker. Thus the claim that Cook authored the letter to Mary Brown is quite plausible, in which case Edwin Coppoc paid dearly for the friendship of his cellmate.[14]

✸ ❄ ✸

As Brown's execution date approached—Thursday, December 2—Charleston was turned into a literal armed camp. Alarmed by wild rumors of an impending abolitionist rescue mission, Governor Wise had mobilized a force of over three thousand militia, soldiers, and cadets to guard the execution site. General William Taliaferro of Virginia was in charge of the overall operation, while Robert E. Lee led a contingent of federal troops and Thomas Jackson (not yet called "Stonewall") commanded several hundred cadets from the Virginia Military Institute. All strangers were prohibited from entering Charlestown, and the roads and trestles were closely watched. Most northern observers—including President Buchanan—thought the precautions were overblown, but Governor Wise truly believed they were necessary. "An attempt will be made to rescue the prisoners," he declared, "and if that fails, then to seize the citizens of this State as hostages and victims in case of an execution."[15]

Once the scaffold was built and other preparations completed, General Taliaferro informed Brown that it was nearing time to leave the jail. Brown had only a few farewells to make that morning. He handed his silver watch to the jailor, John Avis, in thanks for the kind treatment he had received while imprisoned. He was then taken to see the other prisoners.

As befit a military leader, Brown greeted most of his men warmly, if sternly. He first visited Green and Copeland, who were chained together in a cell on the jail's upper story. He told "the two faithful colored men" to "stand up like men, and not betray their friends." He handed them each a quarter, saying that "he had no more use for money."[16] Brown's gesture was probably more affectionate and less odd than it now seems. There was nothing more he could do for the two condemned men, and the present of even a small amount of money may have expressed his hope that they might yet be reprieved. The description of Brown's last meeting with Green and Copeland was reported widely at the time, and no contemporary observer commented negatively on Brown's monetary gifts.

Brown's affection and generosity did not last long. He was taken next to the cell where Cook and Coppoc were manacled to one another. From the moment he entered the cell, the old man glared disdainfully at Cook, "toward whose want of good faith he was not disposed to be indulgent." Lack of indulgence was the least of it. A more critical journalist noted that Brown had "nothing but sharp & scathing words" for Cook, accusing him of "falsehood & cowardice."

"You have made false statements," scowled Brown.

"What do you mean?" asked Cook.

"Why, by stating that I sent you to Harper's Ferry." In his confession, Cook wrote that he had objected to the posting in Virginia and that he had wanted to go to Kansas instead. Brown considered that an insult, having always insisted that every man had joined his army voluntarily.

Cook then said—as he had at his trial—that he had not come as a spy to Harper's Ferry, but only to discover whether there had been any premature "disclosures" of Brown's plan.

"No, sir," snapped Brown. Cook had indeed been a spy, although a disastrously unreliable one. Cook had grievously "deceived and misled him in relation to the support he would receive from the slaves." From Cook's reports, Brown had concluded that they were ripe for insurrection, only to learn too late that the "representations were false."

Cook attempted to deny the charge, but there was little he could say. With one fierce glance, Brown silenced his former comrade.

Thoroughly intimidated, Cook dropped his head. Perhaps he was ashamed, or perhaps he just did not care "to prolong a dispute with a man on his road to the gallows." When he finally spoke, Cook could only say, "Captain Brown, we remember differently."

Brown had the last word, telling Cook that his "memory must be treacherous, but it would do no good to talk about that." In an obvious reference to Cook's confession, Brown added that "we had gone into a good cause, and not to deny it now."[17]

Turning to Edwin Coppoc, Brown's attitude at first remained severe. "You also have made false statements," he said, referring to Coppoc's sentencing statement that he had been unaware of Brown's plan for insurrection. But then the old man's tone softened. "I am glad to hear you have contradicted them," he said. Coppoc's jailhouse letters had been filled with condemnations of slavery and, unlike Cook, he had never acceded to any criticism of abolitionism. But neither had Coppoc retracted the claim that Brown had misled him into joining a rebellion when he had only intended to participate in a slave rescue. Nonetheless, Brown was forgiving, no doubt because he knew that Coppoc's statement had been completely true: Brown had indeed concealed his objectives from most of his recruits, informing them of the dangerous scope of the plan at the last possible minute. Brown handed the young Quaker a quarter and shook his hand before leaving the cell.[18]

Brown's final visit was with Aaron Stevens, whom he greeted most warmly of all. Brown had never been close to the other four prisoners, but he had known Stevens well since their days together in Kansas and he respected him greatly. Stevens had joined Brown in the Missouri rescue—when they freed eleven slaves in a dress rehearsal for the greater mission in Virginia—and he had proven his worth by killing a slave owner who objected to the liberation of a young girl. As the only one of Brown's men with military experience, Stevens had served as drillmaster at the Iowa training camp and second-in-command at Harper's Ferry.

Stevens was overcome with emotion when Brown entered his cell. "Good bye, Captain, I know you are going to a better land," he said tearfully.

"I know I am," replied Brown. Although it had been six weeks since the raid, Stevens had not yet recovered from his terrible wounds, and Brown therefore encouraged him to "bear up, as you have done." Stevens got the last of Brown's quarters, and as the two men embraced Brown reminded Stevens "never to betray your friends." Brown was given neither to irony nor elegy, so his parting comment must have been simply a kindness to his companion in arms. Stevens had, in fact, been the first of the raiders to betray his comrades, having provided the names of the fugitives to Governor Wise in the armory paymaster's office. Brown had been present at the time, so he knew of Stevens's admission, but he was now willing to excuse his friend's moment of weakness. Such forgiveness was uncharacteristic of Brown, who saw himself as an austere prophet, but there could be no doubting Stevens's bravery under fire or his devotion to abolitionism. As he left the cell, Brown handed Stevens a note with a quote from the book of Proverbs: "He that is slow to anger; is better than the mighty; and that ruleth his Spirit, than he, that taketh a city."[19] At some point, even prophets must call an end to chastisements.

Brown continued to deny that he knew Albert Hazlett and therefore refused an opportunity to meet with him. Still calling himself William Harrison, Hazlett remained hopeful that he could persuade the prosecutors that he had been misidentified. Brown and the other prisoners played along, however unconvincingly, leaving Hazlett alone in his cell.

By the time Brown had taken leave of his comrades it was close to 11:00 a.m., and General Taliaferro informed him that the time had come. Brown was perfectly calm as he was escorted from the building by Captain Avis and Sheriff James Campbell. As he walked down the jailhouse steps, Brown handed a note to one of the guards. It was oddly punctuated, but his message was unmistakable:

> I, John Brown am now quite *certain* that the crimes of this *guilty land: will* never be purged *away;* but with Blood. I had *as I now think: vainly* flattered myself that without *very much* bloodshed; it might be done.[20]

With his arms pinioned, Brown was taken by open wagon to the execution site. Along the way, he spoke with Avis about the beauty of the Virginia landscape, and he again thanked the jailor for all of his kindness. On the scaffold, Brown's legs were tied together and a white hood was slipped over his head. He did not flinch as the noose was placed around his neck, although he asked the hangman to be quick about his work. Spectators had been kept far from the gallows, but several hundred militia and military cadets—including the actor John Wilkes Booth—watched anxiously while Brown stood "erect & as motionless as if he had been a statue." Finally, Colonel J. T. L. Preston gave the order. As the trapdoor swung open, Preston shouted, "So perish all such enemies of Virginia! All such enemies of the Union! All such foes of the human race!"[21]

❋ ◉ ❋

The day of John Brown's execution was solemnized as "Martyr's Day" in cities and villages throughout the North. Now fully beatified in abolitionist circles, Brown was honored by ringing church bells, crowded prayer meetings, public rallies, and hundred-gun salutes. Ministers, editors, laymen, and poets—both black and white—extolled his virtues as a liberator while ignoring, or perhaps silently endorsing, the deaths he had caused in Virginia (and Kansas and Missouri). The Wylie Street African Methodist Episcopal Church of Pittsburgh declared Brown "a hero because he was fearless to defend the poor [and] a Christian because he . . . remembered those in bonds as bound with them." An African-American congregation in Detroit likewise eulogized Brown as "our temporal redeemer whose name shall never die" and resolved to "concentrate our efforts in keeping the Old Brown liberty-ball in motion." Speaking before four thousand people in Boston's Tremont Temple, William Lloyd Garrison came as close as possible to abandoning his own pacifism. "I am a non-resistant," he said, "yet, as a peace man—an 'ultra' peace man—I am prepared to say, 'Success to every slave insurrection in the South.'"[22]

No words could have been better calculated to stoke anger in the South, where the ever-present fear of slave rebellion had reached panic levels following the Harper's Ferry invasion. It did not matter that only a minority of northerners actually admired Brown; every statement of sympathy or approval (of his goals, if not his means) was taken as a threat to southern civilization and therefore to the stability of the Union.

One consequence of the fury was a wave of violence—aimed almost indiscriminately at suspected abolitionists, unwary northerners, free blacks, recalcitrant slaves, and anybody else who could be remotely associated with John Brown—that swept across the slave states. Beatings and other abuse were common, including "scourging, tar-and-feathering, shaving the head" and even lynching. The perpetrators were unapologetic. One Georgia newspaper justified the violence, explaining, "We regard every man in our midst an enemy to the institutions of the South, who does not boldly declare that he believes African slavery to be a social, moral, and political blessing." A Virginia postmaster was threatened with imprisonment, or worse, if he continued to distribute the *New York Tribune*, leading him to observe that the entire state was "in the midst of a Reign of Terror [in which] all men of Northern birth now here are under surveillance." The terror was visited most intensely on the black population. Slaves who showed the slightest sign of rebelliousness or defiance "were dispatched quickly, often by being hanged or burned alive." Within a week of Brown's execution, the Mississippi legislature passed a bill requiring all free blacks to leave the state or risk being sold into slavery.[23]

The political consequences were even more pronounced as firebrands seized upon Brown's insurrection—and what they regarded as northern approval—to further their long-held goal of secession. On the day of Brown's funeral, Jefferson Davis invoked the Harper's Ferry raid as proof that the "General Government" could no longer protect slaveholders "in our property." Thus, he declared, "to secure our rights and protect our honor we will dissever the ties that bind us together, even if it rushes us into a sea of blood."[24]

Another leading secessionist was Edmund Ruffin, a wealthy Virginia planter who had attended Brown's execution and who would later fire one of the first shots at Fort Sumter. For years, Ruffin had been frustrated by the persistence of Unionism in Virginia, even among the slaveholding aristocracy. He therefore saw Brown's raid as a providential warning that would at last "stir the sluggish blood of the south." Following Brown's execution, Ruffin was both appalled and elated by "the very general sympathy of the northern people" for the abolitionist murderer. In his view, the northern reaction proved the existence of an "abolitionist conspiracy [that] afforded the best practical ground of dissolution that the south ever had." It was time to seize the opportunity. "We ought to agitate & exasperate the already highly excited indignation of the south," he wrote.[25]

Thus was John Brown's ultimate triumph. Although not quite according to plan, he and his "tiny revolutionary terrorist cell succeeded in producing a general panic that propelled" even moderate southerners into confrontation with the north. As Henry David Thoreau put it,

"No theatrical manager could have arranged things so wisely to give effect to his behavior and words."[26]

In Jefferson County, however, the drama was not yet complete.

❖ ◉ ❖

Cook and the other prisoners were deeply saddened by their commander's death. Brown had been their leader throughout every ordeal, and his unshakeable commitment to the "indispensability of their mission" had sustained the courage of even those who had sometimes strayed from the cause. With Brown departed and realistic hopes of pardon lost as well, a pall fell over the remaining inmates of the Charlestown jail. Cook and Coppoc, who had once been the most expansive of the prisoners, now appeared to have "no thought of averting their fate."[27] But even among condemned men appearances can be deceiving.

On Tuesday, December 13, Governor Willard and Fanny Cook Crowley arrived in Charlestown, accompanied by Daniel Voorhees, for their final visit with Cook. As their carriage pulled up to the Carter House Hotel, they were surrounded by curious onlookers who were eager to get a look at Cook's sister. If the gawkers hoped for a glimpse of pathos, they were rewarded when the party stepped down from the coach. Fanny Crowley was "bowed down" with grief, and Willard seemed overcome with sorrow. Later that day another sister, Cynthia Sophia, arrived along with her husband, Dr. A. S. Staunton, and their two-year-old son. Mrs. Staunton showed a "heavy weight of woe" that contrasted sharply with the "bright happy-faced boy" in her arms. The child, of course, had no idea of the unfolding tragedy, and he was the only member of the extended Cook family who was not in visible despair.[28]

The family meeting in Cook's cell that afternoon was a "scene of grief and anguish scarcely to be described," as the Cook sisters sadly embraced the lovely boy they remembered from childhood. Voorhees and Staunton were stoic, but Willard dissolved in tears when he attempted to deliver a message from Caroline. Weeping as though he was saying good-bye to his own son, Willard's "lamentations could be heard throughout the building." Finally, at about 6:00 p.m., Willard decided that it was time to retire for the evening. The sisters promised to return the next day, and they wished their brother an affectionate good night.[29]

Back at the hotel Willard informed the ladies "that he deemed it best for them to leave for their homes" without returning to the jail. He feared that the emotional strain would be too great if they "were to witness the last hours of the poor unfortunate" Cook, whom he thought ought to be left alone for his final preparations. Willard asked each woman to write a short farewell note, which he promised to deliver, and he arranged for a carriage and baggage wagon to take them to the railroad station. The deeply disconsolate family members left the following morning, bidding farewell, as one observer put it, "to a place which will always be surrounded with painful recollections." Strangely enough, Cook seemed hardly upset at his relatives' departure, leading one reporter to remark upon his apparent lack of feeling.[30]

Coppoc had his own visitors on Tuesday. From Ohio came Joshua Coppoc and John Butler, with whom Edwin had lived as a child. Thomas Winn also arrived, bearing a large pound cake, as a representative of the Springdale Quakers. Together they met with Rev. North, who announced his approval of the Quakers' "Christian deportment."

On Wednesday, December 14, the Charlestown jail resembled a revival meeting. No fewer than four local ministers, from Presbyterian and Methodist Episcopal churches, arrived to meet the spiritual needs of the prisoners. All of the condemned men participated in the services, giving their "unqualified assent to the conviction of religious truth" and expressing their hope of salvation in the world to come.[31]

There is no reason to think that John Cook ever attended church during his six years in Kansas and Virginia. According to a friend, Cook's "theology was of a mongrel sort," closer to deism than to any denomination, but he had apparently experienced a jailhouse conversion. Among the prisoners, he was the loudest in the "profession of a change of heart, and in the hope of Divine forgiveness." He and Coppoc "freely admitted their guilt, and acknowledged their doom as a just one." Rev. North was delighted at the change in Cook's disposition. One day earlier, following his sisters' departure, he had appeared impassive and nearly numb, but he now seemed almost ecstatic in his embrace of Christianity.[32]

Only later would the ministers learn, along with everyone else in Charlestown, that Cook and Coppoc were "playing opossum." Their great show of faith was meant to hoodwink the jailors and conceal their intentions, rather than to save their souls. Even as Cook knelt in prayer his mind was "fixed on hopes of life and liberty rather than death and eternity."[33]

▪ ◉ ▪

Thursday, December 15, passed uneventfully inside the jailhouse. All visitors had departed, and Captain Avis ordered the building closed to outsiders. Cook wrote a short letter to the family with whom he had boarded in Springdale, sending his love and expressing his hope to meet them "beyond Death's River." He had evidently come to good terms with his fellow prisoners, as he added on the reverse side of the letter that "Stevens and Coppoc send their love," and he signed his name with a flourish—"Ever and truly yours, John E. Cook."[34]

The streets of Charlestown were far from quiet. Unlike Brown's hanging, the executions the following day would be open to the public. Hundreds of visitors from other parts of Virginia "were flocking in to witness the last act of the Harper's Ferry tragedy." Many of them came early, worried that they might be stopped or delayed by sentries along the road, but security for the event turned out to be lax and "little difficulty was experienced in getting in town."[35]

Following the arrival of the afternoon train, which carried a contingent of eastern newspaper reporters, the various militia companies held a dress parade, featuring polished arms and precision marching. Under the command of Lieutenant Israel Green of the United States Marines—the man who slashed Brown into submission at the armory—

the four battalions went smartly through their maneuvers. Their "bright bayonets and gay uniforms" delighted the large number of well-dressed ladies in attendance and earned the approval of General Talia-ferro, who reviewed the troops while mounted on "a spirited charger."[36]

By nightfall the troops had retired to their quarters and the strag-gling out-of-towners were busy seeking lodging for the evening. The Carter House, so recently vacated by Governor Willard and the Cook sisters, was serving supper to the fifth or sixth round of guests, and the bar rooms were crowded with patrons who celebrated "the resignation of the prisoners to their fate." In sharp contrast to Brown's execution, "all apprehensions of an intended rescue had long since been banished." The public mood was relaxed and almost festive in anticipation of the next day's events.

Just as the last meal was being served at the Carter House, Charles-town's calm was shattered by the sound of gunfire and the "whole town was thrown into commotion." An alarm was sounded in the vicinity of the jail, and soldiers rushed into the streets, as also did some brave, or foolishly curious, civilians. The surprised and sleepy—and in many cases drunken—militiamen aimed their rifles at shadows and jumped at every unexpected sound, making it "dangerous for a citizen to go out to ascertain the cause of the excitement." Rumors spread quickly through the taverns and homes, and "it was at one time thought that the prisoners had overpowered their guards" or that the long-feared second abolitionist invasion had begun. In the words of one observer, the turmoil "was beyond anything that had yet occurred during our ever memorable era of military occupation."[37]

Cook and Coppoc had attempted an escape.

❊　❂　❊

Shortly after 8:00 p.m., a militia sentry—aptly named Thomas Guard, who was a tailor in civilian life—observed a figure standing on the jail-house parapet. It was John Cook, who had somehow gotten free from his cell. Then another man's head appeared, peeking over the wall. That was Edwin Coppoc, slowly following his more daring comrade. Guard shouted an order to stop, followed by a warning shot. Coppoc retreated, but Cook looked as though he was about to jump from the wall. Officer Guard fired again and called out his "intention of impaling him on his bayonet." Realizing that the gunfire would soon draw additional sentries, Cook surrendered and was taken back into the jail yard.[38]

General Taliaferro arrived at the jail within minutes of the arrest, having rushed to the scene at the moment the alarm was given. He immediately took command of the premises—an order that was soon confirmed in a wire from Governor Wise—and directed his men to chain down Cook and Coppoc and watch over them until they were executed. That development was hugely embarrassing to Captain Avis, who until that night had resisted "all interference of the military with the interior discipline of the jail," including Taliaferro's request to station troops inside the building itself. It was a point of pride with Avis that he had preserved the civilian character of his jail even while the rest of the town was under virtual martial law. Now, however, the humane jailor found himself accused of incompetence (which was more or less true) and suspected of having perhaps accepted a bribe (which he most definitely had not).[39]

Once Cook and Coppoc were securely in custody, it did not take long to figure out what had happened. Using their bedclothes to muffle the sound, the two prisoners had managed to chisel through the wall of their cell in a spot that was concealed by a bed frame. They had removed the outer plaster and then a sufficient number of bricks to create a man-sized "aperture," hiding the bricks and dirt in their stove. Following the last inspection of the night, they had pulled the bed aside and slipped through the opening, which was about fifteen feet above ground. The outer wall was even higher, and at first it seemed impossible to scale. "That difficulty, however, was soon overcome with the aid of the timbers of the scaffold on which Capt. Brown was hung, and which were intended also for their own execution."[40] If Officer Guard had not been making his rounds at the precise moment when Cook reached the top of the wall, it would have been an easy matter for the prisoners to drop to the street and head for the safety of the nearby Shenandoah Mountains.

That much was apparent from an examination of the cell. Upon interrogation, Cook proved willing to provide all of the surrounding details. He and Coppoc had been at work on their escape plan for at least ten days. It began when a guard had innocently forgotten to retrieve a knife that he had given Cook to cut a lemon. With the knife, Cook and Coppoc were able to remove a screw from their bedstead, which they fashioned into a chisel. They obtained a smaller blade from Shields Green—jailhouse precautions were evidently slack on the matter of cutting tools—and used it to "make some teeth in the Barlow knife." That enabled them to saw through their chains, although the shackle rings still remained around their ankles. They had used torn clothing and the ends of their trousers to deaden the clanking sound when they clambered out of the cell.[41]

For the first time since his extradition from Chambersburg, Cook was openly defiant. With no prospect of pardon and freed from the influence of Willard and Voorhees, there was no longer any reason for Cook to pretend to be remorseful or cooperative. His only regret was that he had not "throttled the guard" and made his way over the wall. With a head start into the mountains, he declared, no militia could have caught him. He knew how to travel at night, and they did not.

Cook did express some remorse for the difficulty that his escape attempt had caused for Captain Avis. He apologized sincerely to the jailor and volunteered to write a letter absolving him of blame. The note, written in Cook's "beautiful style of penmanship," was given to a southern reporter and published widely. Cook explained that he and Coppoc wanted "to make a fair statement in regard to the ways and means of our breaking jail . . . from a sense of our duty to the Sheriff of the county, and jailor and jail guard. We do not wish that any one should be unjustly censured on our account." Cook provided a brief description of the means of the escape and stressed that he and Coppoc had "received no aid from any person or persons whatever."[42]

Cook also explained that he and Coppoc had originally planned to make their escape on Wednesday, only to change their minds because Willard and the other relatives were still in town that day. "I knew that it would reflect on them," he wrote, "and we postponed it." Cook added that he had urged Coppoc to go alone on Wednesday, but he refused and they decided together to wait. It is hard to know how much of Cook's rendition is true. It is understandable that he would not have wanted to escape while his family was in Charlestown, but why would he have urged Coppoc to flee alone on Wednesday? Once discovered, Coppoc's disappearance would have doomed Cook, who obviously would have had no chance of escaping the following day. Moreover, there would have been no reason for Cook to think that Wednesday was a better day than Thursday to make the escape. The account of his self-sacrificing offer to Coppoc seems very much like one of Cook's boastful fabulations, not unlike his story of deceiving the Kickapoo Rangers or his assurance to Brown that Maryland political figures could be recruited for the insurrection or even his claim at sentencing that he had once been "a pro-slavery man." Cook exaggerated at almost every opportunity, and we will never know Coppoc's side of this particular story.[43]

❖ ✲ ❖

Reveille sounded at dawn on Friday, December 16, and soon the streets of Charlestown were filled with soldiers, most of whom had been on duty all night or "sleeping on their arms." The first executions would not be for several hours, but there were many preparations to be made. The scaffold had to be erected; the prisoners had to be readied; and, given the previous night's excitement, belated security measures had to be employed. Country folk from the surrounding counties and strangers from as far as Baltimore continued to arrive—most of them unaware of the dramatic escape attempt—only to be stopped by nervous soldiers at the outskirts of town. Those who could not give a satisfactory "account of themselves or get some citizen to vouch for them" were taken to a guardhouse and confined until after the executions. Most of the travelers were allowed to proceed, but anyone who expected a good time would soon be disappointed. "The heavens were overcast, the air raw and bitter," and it appeared that an "equinoctial storm" was about to descend on the valley. The apprehensive public mood was in keeping with the threatening weather.[44]

Once again, a deputation of the Charlestown clergy came to the jail, but this time there would be no false declarations of remorse. The Presbyterian Rev. North, accompanied by Rev. Henry Waugh of the Methodist Church, first visited Shields Green and John Copeland, who were scheduled to be hanged in the morning. As usual, most of the press paid little attention to the black prisoners, with the *New York Tribune* mentioning only that ministers led an impressive religious ceremony in their cell. The local *Shepherdstown Register* was somewhat more expansive, reporting that Shields Green wanted to "pray and prepare for another world," while John Copeland spoke out more forcefully. "If I am dying for freedom," he said, "I could not die in a better cause—I would rather die than be a slave."[45]

The final services for Cook and Coppoc were far better attended. A third minister was present—Rev. Leech, whose denomination was not reported—along with fifteen or twenty others, all of whom were eager to hear the prisoners' last words. Prompted by Captain Avis, Cook said that he was thankful for the kindness he had been shown by the jailor, and he also thanked by name the various clergymen who had visited him "and others who had manifested such interest in his welfare." As before, Coppoc let Cook speak for him, saying only "them's my sentiments too, gentlemen."

Cook remembered his manners, but he had also rediscovered his ideals. Taking advantage of the large audience, he departed from the apologetic script to assert that "a negro was as good as a white man," and he called upon Virginians "to take into consideration freedom and slavery, and to reflect upon it well." Cook declared that "slavery was a sin" and he was "prepared to die in such a cause, and thought he had done nothing to regret so far as principle was concerned."

With far more prescience than anyone could have realized at the time, Cook predicted that slavery "would be abolished in Virginia in less than ten years."[46]

※　✸　※

Shortly after 10:30 that morning, General Taliaferro arrived at the jail, ready to escort Green and Copeland to the gallows. A contingent of about twenty-five troops formed a hollow square at the jailhouse door, as Sheriff Campbell and Captain Avis led the prisoners out of the building and down the steps. An open wagon holding two poplar coffins drew into the middle of the square, and Campbell helped the two prisoners take their seats on the caskets. With their arms pinioned, Green and Copeland appeared downcast, and "wore none of that calm and cheerful spirit evinced by Brown under similar circumstances." By 10:45, the cortege was under way, flanked by riflemen on either side as it passed through the crowded street. It took less than ten minutes to reach the hanging ground, where the two prisoners were led up the scaffold steps to the center of the platform. Copeland remained quiet, but Green is said to have trembled with fear and prayed out loud.

Following a minister's obligatory prayer, Copeland attempted to speak to the large crowd. Condemned men were routinely allowed a final address in the nineteenth century, and Copeland therefore expected to make one last statement about the injustices of slavery. But that privilege was apparently denied to black men in Virginia. The hangman intervened, pulling hoods down around the heads of the prisoners and affixing ropes around their necks. The trap was drawn at a few minutes after eleven o'clock, and the two men were "launched into eternity." Green appeared to die instantly, his neck having been broken by the fall, but Copeland was slowly strangled and he "writhed in violent contortions for several minutes."[47]

Green and Copeland were allowed to hang for half an hour, until they were cut down and pronounced dead by a physician and readied for burial on the execution ground. Governor Wise had evidently denied the petition of the Philadelphia "committee of colored persons," as well as a similar request from John Copeland's father, and no plans had been made to send the bodies north for the requested respectable interment. In fact, it was expected that Green and Copeland would rest only briefly in their graves. A group of medical students from nearby Winchester attended the hanging, and it was understood that they would not leave the dead men buried for long. With the apparent approval of the authorities, Green and Copeland were allowed to "remain in the ground but a few moments, before they were taken up and conveyed to Winchester for dissection."[48]

While Green and Copeland were still hanging from the gallows, a courier was sent to inform Cook and Coppoc that only about an hour remained before they would have to depart. Taliaferro's retinue took somewhat longer to reach the jail as it first had to load two more coffins onto the wagon. At 12:30 p.m. the military escort was fully in place, waiting for the prisoners to finish their last preparations.

❈ ❂ ❈

Cook and Coppoc had spent the intervening time washing themselves and dressing in clean clothes. Each man wrote a final letter—Cook to his wife and Coppoc to his uncle—which they finished just as Avis came to collect them. Asked if he had any last wishes, Cook asked the jailor to dispose of "one or two articles which he had in his possession." He requested that a small breast pin remain on his shirt until after the execution, and then "given to his little boy if he shall live." He also told Avis that his pocket held a "daguerreotype and a lock of my little boy's hair," and requested that it be sent to his wife.[49]

By then it was time to leave. Both men asked that their arms be only loosely pinioned, and Avis gently complied. A blue cloak, called a talma, was thrown over Coppoc's shoulders, and a darker one was placed on Cook, as though some sort of formal dress was necessary for the trip to the scaffold.

Coppoc was shaking with emotion as he left the cell. Cook appeared outwardly calm, but an occasional tremor betrayed his fear. Someone commented that it must be hard to die, to which Coppoc replied, "It is the parting from friends, not the dread of death, that moves us." At the end of the corridor, the prisoners were taken to the cell of Stevens and Hazlett, where they were allowed to say farewell. Stevens had been Brown's adjutant and drillmaster, but he showed no lingering resentment toward Cook. Warmly shaking hands with both of his comrades, Stevens said, "Good bye friends! Cheer up! Give my love to my friends in the other world." Cook and Coppoc also shook hands with Hazlett, although they maintained the pretense that they did not know him.[50]

With their arms bound, Cook and Coppoc had to be helped into the waiting wagon, where they took seats upon their own coffins. Reports of their demeanor differ greatly. According to one account, the prisoners were impassive and downcast, and they "seemed to take but little notice of anything as the procession slowly moved to the field of death." Another observer said that they were responsive to the spectators, although each in his own way. "Cook recognized a face, bowed, and said, 'Remember me to all my friends at the Ferry,'" while Coppoc "looked wildly around upon the crowd" as though he was still hoping for news of a commutation.[51]

However well they endured the short ride, both Cook and Coppoc regained their composure before reaching the gallows. They ascended the steps "with a determination that was scarcely surpassed by Capt. Brown." A brief prayer was offered, but neither of the condemned men made "any direct profession of religion." Before they were hooded, Cook reached for Coppoc's hand and continued to hold it as the ropes were placed around their necks. If there had been any recriminations between the two men, they had been set aside on their last day. Turning toward Coppoc, Cook softly said "God bless you," and then in a loud tone, "Be quick—as quick as possible." The hangman obliged, dropping the trap after only four or five minutes on the scaffold. Both men died easily, their necks broken by the fall.

The bodies remained hanging for thirty minutes before they were cut down and laid in coffins. Coppoc was put into a walnut casket, supplied by the local undertaker, to be shipped to his mother in Iowa. Cook's family had provided a more elegant coffin, with instructions that it be shipped to "Ashbel P. Willard and Robert Crowley, No. 104 William Street, New York, care Adams Express." In the Jefferson County Register of Deaths, Cook's occupation was listed as "adventurer."[52]

※ ✸ ※

Before leaving his cell, Cook had given the jailors a final letter to his wife, and he also left a sheaf of papers behind on the table. Some of the pages were notes in Cook's own hand, but there was also a memorandum in different handwriting: "Give me an accurate description, as possible as you can of the *age* and *personal appearance* of Owen Brown, Barclay Coppic, and J. T. Merriam," read the note, which was signed in pencil by Captain John Avis. It appears that Cook may at first have balked at Wise's (and Voorhees's) request for information about his fugitive friends, and the compassionate jailor was not above exerting some pressure on behalf of the prosecution.

Below Avis's request, Cook had written his own message: "Revealed the secret only to a woman and that under a solemn pledge of secrecy." Cook's attempt at self-exoneration was undated, and there is no way to know for whom it was intended, but it must have been the last tale he ever told.[53]

TWELVE
Forgiveness

John Cook's body was not easily laid to rest. The Adams Express Company did its job promptly and efficiently, delivering the coffin just before midnight on Saturday, December 17, at a railroad terminal in Jersey City, but things did not go well afterward. Willard and Crowley were waiting with a hearse at the depot, but they had second thoughts about transporting the notorious Cook's remains in so visible a vehicle. Fortunately, they were able to arrange quickly for a freight wagon, in which they proceeded to the Hudson River. The ferry operator, however, refused to take them across to New York because they had not obtained the appropriate permit to take the body through the city. Willard and Crowley pleaded with the operator, who finally relented upon their "assurances that the permit should be forthcoming in the morning." They crossed Manhattan without incident, but they encountered a similar objection from the Williamsburg ferryman, who only reluctantly agreed to take them on board.

By the time they crossed the East River it was nearing 4:00 a.m., and the weary brothers-in-law directed the driver to go directly to the undertaker's parlor. Still before dawn, the mortician, Dr. Holmes, opened the coffin to see the condition of the body. As expected following an execution, there were pronounced ligature marks on Cook's broken neck, his face was distorted from strangulation, and much of his body appeared bruised due to "extravasation of blood." Considerable work would be needed to prepare the corpse for viewing. Cook's body was injected with embalming fluid and placed upright so that the blood could drain from his face.

Word spread quickly that the remains of Captain Cook had arrived in Brooklyn, and hundreds of people called at the undertaker's in hope of seeing one of the notorious Harper's Ferry insurgents. Some claimed to have been Cook's acquaintances when he lived in Williamsburg and others were clearly just voyeurs, but all were turned away. Cook's face was so badly discolored that it was "not thought advisable to expose it" until he had been fully embalmed.[1]

Virginia Kennedy Cook had been living in Haddam with John's parents, but she had come to Brooklyn for her husband's interment. She too was denied permission to see the body until it could be made more presentable. The undertaker assured Virginia that the body would be ready in time for an open casket wake, which he expected to take place the following day. The embalmer's work was duly finished on schedule, but the funeral would be delayed.

The Crowleys had assumed that the funeral service would be held at Rev. Elder Porter's Reformed Dutch Church, where they had worshipped for fifteen years and where Cook sometimes taught Sunday school during his clerkship for attorney Stearns. Rev. Porter himself had agreed to preach the sermon, and the Crowleys were so certain of the funeral's location that they printed a circular that was distributed to other ministers and congregations in Brooklyn. The only remaining formality was the consent of the Consistory, a governing body on which Robert Crowley had served since 1852. To Crowley's great shock and dismay, however, permission was withheld. The ostensible reason for the denial was that "undue excitement might be created, endangering the temporal and spiritual interests of the church," but in fact the Consistory members did not want to risk offending the proslavery Democrats who controlled politics and commerce in New York City. There was even a possibility that the funeral might be disrupted, as had been an abolitionist meeting at Cooper Union the previous week. Crowley protested strongly, pointing out that only a minority of the church's members objected to the funeral. That was true, but irrelevant to the Consistory, among whom economic and political considerations could not be ignored. As a concession, it was proposed to allow the "obsequies in the church, if the body was not brought there." But that was unacceptable to the Crowleys, who wanted "the body to be in the church, and there to receive a Christian burial according to the customary forms."[2]

Robert Crowley was deeply offended. As a pillar of his church, he had expected no difficulty obtaining the last rites for his errant brother-in-law. Fanny Cook Crowley was even more profoundly grieved at the action of the church, leading one of her close friends to observe that "the blow was felt even more keenly than that of the unfortunate death of [her] relative." That was obviously an overstatement. Nothing mattered more to Fanny than the loss of her brother, but the hard-heartedness of the church trustees made her tragic situation even worse.

Although no friend of abolitionism, Robert Crowley had already gone to extraordinary lengths for John Cook—traveling twice to Charles-town at his beloved wife's behest—and he was not willing to stop short of an appropriate grave. With little time left to make the necessary arrangements, Crowley approached Rev. Tompkins of the nearby New England Church, but he was again turned away by a vote of the trustees. In a more generous spirit, the small South Baptist Church offered the use of its hall, but the facility was not large enough to accommodate all of the legitimate mourners. A solution was only found when a wealthy neighbor offered the use of his private home, located in a fashionable section of Williamsburg.

Cook's funeral was finally held on the morning of Tuesday, December 20, with the body displayed in an open casket. Cook was dressed in a black suit, and a daguerreotype locket—no doubt the one he had mentioned to Captain Avis as he prepared for execution—hung around his neck. Despite the embalmer's best efforts, Cook's face was still badly discolored. His features, however, showed a firm expression, and his blond hair and mustache made him seem almost lifelike.

The extended Cook family gathered around the coffin. Nathanial Cook, the stout patriarch, had arrived from Connecticut on Sunday, although his wife Mary remained behind in Haddam. At age seventy-two, Mary Cook might have been too infirm to travel—she would die in 1862—or she might simply have been overcome with sorrow at the loss of her son. Most of the Cook siblings were also in attendance, Caroline, Catherine, and Cynthia Sophia all having traveled from Indiana in the company of Ashbel Willard.

Virginia Kennedy Cook found herself almost a stranger among so many New England Puritans. To outsiders, it seemed as though she was making "her first acquaintance with the Northern relatives of her husband . . . at his grave," although in fact she had been living with them for nearly two months. Her evident discomfort was due to her awkward situation. Impoverished and completely dependent upon the Cooks and Crowleys for support, Virginia had lied about the date of her wedding—claiming to have been married in July 1858, almost a year earlier than the actual date—in order to conceal the circumstances of her son's conception. However proper she tried to appear, Virginia was intimidated by Fanny Cook Crowley, who was forceful in any situation and must have seemed overbearing to the self-conscious and unrefined country girl.[3] The tension between Virginia and the Crowleys would increase over the following years, but on such a grim occasion it only rippled beneath the surface.

Nathanial Cook said a few words about his son, stressing his religious education and love for his family, but the main eulogy was delivered by a Rev. Caldicott. The minister referred only obliquely to Cook's abolitionism, saying there was "abundant evidence that the departed was a child of God." Caldicott also read from the Bible as well as from some of Cook's prison letters. He concluded the emotional service by reciting lines from Cook's last poem:

And again in heaven united,
'Mid those fair Elysian bowers,
We'll perfect the love we plighted
In this darkened world of ours.

The "darkened world" was (and is) a common Christian allusion, but Cook had also frequently used it as a reference to slavery. In an August 1859 letter from Harper's Ferry, for example, he had rejoiced that the "Egyptian darkness" would soon give way to a "light breaking in this southern sky," meaning that the abolitionist insurrection would soon begin. Among those in attendance at the funeral, it is likely that only Virginia Cook wondered about the possible double meaning of the verse, or perhaps she simply prayed along with the others. When the service ended, Virginia was allowed to retrieve the locket and breast pin from the body before the casket was closed. The pallbearers then removed the rosewood coffin, which was mounted with silver headed screws and handles, and with a silver plate on the lid that read, "John E. Cook, died Dec. 16, 1859." Cook was buried at the nearby Cypress Hill Cemetery. He was later moved to the Crowley family plot at Brooklyn's stately Greenwood Cemetery, where his remains rest today.[4]

※　❂　※

John Cook had gone from obscurity to infamy to death in only two months' time. For ten days—from the collapse of the Harper's Ferry raid until his capture in Chambersburg—he was among the most wanted fugitives in the history of the United States. Following his execution and burial, however, Cook's notoriety quickly waned. He was mourned by his relatives and their friends as a wayward and misguided child, but not as a hero. Although they took some solace that he had sacrificed his life in pursuit of a selfless cause, they expressed no pride in his "attempt to incite servile insurrection." At best, they regretted that Cook had yielded "to a visionary philanthropy for a race incapable of appreciating the privileges [he] desired to confer upon it," while hoping that his terrible example would stand as a warning to others.[5]

If Cook's abolitionism drew little sympathy from his family, his defection at first drew only scorn within the antislavery movement. Many considered Cook to be a coward and a traitor or, in the eyes of Thomas Wentworth Higginson, a "recreant." Frederick Douglass, for example, castigated Cook as the only one of Brown's men who "sought to save his life by representing that he had been deceived, and allured by false promises." George Sennott, the attorney who spoke most powerfully against slavery at the Charlestown trials, said that "Cook failed in courage, and has gained by it the contempt of all mankind." Sennott was proud that his own clients—John Copeland, Shields Green, and later Aaron Stevens—had not repudiated the cause. All save Cook had faced death like heroes. "It is better to die like Brown," wrote Sennott, rather than "whine like a sneak and a scoundrel like Cook."[6] Sennott's reaction was visceral. Unlike other abolitionists who maligned Cook, Sennott had actually seen him in action, and the attorney was acutely aware that Cook's confession had endangered others.

Fortunately, Cook's confession had cost no additional lives, and it had not ultimately resulted in any further arrests.[7] Cook had neither saved himself from the gallows nor advanced the designs of Governor Wise and the Virginia prosecutors. Thus most abolitionists saw little to be gained by vilifying Cook, and some saw good reasons to forgive him.

In the immediate aftermath of the Harper's Ferry raid, most northern abolitionists and Republicans had attempted to distance themselves from John Brown. Governor Salmon Chase of Ohio, who hoped to be the Republican presidential nominee in 1860, denounced Brown's "insane attempt" and called him a rash criminal. Others called Brown "an old idiot" who deserved to hang, a "lawless brigand," a "fanatic," and most frequently a "madman." Even William Lloyd Garrison's *Liberator* called the raid "misguided, wild, and apparently insane." In the weeks between his arrest and execution, however, Brown's letters and interviews—and most of all his final speech to the court—actually "eradicated all such misgivings," and he came to be seen far more favorably in the North. Within days of Brown's conviction and sentencing, Ralph Waldo Emerson rhetorically completed Brown's transformation from pariah to hero:

> That new saint, than whom none purer or more brave was ever led by love of men into conflict and death,—the new saint awaiting his martyrdom, and who, if he shall suffer, will make the gallows glorious as the cross.[8]

The beatification of Brown also affected attitudes toward the other survivors of the raid. As a hero, he must have led heroic men, six of whom had been imprisoned with him in Charlestown. In truth, Brown had been so desperate for troops that he accepted every man who volunteered, no matter how erratic or unsuited to the task. But such poor judgment of character was not the attribute of a true saint, and Brown's old friends and new admirers therefore proved willing to overlook or excuse the failings of his comrades in arms. Thus began the rehabilitation of John Cook.

Cook's failings, to be sure, had been well known and pronounced, but most of the other captured raiders also broke ranks with Brown at some point. Stevens had provided the Virginia authorities with the names of his fugitive colleagues; Coppoc and Green complained loudly that Brown had misled them; and Copeland made his own confession to federal marshals from Ohio, disclosing the names of the Oberliners who financed his travel to Harper's Ferry. Only Hazlett kept completely mum, and that was because he refused to acknowledge that he knew Brown at all. But never mind the full and partial confessions. Brown's growing legend could be better served if his men were celebrated along with him, even if that meant treating Cook's confession as the product of forgivable weakness rather than a calculated betrayal.

It could have turned out differently. There was certainly a place in Brown's legend for a true Judas figure, and it may simply have been fortuitous that Cook was not assigned that role. If one of Brown's more prominent defenders—say, Ralph Waldo Emerson or Wendell Phillips—

had publicly excoriated Cook, then perhaps others would have done so as well. It appears, however, that it was more convenient to extol Brown's virtues, which were said to include compassion and leadership, than to explain how a traitor had been sent on so many important missions. It could also be said that Cook's confession had been wrung from him by Willard and Voorhees, and that he might have been steadfast if represented by an antislavery lawyer such as Hiram Griswold or George Sennott. After all, Cook's betrayals ended as soon as Voorhees left town. A more determined turncoat could have continued bargaining for his life by identifying Albert Hazlett, but Cook, to his credit, took no advantage of that opportunity.

For at least the time being, it seemed that abolitionism was best served by an uncomplicated narrative of righteousness. Saintly John Brown dominated the story, and his twenty-one confederates occupied the background as trusty minions with few real motives of their own. Cook did not fit quite so neatly into the story, but that problem was easily resolved through forgiveness. Osborne Anderson, the only African-American survivor of the raid, said that he had no "intention to dwell upon the failings of John E. Cook" whose "very weakness should excite our compassion." Recognizing that Cook had been under merciless pressure to confess, Anderson absolved him of treachery to the cause. Anne Brown wrote to Thomas Wentworth Higginson in the same vein, expressing "pity and sorrow" for Cook and "uttering the hope that allowances might be made for his conduct."[9] She would repeat that sentiment for the rest of her life, and most of Brown's friends, including his early biographers, would do the same.

In early 1860, James Redpath published the first full biography of John Brown. It was a work of hagiography, with half of the royalties going to Brown's surviving family. A committed abolitionist and a friend of Brown's from his Kansas days, Redpath did not disguise his motive for writing the book. "I loved and reverenced the noble old man," he wrote in the introduction, adding, "I think that John Brown

did right in invading Virginia and attempting to liberate her slaves."
Redpath made a point of downplaying anything negative or disagree-
able about Brown's relationship to Cook or the other recruits, even if
that meant denying known facts, or omitting them, or adding new ones.
For example, Redpath claimed that no cross words had ever passed between Brown and Cook at the Iowa training camp, and he denied that
any of the men had protested when Brown first revealed his intention
to invade Virginia. He also denied that John Copeland had confessed
to the federal marshal from Ohio, even though reports of Copeland's
interrogation had already been published. Redpath made no mention
of Brown's harsh rebuke of Cook on the way to the gallows, but he did
recount an inspiring scenario in which Cook watched Brown's hanging
from the jail. Cook's reaction, according to Redpath, showed his great
"agony of mind" at the death of his leader:

> From the window of his cell, Cook had an unobstructed view of
> the whole proceedings. He watched his old Captain until the trap
> fell and his body swung into mid air, when he turned away and
> gave vent to his feelings.

That was a poignant vignette, reinforcing as it did the themes of solidarity and reconciliation among the condemned men. But it never happened. Cook himself later wrote a letter about Brown's execution, in
which he said nothing about watching the hanging—which in any case
would have been impossible from his cell.[10]

Redpath's was neither the first nor the last attempt to harmonize
John Cook's faithlessness with the image of John Brown as a warrior-
saint. As years passed, a legend emerged that Cook had repudiated
Daniel Voorhees's proslavery defense, calling out "It's a damned lie" in
the middle of the final argument. There was no truth to the story, but it
conveniently fit the belief that Brown had chosen only upright men.[11]

In 1886, Anne Brown still remembered Cook with a combination of
disdain and affection. "Cook was very impulsive and indiscreet," she

wrote, "but I can never believe that he ever intentionally wronged father in word, thought or deed. After seeing and knowing Cook's wife,
I think he did far better, and showed more honor and manliness than
most men would have under the circumstances."[12]

Some years later, Anne wrote a similar letter to Richard Hinton,
who was then preparing his highly sympathetic biography, *John Brown
and His Men.* "I am anxious to have you give John E. Cook a much better character than anyone has done heretofore," she advised. In Anne's
opinion, the confession had been extorted by Andrew Hunter for the
purpose of provoking Brown himself into making intemperate statements. "I never blamed Cook," she said, because he was "young and
wanted to live. . . . People who never are known to offer themselves as
martyrs to a cause, will clamor loudly for steadfast bravery in those
who do suffer for a cause as a good principle."[13]

Hinton did not need much convincing. Although his book is thorough
and well documented, his pronounced bias in favor of John Brown led
him frequently to sanitize the record, including his treatment of John
Cook. Hinton did not mention the circumstances of Cook's hurried wedding, and he suppressed Cook's important role in providing the information that allowed Governor Wise to offer rewards for Owen Brown,
Barclay Coppoc, Charles Tidd, and Francis Merriam. Hinton also denied
that Brown had scolded Cook when they met for the last time. Contrary to all other accounts, Hinton said that Brown had embraced Cook
warmly and bid him an affectionate farewell.[14]

Anne Brown was surely right that Cook never set out to be a traitor.
He confessed only under duress, and he would not have been nearly
so forthcoming without the intervention of Willard and Voorhees. But
Anne might well have been less indulgent if she had known the full extent of Cook's cooperation with the authorities. He confessed not once
but several times over a period of many days, readily embellishing his
account to meet the needs of the prosecution. Unbeknownst to Anne, or
to any of her relatives, Cook had provided a description of Owen Brown

that could have served to hang him. If Voorhees's proslavery advocacy had been more successful—if Cook had been pardoned or reprieved—it is nearly impossible to imagine that he would have been so kindly remembered by northern abolitionists. It was far easier to forgive a dead recreant than a live collaborator. As it happened, the loss of his life saved Cook's reputation.

※　❂　※

Lacking Brown's ascetic strength, Cook had allowed a cagey prosecutor and a politically ambitious defense lawyer to manipulate him into making a purportedly full confession. He had been led to believe that he could save himself by implicating others, but that turned out to be a false promise. Cook named too few names and provided too few details to be helpful in the prosecution of Brown's northern backers, and once his usefulness was exhausted he was condemned all the same. He had attempted to take advantage of every experience life had to offer— from adventure to intimacy—but self-regard proved to be his downfall. He could not stand firm as an idealist, nor could he become an effective collaborator. Only when he finally approached the gallows was he able to recapture some of the fervor that had first led him to abolitionism. John E. Cook became a casualty of the coming Civil War. However reluctantly, he too shed his blood for a noble cause.

※　❂　※

Daniel Logan and Cleggett Fitzhugh were well paid for capturing John Cook. On November 17 they received a check for $1,000, which they quickly acknowledged in a letter to Governor Wise. In addition, Lewis Washington arranged for each man to receive a rifle with an engraved inscription commemorating their "efficient service in capturing . . . John E. Cook one of the band under the command of John Brown."[15]

The other rewards, however, went uncollected. Owen Brown, Charles Tidd, Francis Merriam, and Barclay Coppoc all reached safety, although not easily. At first they lurked in the vicinity of Chambersburg, somewhat foolishly hoping to obtain a little food at the Ritner boardinghouse. Coppoc and Tidd went so far as to knock at Mrs. Ritner's window at night, but she shooed them away with a warning that armed men were watching her house. Still nearly starving, the fugitives realized that Merriam was too weak to proceed on foot and that he would have to risk traveling by rail. In a makeshift disguise, Merriam boarded an eastbound train that took him to Philadelphia. The other three men continued walking toward the northwest, in search of shelter among friends. It took them nearly another month to reach Center County, Pennsylvania, where Owen was able to contact several relatives who provided the fugitives with food and money. From there, Owen went on to Ohio's Western Reserve, Coppoc made his way back to Springdale, Iowa, and Tidd headed first to Chatham and then to Boston. Osborne Anderson—who was never identified and for whom there was no reward—escaped with the help of the free black community in Chambersburg and elsewhere in Pennsylvania. He returned to his home in Chatham, and in 1861 he published *A Voice from Harper's Ferry*, which included an important account of Brown's African-American allies.

Only Barclay Coppoc was seriously pursued by the Virginia authorities. Acting in part on the information provided by Cook, Governor John Letcher (Wise's successor) sent a requisition to Iowa for Coppoc's arrest and extradition. Fortunately, Iowa Governor Samuel Kirkwood had antislavery sympathies, and he refused the requisition on a technicality. Although a new indictment was later issued in Virginia, Coppoc's friends managed to protect him and no arrest was ever made.

Despite the jockeying at Cook's trial, neither Aaron Stevens nor Albert Hazlett was turned over to the federal court. President Buchanan declared the question of federal jurisdiction "a matter quite indifferent to me," leaving the disposition of the cases to Virginia justice.[16] Both Stevens and Hazlett (the latter still claiming to be "William Harrison") were tried and convicted in the Jefferson County Circuit Court; neither repented his involvement with John Brown; both were hanged in Charlestown on March 16, 1860.

Barclay Coppoc, Charles Tidd, and Francis Merriam all served in the Civil War, although only Merriam survived. Tidd died of disease, and Coppoc was killed when his troop train was derailed by Confederate saboteurs in Missouri. Despite his infirmities, Merriam was made an officer in command of black troops in South Carolina. He died in 1865, six months after the war's end. Although Osborne Anderson did not join the Union Army, he helped recruit United States Colored Troops in Indiana and elsewhere. Anderson died of pneumonia in 1872.

Owen Brown spent the rest of his life as a semi-recluse, living first on an island in Lake Erie and later on a southern California mountaintop known as Brown's Peak. He died in 1889, the last surviving soldier of John Brown's insurrectionary army. Anne Brown also moved to California, where she married and raised her children in Humboldt County. Only sixteen when she kept house for the "invisibles" at her father's Maryland headquarters, she lived until 1926.

Alexander McClure and Daniel Voorhees both rose to prominence during the Civil War. McClure was one of Abraham Lincoln's major supporters, serving as a military recruiter and an organizer for Lincoln's reelection campaign in 1864. After the war, McClure lived in Philadelphia, where he founded and edited the *Philadelphia Times*. He also wrote numerous books, concentrating on history and biography, as well as several memoirs. In 1901 he published *Abe Lincoln's Yarns and Stories*, which he called "a complete collection of the funny and witty anecdotes that made Lincoln famous as America's greatest story teller." McClure died in 1909, some years after he sold his newspaper to Adolph Ochs (of the *New York Times*).

Far from being politically damaged by his representation of John Cook, Daniel Voorhees was catapulted to fame by his eloquent closing argument. He was elected to Congress in 1860, where he became one of Lincoln's greatest adversaries during the Civil War. As a leading

"Copperhead," he was constantly suspected of subversion, and he once narrowly avoided arrest when a search of his Indiana law office discovered literature from the pro-Confederate Knights of the Golden Circle. Remaining popular in Indiana, Voorhees was elected to the Senate in 1876, where he served until his death in 1897. Voorhees continued to try cases throughout his political career, specializing in the defense of spurned women who had killed their lovers.

Voorhees and McClure were surely aware of each other during the decades of their national prominence, and they may have had occasion to meet. It is possible that they exchanged reminiscences of representing John Cook, as Voorhees passed through Philadelphia on trips between Indiana and Washington, D.C. But if so, neither man appears ever to have mentioned it afterward.

Ashbel Willard did not live to support any Democratic candidate in the 1860 election. His health declined rapidly following Cook's funeral, and he succumbed to a pulmonary hemorrhage in October 1860, becoming the first governor of Indiana to die in office.

※　◉　※

Life was difficult for Virginia Kennedy Cook following her husband's funeral. At first she returned to Haddam to live with John's parents. Nathanial Cook treated her well, but Mary Cook, whose health was failing, was short-tempered and resentful. Perhaps it was natural for a grieving mother to blame her misfortune on her daughter-in-law, but Mary Cook's treatment of Virginia was remarkably harsh. "You had not a word of warning for us when you knew our son was in danger," she scolded, "but you could find us quickly enough when you wanted help yourself."[17]

It was true that Virginia needed assistance for herself and her son—who was, after all, Mary Cook's grandchild—but she was not willing to remain in Haddam in such inhospitable circumstances. She departed as soon as possible, staying for a while with the Crowleys in Williamsburg before returning in late 1860 to her mother's boardinghouse. Sadly, Virginia was not able to resettle in Harper's Ferry. The memory of Brown's raid was still fresh and the "local feeling against her was so bitter" that she was forced to leave town after only a few months. Still desperate to find a home for herself and her son, she returned briefly to Williamsburg before spending the summer of 1861 at the Brown family seat in North Elba, New York. By autumn, Virginia still had no permanent place to live. Reluctant to stay with the Crowleys—who, for all their generosity, seemed to disdain her "rusticity"—she turned to Wendell Phillips for assistance.

Fortunately, the abolitionist community was more helpful to Virginia—or perhaps merely less judgmental—than her own in-laws. Phillips found both lodging and employment for her in Boston. At first she worked in the office of Dr. Samuel Howe, who showed admirable forgiveness for John Cook's betrayal. Before long, Virginia obtained a position as a compositor for the *Pine and Palm*, a weekly newspaper "devoted to the interests of freedom and of the colored races in America." Edited by Brown's biographer James Redpath, the *Pine and Palm* shared an office building with *The Liberator*, which gave Virginia the opportunity to meet many of Boston's most prominent abolitionists.

Virginia remained in Boston until 1865, when she married a returning Union Army veteran named George Johnston. When the young couple decided to move west, Robert Crowley asked if John, Jr., could live with him in Brooklyn. Virginia reluctantly agreed, believing that the Crowleys could give her son an "educational advantage [that] exceeded anything that she could hope to do for him." Virginia relocated with her husband to Chicago, where she gave birth to several more children, including a daughter named Grace and a son named George, Jr. She remained in Chicago until her death in 1916.

In 1908, an obscure figure surfaced in Baltimore, claiming to be a previously unacknowledged son of John E. Cook and a woman named Tydings, who had lived in Martinsburg, Virginia. Calling himself W. F. S. Cook, he wrote letters to Brown biographer Oswald Garrison Villard, as well as to Brown's daughter Anne, demanding recognition. Although he did not deny that Cook had married and fathered a son with Virginia Kennedy, he disparaged her morals and blamed her for subverting the relationship between Cook and his own mother (whose first name he never mentioned and who was said to have died of sorrow in 1860). Villard made a few efforts to investigate the allegation, but it was flatly dismissed by members of the Cook and Brown families who suggested that W. F. S. was mentally disturbed. Perhaps that was so. Nonetheless, the letters of W. F. S. Cook did include internal evidence that he had grown up in the environs of Harper's Ferry, where John E. Cook would not have been an obvious hero for an out-of-wedlock child. Why would an orphan in the Reconstruction era South seize upon Cook as his father unless he had been told as much by his mother's relatives? And why would a family ever assert such a seemingly embarrassing connection to a locally despised man unless there was some reason behind the claim? John E. Cook was certainly capable of fathering a child in Martinsburg while concurrently courting Virginia Kennedy in Harper's Ferry, but more than that we will never know. Following his rejection by Villard, W. F. S. Cook vanished from history with the mystery of his parentage unsolved.

There was no such mystery about the paternity of John Cook, Jr., who remained with the Crowleys through most of his adolescence and into young adulthood. By 1880, he was working in Richmond as a salesman for his uncle's needle business. When interviewed by a researcher in 1908, Virginia complained that the Crowleys had not kept their promises and that John, Jr., had become "burdened down with an improvident, coarse wife and swarms of children and [had] fallen into hopeless poverty." By then, however, John, Jr., was almost fifty years old—and not poverty stricken—so it seems most likely that Virginia's lament was occasioned by some falling out with her son rather than by a long-ago broken promise of Robert Crowley's.[18]

John, Jr., himself appears to have remained on good terms with the Crowleys, although he chose not to continue selling needles. He settled instead on a career in finance, and he eventually held a comfortable position in the Connecticut office of the Prudential Insurance Company. In a note to Brown biographer Oswald Garrison Villard, John regretted that he had no letters or keepsakes from his father. But he did have—very much like his father—beautiful cursive handwriting.[19]

APPENDIX

Personnae

JOHN ALLSTADT. A Virginia slave owner who was taken hostage by John Cook. His son, also named John Allstadt, was taken hostage at the same time.

OSBORNE ANDERSON. One of John Brown's raiders; a free black man from Canada, he escaped from Harper's Ferry and later wrote a memoir about the raid.

JOHN AVIS. The Jefferson County jailor, he was known for his humane treatment of John Brown, John Cook, and the other prisoners.

FONTAINE BECKHAM. The mayor of Harper's Ferry, he was killed during the raid.

LAWSON BOTTS. A Virginia lawyer appointed to represent John Brown, he later volunteered to represent John Cook.

ANNE BROWN. A daughter of John Brown; at age sixteen, she kept house for the "invisibles" at Brown's Maryland farmhouse headquarters.

FREDERICK BROWN. A son of John Brown; killed by border ruffians in Kansas.

JASON BROWN. A son of John Brown; he did not join the Harper's Ferry raid.

JOHN BROWN. Commander in chief of the Provisional Government of the United States; he led the raid on Harper's Ferry and was later executed in Charlestown.

JOHN BROWN, JR. A son of John Brown; he did not join the Harper's Ferry raid.

OLIVER BROWN. A son of John Brown; killed at Harper's Ferry.

OWEN BROWN. A son of John Brown, he escaped to safety from Harper's Ferry along with Charles Tidd, Barclay Coppoc, and Francis Merriam.

SALMON BROWN. A son of John Brown; he did not join the Harper's Ferry raid.

WATSON BROWN. A son of John Brown; killed at Harper's Ferry.

JAMES AND TERRENCE BYRNE. Maryland slave owners, they were taken hostage by John Cook.

JAMES CAMPBELL. The sheriff of Jefferson County, he oversaw the executions of Brown and others.

SAMUEL CHILTON. A prominent lawyer from Washington, D.C., he was paid $1,000 to represent John Brown.

CATHERINE COOK. A sister of John Cook.

MARY AND NATHANIEL COOK. John Cook's mother and father.

VIRGINIA KENNEDY COOK. John Cook's wife and the mother of his child, John, Jr.

JOHN COPELAND. One of John Brown's raiders; a free black man from Oberlin, Ohio, he was captured at Harper's Ferry and hanged in Charlestown.

BARCLAY AND EDWIN COPPOC. Quaker brothers from Springdale, Iowa, who enlisted in Brown's army. Barclay escaped in the party with Owen Brown; Edwin was captured at Harper's Ferry and hanged at Charlestown.

FRANCES (FANNY) COOK CROWLEY. An older sister of John Cook's; she was married to the wealthy merchant Robert Crowley and she often came to the assistance of her younger brother.

ROBERT CROWLEY. John Cook's brother-in-law; he came to Cook's aid in Charlestown and later arranged Cook's funeral.

LIND CURRIE. A Maryland schoolmaster, he was briefly held prisoner by John Cook.

FREDERICK DOUGLASS. A leading black abolitionist, he declined to join John Brown's provisional army. Douglass was implicated by John Cook.

CLEGGETT FITZHUGH. A bounty hunter who captured John Cook in Pennsylvania.

JOSHUA GIDDINGS. A Republican congressman from Ohio; the Virginia authorities tried but failed to implicate him in Brown's raid.

HIRAM GRISWOLD. An antislavery lawyer from Cleveland, he represented John Brown and Edwin Coppoc in Charlestown.

SHIELDS GREEN. An escaped slave who joined John Brown's army, he was captured at Harper's Ferry and hanged in Charlestown.

THOMAS GREEN. A lawyer and the mayor of Charlestown; he was appointed to represent John Brown and he later volunteered to represent John Cook.

THOMAS GUARD. The aptly named sentry who prevented John Cook and Edwin Coppoc from escaping jail.

CHARLES HARDING. The elected commonwealth attorney for Jefferson County, he was nominally in charge of the prosecution of John Brown, John Cook, and other Harper's Ferry defendants.

ALBERT HAZLETT. One of John Brown's raiders, he initially escaped but was later captured in Pennsylvania. Although insisting that his name was "William Harrison," he was identified and hanged in Charlestown.

THOMAS WENTWORTH HIGGINSON. A radical abolitionist clergyman from New England, he was one of Brown's financial backers and a member of the self-named Secret Six.

RICHARD HINTON. A comrade of Brown's in Kansas, he did not join the provisional army at Harper's Ferry. He later wrote an admiring biography of Brown, in which he omitted compromising details about John Cook.

SAMUEL HOWE. One of Brown's financial backers (a member of the Secret Six), he was implicated by John Cook's confession as one of Brown's possible aiders and abettors.

GEORGE HOYT. A Boston lawyer who represented John Brown.

ANDREW HUNTER. A prosecutor at the Charlestown trials of John Brown, John Cook, and others. Although he was formally appointed by Governor Wise only to assist Charles Harding, he was in fact the lead prosecutor.

THADDEUS HYATT. A New York industrialist and antislavery activist, he was implicated by John Cook's confession as one of Brown's possible aiders and abettors.

MATTHEW JOHNSON. The United States marshal for Cleveland, he interrogated John Copeland in the Charlestown jail.

JAMES MONROE JONES. A black gunsmith with whom Cook boarded during the Chatham conference.

JOHN KAGI. John Brown's adjutant; killed at Harper's Ferry. Also known as J. Henry, John Henri, and similar pseudonyms.

FRANKLIN KEAGY. A border at Ritner's boardinghouse in Chambersburg and a benefactor of Virginia Kennedy Cook and her son.

WILLIAM KELLY. The Virginia detective who escorted John Cook from Chambersburg to Charlestown; he conducted the first formal interrogation of Cook.

MARY ANN KENNEDY. John Cook's mother-in-law. Along with her son James, she attended every day of Cook's trial.

LEWIS SHERIDAN LEARY. One of Brown's raiders. A free black man from Oberlin, Ohio, he was killed at Harper's Ferry. He was the biological grandfather of the poet Langston Hughes.

WILLIAM LEEMAN. One of Brown's raiders; killed at Harper's Ferry.

DANIEL LOGAN. A bounty hunter who captured John Cook in Pennsylvania.

JULIA LOUISA LOVEJOY. John Cook's neighbor in Lawrence, Kansas.

JAMES MASON. A United States senator from Virginia; he helped interrogate John Brown and later participated in procuring John Cook's confession.

MARY AND GEORGE MAUZY. Two Harper's Ferry residents whose correspondence included comments about John Cook.

ALEXANDER KELLY MCCLURE. John Cook's lawyer in Chambersburg, Pennsylvania, he was not able to thwart Cook's extradition to Virginia.

JOSEPH MCDONALD. The attorney general of Indiana, he assisted in Cook's defense at trial.

FRANCIS MERRIAM. One of John Brown's raiders, he escaped from Harper's Ferry in the party with Owen Brown.

SHUBEL MORGAN. A pseudonym of John Brown's.

DANGERFIELD NEWBY. A free black man who joined Brown's army in the hope of rescuing his enslaved wife and children; he was the first raider killed at Harper's Ferry.

N. GREEN NORTH. Pastor of the Charlestown Presbyterian Church, he ministered to Cook and the other prisoners.

RICHARD PARKER. The judge in the Charlestown trials of John Brown, John Cook, and others.

RALPH AND SAMUEL PLUMB. Abolitionist brothers from Oberlin, Ohio, who provided the funds for John Copeland and Lewis Sheridan Leary to join John Brown.

JAMES REDPATH. John Brown's first biographer, he also employed Virginia Kennedy Cook following John Cook's execution.

SAMUEL REISHER. The Pennsylvania judge who ordered Cook's rendition to Virginia.

MARY RITNER. The keeper of a boardinghouse in Chambersburg, Pennsylvania that was frequented by Brown and his men. Virginia Kennedy Cook stayed at Ritner's during the days just before and after the Harper's Ferry raid.

FRANKLIN SANBORN. One of Brown's financial backers (a member of the Secret Six), he was implicated by John Cook as a possible aider and abettor of Brown's.

GEORGE SENNOTT. An abolitionist lawyer from Boston, he represented

Shields Green and John Copeland, and later Aaron Stevens, in Charlestown.

HAYWARD SHEPHERD. A free black man in Harper's Ferry, he was the first person killed by Brown's raiders.

GERRIT SMITH. One of Brown's financial backers (a member of the Secret Six), he was implicated by John Cook as a possible aider and abettor of Brown's.

ISAAC SMITH. A pseudonym of John Brown's.

CYNTHIA SOPHIA COOK STAUNTON. A sister of John Cook's, she visited him in jail along with her husband and infant son.

JOHN STEARNS. A Brooklyn lawyer who employed John Cook as a clerk.

AARON STEVENS. John Brown's drillmaster; he was captured at Harper's Ferry and brought to trial and then hanged in Charlestown.

ELMIRA STEPTOE. A Charlestown grandmother who testified as a character witness for John Cook.

WILLIAM TALIAFERRO. A general in the Virginia State Militia, he commanded troops at Harper's Ferry and Charlestown.

LUCY THOMPSON. A young girl who testified as a character witness for John Cook.

WILLIAM AND DAUPHIN THOMPSON. Two of Brown's raiders—related to him by marriage—both of whom were killed at Harper's Ferry.

CHARLES PLUMMER TIDD. One of Brown's raiders who escaped from Harper's Ferry in the party with Owen Brown. His constant quarreling with Cook during their escape attempt may have been a cause of Cook's capture.

GEORGE TURNER. A Virginian killed during the Harper's Ferry raid; it was thought that he may have been shot by Cook, although that was never proven.

EMLEN (ELIZABETH) VARNEY. A young Quaker girl in Springdale, Iowa, she was the confidant of one of Cook's lovers.

MOSES VARNEY. Patriarch of the Springdale Quakers, he attempted to expose Brown's plan as a means of preventing the fiasco.

DANIEL VOORHEES. John Cook's lead defense counsel.

LEWIS WASHINGTON. A prominent Jefferson County slave owner and a great-grandnephew of George Washington; he was taken hostage by John Cook.

ASHBEL WILLARD. Governor of Indiana and John Cook's brother-in-law, he attempted to secure a pardon from Virginia's Governor Wise.

CAROLINE COOK WILLARD. A sister of John Cook, she was married to Governor Ashbel Willard of Indiana.

HENRY WISE. The governor of Virginia during the Harper's Ferry raid and the subsequent trials.

SAMUEL YOUNG. A Virginian who was badly injured during the Harper's Ferry raid; a published edition of Cook's confession was sold for his benefit.

NOTES

INTRODUCTION

1. Mary E. Mauzy to Eugenia Burton, December 18, 1859, Stutler Collection, West Virginia State Archives (spelling original).

2. DeWitt, *Life* at 26. Hinton, *Old John Brown* at 734–35.

3. *Virginia Free Press*, November 17, 1859. *Valley Spirit*, November 2, 1859. George Gill interview notes (undated), Hinton Papers, Kansas State Historical Society. A fine exemplar of Cook's handwriting can be found in John Edwin Cook to James Redpath, from Charlestown, Va., Jail, December 11, 1859, Horatio Nelson Rust Collection, Bancroft Library.

4. Salmon Brown to William E. Connelley, December 2, 1913, Stutler Collection, West Virginia State Archives (spelling original). Owen Brown's Springdale Log, March 1858, Villard Papers, Columbia University Library; *Richmond Daily Whig*, October 29, 1859; Reynolds, *John Brown* at 246.

5. Horwitz, *Midnight Rising* at 157.

6. Quoted in Reynolds, *John Brown* at 328.

7. Harriet Newby to Dear Husband, April 11, 1859, Library of Virginia. John Mercer Langston, *Virginia Plantation* at 191. John Copeland to Dear father & mother, November 26, 1859. Oberlin College Archive.

8. The partial exception is John Wayland's 1961 monograph *John Kagi and John Brown*. At 128 pages, it is, as the author acknowledged, basically an extended magazine article. Villard, *JB's Men* at 369. Rampersand, *Langston Hughes* at 6.

CHAPTER 1. KANSAS

1. Some sources give his birth year as 1830, but Cook's tombstone, erected by his family, gives the date as May 12, 1829.

2. Phila Parmalee, "The Cook House" and "We Trust Those to Whom We Gave the Charge," undated typescripts, Haddam Historical Society.

3. Nathaniel Cook account books, 1845–47, Haddam Historical Society.

4. *Richmond Enquirer*, December 23, 1859.

5. Isaac Arnold, Sr., to Isaac Arnold, Jr., October 27, 1859, Haddam Historical Society. Isaac Arnold, Jr., to Isaac Arnold, Sr., November 13, 1859, Haddam Historical Society.

6. Richard Hinton, who knew Cook personally, places him at Yale, and other Brown biographers agree. Hinton, *JB's Men* at 466; Oates, *Purge This Land* at 219; Abels, *Man on Fire* at 158. Almost fifty years after his death, Cook's widow told an interviewer that he had attended "Haddam University." There has never been such an institution as "Haddam University," however, and it appears that Cook's widow, a Virginia native with little education, had simply confused Cook's home town for the site of his law studies.

7. *New York Times*, October 24, 1859.

8. Hinton, *JB's Men* at 460; *New York Times*, October 24, 1859; P. G. Cutler to Governor Wise, November 25, 1859, Villard Papers, Columbia University Library.

9. "Cook to My Dear Brother & Sister," July 3, 1859, Hinton Collection, Kansas Historical Society; John Edwin Cook to James Redpath, December 11, 1859, Hinton Papers, Kansas State Historical Society. *New York Times*, October 24, 1859.

10. For Beecher's interest in Sir Walter Scott, see Debby Applegate, *Most Famous Man* at 88, 123, 124; for Cook's interest, see "Interview with Mrs. Virginia Kennedy Cook Johnston, Chicago, Nov. 2, 3 1908" (hereafter Virginia Kennedy Cook Johnston interview), Villard Papers, Columbia University Library.

11. Applegate, *Most Famous Man*, passim; Reynolds, *Mightier Than the Sword* at 13. See also, "Henry Ward Beecher," http://www.plymouthchurch.org/our_history_henry-wardbeecher.php.

12. James Brewer Stewart, *Abolitionist Politics* at 37, 158.

13. David O. Stewart, *Summer of 1787* at 68.

14. Max Farrand, *Records* at 1:486 and 3:254.

15. James Brewer Stewart, *Abolitionist Politics* at 10.

16. Henry Mayer, *Man on Fire* at 61–62.

17. William Lloyd Garrison, Address to the American Colonization Society, July 4, 1829, in Cain, *William Lloyd Garrison* at 61–70.

18. *The Liberator*, January 1, 1831. Fehrenbacher, *Dred Scott* at 119.

19. Mayer, *Man on Fire* at 112.

20. McCarthy and Stauffer, *Prophets* at xxi.

21. Jones, *Amistad* at 202. David Brion Davis, *Inhuman Bondage* at 24.

22. Amos Lawrence to Giles Richards, June 1, 1854, quoted in James McPherson, *Battle Cry* at 120.

23. Rev. Porter also took a quite evident jab at Henry Ward Beecher, blaming "preachers and politicians" for encouraging young men such as John Cook to join the war in Kansas. Villard, *John Brown* at 466–67. By one account, fewer than eight hundred white settlers lived in the Kansas Territory as of May 1854. Etcheson, *Bleeding Kansas* at 29. There were of course many more Native Americans, but they were not permitted to vote.

24. Quoted in Reynolds, *John Brown* at 141.

25. Quoted in Goodrich, *War* at 9.

26. "The Kansas Emigrants," in Whittier, *Poetical Works* at 146.

27. Higginson, *Cheerful Yesterdays* at 198–99, 201, 228.

28. Mary E. Mauzy to Eugenia Burton, December 18, 1859, Stutler Collection, West Virginia Archives (orthography original). *Richmond Enquirer*, December 23, 1859. Hinton, *JB's Men* at 467.

29. "My First Panther Hunt," undated story by Edwin Cook, Hinton Papers, Kansas State Historical Society.

30. Hinton, *JB's Men* at 467; Hinton, *Old John Brown* at 735. DeWitt, *Life* at 23–26; undated clipping, Villard Papers, Columbia University Library.

31. Goodrich, *War* at 114–15.

32. Quoted in Goodrich, *War* at 90, 115.

33. DeWitt, *Life* at 23–26; Salmon Brown interview, October 11–13, 1908, Villard Papers, Columbia University Library.

34. Cook to Redpath, Charlestown Jail, Va., December 11, 1859, Hinton Papers, Kansas State Historical Society. *Hartford Courant*, September 1, 1856. De Witt, *Life* at 24. Gill interview, Hinton Papers, Kansas State Historical Society.

35. Reynolds, *John Brown* at 117. Sumner, "The Crime against Kansas," Cong. Globe, 34th Cong., 1st sess., App. 529 (1856). McPherson, *Battle Cry* at 150–51.

36. Quoted in McPherson, *Battle Cry* at 152. Quoted in Reynolds, *John Brown* at 158–59. Other historians question whether Brown could have learned so quickly of Sumner's beating. The story of Brown's reaction was told by Salmon Brown, who may have misremembered when he recounted the events for Oswald Garrison Villard in 1908. Villard, *John Brown* at 154; Abels, *Man on Fire* 62–63.

37. Thomas Wentworth Higginson, quoted in Wells, *Preceptor* at 101.

38. Quoted in Reynolds, *John Brown* at 174–75, 176, 178.

39. Quoted in Reynolds, *John Brown* at 176. Quoted in Horwitz, *Midnight Rising* at 59.

40. Salmon Brown to William E. Connelley, December 2, 1913, Stutler Collection, West Virginia State Archives; Salmon Brown to William E. Connelley, November 6, 1913, Stutler Collection, West Virginia State Archives; Salmon Brown interview, October 11–13, 1908, Villard Papers, Columbia University Library.

41. Goodrich, *War* at 166. Van Gundy, *Reminiscences* at 16.

42. Van Gundy, *Reminiscences* at 21–22, 24. Cook did not participate in all of the Neosho raids. Writing more than fifty years later, Salmon Brown confirmed that Cook had robbed "Bernards Store [which] had been notorious as head quarters for the border ruffians" but denied that Cook had been responsible for a different robbery. Salmon Brown to William E. Connelley, November 6, 1913, and December 2, 1913, Stutler Collection, West Virginia Archives (spelling original).

43. "My First Panther Hunt," undated story by Edwin Cook, Hinton Papers, Kansas State Historical Society.

44. Julia Louisa Lovejoy, letter to the editor, November 24, 1859, *Kansas Historical Quarterly* 16 (February 1948): 72–73.

45. DeWitt, *Life* at 26. Undated clipping, Villard Papers, Columbia University Library; *Hartford Courant*, September 1, 1856.

46. *Richmond Daily Whig*, October 29, 1859; Owen Brown's Springdale Log, March 1858, Villard Papers, Columbia University Library; Reynolds, *John Brown* at 246. Salmon Brown to William E. Connelley, December 2, 1913, Stutler Collection, West Virginia State Archives (spelling original).

47. Julia Louisa Lovejoy, letter to the editor, November 24, 1859, *Kansas Historical Quarterly* 16 (February 1948): 72–73.

48. Hinton, *JB's Men* at 469.

49. Commissions were quite freely distributed in the antislavery militias; Brown's company of twenty-two men at Harper's Ferry would include five captains and four lieutenants in addition to Brown as commander in chief. Cook, *Confession* at 5–6.

50. Reynolds, *John Brown* at 244–45. Owen Brown's Springdale Log, March 1858, Villard Papers, Columbia University Library. Luke F. Parsons to "Dear Friends Redpath and Hinton," December 1859, Territorial Kansas Archive. James Redpath and Richard Hinton had been colleagues of Brown (and of Par-

sons and Cook) in Kansas. In December 1859, in the aftermath of Harper's Ferry, both men were collecting information for biographies of Brown to be used as political tracts in the antislavery movement.

51. Lloyd, "Pedee Quakers" at 714. Undated letter fragment from Ella Frazier, Hinton Papers, Kansas State Historical Society. She also called him a "beautiful pensman," but it probably was not a double entendre.

52. Gill interview notes (undated), Hinton Papers, Kansas State Historical Society. Gill was elected secretary of the treasury at the Chatham conference, but he did not join Brown at Harper's Ferry. "Emlen Varney to Charles Tidd," August 11, 1859, excerpted in *Calendar of Virginia State Papers*, vol. 11 at 348. Emlen appears to have been a nickname for Elizabeth Varney, who was seventeen years old at the time of the 1856 Iowa census. Also during the summer of 1859, a young Iowa Quaker woman named Anna expressed the hope that Brown's men "would always see that the rights of women are respected and protected," which may well have been a reference to certain ungentlemanly behavior in Springdale. *New York Tribune*, October 29, 1859.

53. Owen Brown to Dear Father and Brother, Springdale, February 28, 1858. Horatio Nelson Rust Collection, Huntington Library.

54. Hamilton, *Canada* at 8.

55. "Cook to My Dear Sisters, May 6, 1858, quoted in Richman, *Quakers* at 36. In 1850 the black population in Connecticut was 7,693, concentrated in the cities of Hartford and New Haven, and the total population was over 370,792, meaning that blacks were only about 2 percent of the population. Dodd, *Historical Statistics* at 14–15. Connecticut enacted a gradual emancipation statute in 1784, but it did not fully abolish slavery until 1848. Only 17 elderly slaves remained unemancipated in 1840.

56. Hamilton, *Canada* at 15.

57. "Journal of the Provisional Constitutional Convention, held on Saturday, May 8, 1858," published in *Report of the Select Committee of the Senate Appointed to Inquire into the Late Invasion and Seizure of the Public Property at Harper's Ferry*, 36th Cong., 1st sess., 1860 (hereafter *Senate Report*) at 45–47. Richard Realf testimony, *Senate Report* at 99. Hamilton, *Canada* at 9–10.

58. Hinton, *JB's Men* at 467–68, 473; Reynolds, *John Brown* at 246.

59. Reynolds, *John Brown* at 184; Higginson, *Contemporaries* at 219. *Provisional Constitution and Ordinances for the people of the United States*, Article 40, reproduced in *Senate Report* at 57 (capitalization in original). Salmon Brown to William E. Connelley, December 2, 1913, Stutler Collection, West Virginia State Archives.

60. Villard, *John Brown* at 330. John Cook to My Dear Sisters, June 6, 1858, quoted in Richman, *Quakers* at 42–45.

61. As "his most sociable and loquacious follower, Cook convinced [Brown] that these very qualities would help him assimilate naturally into the community and acquaint himself with its inhabitants and their routines." Carton, *Treason* at 267–68.

62. Richard Realf to John Brown, May 31, 1858, Territorial Kansas Archive, also quoted in Sanborn at 471. Nearly all of the descriptions of Cook were written years or decades after the Harper's Ferry raid and long after he had become infamous for his confession and defection. Realf's letter, however, was contemporaneous and therefore unaffected by later events. It is thus notable that Realf described Cook almost exactly as did everyone else.

63. Cook, *Confession* at 14–15 (italics original).

CHAPTER 2. HARPER'S FERRY

1. It is impossible to tell the story of John Cook without at some point comparing him to Lord Byron. Although Cook's life was played out on a much smaller stage, he likely believed that he had styled himself after Byron's romantic example—as a poet, adventurer, freedom fighter, and seducer of women. Cook may well have known that Byron had once commissioned a yacht called the *Bolivar*, which would make his choice of the Kennedy rooming house even more understandable. In any case, the coincidence provides an opportunity for this inevitable digression.

2. *Richmond Enquirer*, October 21, 1859. Mary E. Mauzy to Eugenia Burton, December 18, 1859, Stutler Collection, West Virginia Archives.

3. *New York Tribune*, October 29, 1859. Quoted in Villard, *John Brown* at 413 and in Reynolds, *John Brown* at 299. *Shepherdstown Register*, December 10, 1859. According to historian David Reynolds, Cook informed Brown that "blacks would swarm in revolt as soon as they caught wind of the raid." Reynolds, *John Brown* at 305. Historian Robert McGlone agrees that Brown's conviction "was reinforced by reports he received from John Cook, the spy he planted in Harpers Ferry a year before the raid." McGlone, *War on Slavery* at 151.

4. Mary Mauzy to Eugenia Burton, December 18, 1859, Stutler Collection. English-born Richard Hinton first befriended John Brown in Kansas in 1856. Hinton was a journalist, but he was also a militant abolitionist whom Brown unsuccessfully attempted to recruit to his training camp in Tabor, Iowa, as well as to the Harper's Ferry campaign. Hinton deeply admired and respected Brown

(he briefly plotted an armed rescue when Brown was imprisoned in Charlestown, Virginia). Reynolds, *John Brown* at 378. Peterson, *John Brown* at 39, 74–75. It is unsurprising, therefore, that Hinton's 1894 biography of Brown, though thorough and extremely important, tended to sanitize the record. Regarding John and Virginia Cook, for example, Hinton did not mention that their child was born only one month after their wedding, and, as noted, his observation about Virginia's premarital chastity seems to have been invented. In December 1859, Mary Mauzy, a local housewife, expressed admiration for Cook's education and manners, even though he had already been exposed as a spy and insurrectionist. Nonetheless, Mrs. Mauzy considered Cook a gentleman, and therefore she "could not imagine how he ever came to marry Jennie Kennedy." Mary E. Mauzy to Eugenia Burton, December 18, 1859, Stutler Collection, West Virginia Archives. The persistent and mysterious W. F. S. Cook, however, claimed that Cook was his father, having impregnated his mother, who lived in Martinsburg, about thirty-five miles from Harper's Ferry. Although there is no strong evidence of that claim, biographer Richard Hinton said several times that Cook visited Martinsburg, including the cryptic statement that he had "lived there . . . with his wife's people." Hinton, *JB's Men* at 275. *Valley Spirit*, October 26, 1859. It was W. F. S. Cook who made the most unkind observations about Virginia Kennedy. Of course, he claimed to be John Cook's son by another woman, and he was therefore angry and resentful at the status accorded to Virginia Kennedy Cook and her child. Although W. F. S.'s claim to paternity cannot be verified, he does appear to have grown up in the Harper's Ferry region where he evidently heard rumors—however true, false, or in between—about Virginia Kennedy. W. F. S. Cook to Oswald Garrison Villard, December 6, 1909; Roland C. Cook to Oswald Garrison Villard, November 30, 1908; Annie Brown Adams to Oswald Garrison Villard, October 26, 1908, all in Villard Papers, Columbia University Library.

5. Mary E. Mauzy to Eugenia Burton, December 18, 1859; George Mauzy to Eugenia Burton, November 10, 1859, Stutler Collection, West Virginia Archives.

6. Virginia Kennedy Cook Johnston interview, Villard Papers, Columbia University Library. Mrs. Kennedy's later partner—perhaps her common-law husband—testified that he was living at the boardinghouse when his "daughter" Virginia became involved with Cook. *Indiana State Sentinel*, December 14, 1859. *Baltimore American*, November 11, 1859; Annie Brown Adams to Richard Hinton, May 23, 1893, Villard Papers, Columbia University Library.

7. *Baltimore American*, November 11, 1859. Even in 1872, a locally produced history of Harper's Ferry reported that Cook "was regarded as a pleasant com-

panion and had married a respectable lady." Joseph Barry, *Annals of Harper's Ferry* (1872) at 50. According to Mary Mauzy, "Cook was perfectly devoted to his child, poor little innocent thing." Mary E. Mauzy to Eugenia Burton, December 18, 1859, Stutler Collection, West Virginia Archives. Even W. F. S. Cook, who claimed to be the abandoned and unacknowledged child of John E. Cook, did not question Cook's devotion to John, Jr., Letter from W. F. S. Cook to Oswald Garrison Villard, December 6, 1909, Villard Papers, Columbia University Library.

8. Virginia Kennedy Cook Johnston interview, Villard Papers, Columbia University Library. "Cook to Dear Friends," August 10, 1859; "Cook to My Dear Brother & Sister," July 3, 1859. Hinton Collection, Kansas Historical Society.

9. Virginia Kennedy Cook Johnston interview, Villard Papers, Columbia University Library. Hinton, *JB's Men* at 257, 276. *Indiana State Sentinel*, December 14, 1859.

10. Quoted in Reynolds, *John Brown* at 262.

11. Quoted in Reynolds, *John Brown* at 265. Forbes later claimed that his only purpose had been to deter Brown's mission, which he thought would be "fatal to the anti-slavery cause," and he denied providing any information to officials of the Buchanan administration. *New York Herald*, October 25, 1859. Whatever his motives, all of Forbes's warnings were ignored at the time.

12. Virginia Kennedy Cook Johnston interview, Villard Papers, Columbia University Library.

13. Annie Brown Adams to Richard Hinton, May 23, 1893, Villard Papers, Columbia University Library. Brown's headquarters is usually referred to as the Kennedy Farm, but I have opted to call it the Maryland farm in order to avoid confusion with the members of the unrelated Kennedy family of Bolivar (who are more important in this account than they have been in any of the Brown biographies).

14. "Statement of Annie Brown, Daughter of John Brown, Written November 1886," Frank Logan/John Brown Collection, Chicago History Museum.

15. Gue, *Iowa Friends* at 110–11; Gue, *History of Iowa* at 24–30. Varney and his friends were alarmed by the suicidal nature of Brown's mission, which they attempted to thwart by sending two anonymous letters to John Floyd, the United States secretary of war. It was their hope that public exposure would cause the insurrection to be canceled, but Floyd discounted the letters as a hoax. John Floyd testimony, *Senate Report* at 250–52.

16. "Statement of Annie Brown, Daughter of John Brown, Written November 1886," Frank Logan/John Brown Collection, Chicago History Museum.

17. When Anne Brown spoke to Higginson after the Harper's Ferry attack,

she singled out Cook as the only unprincipled man whom she observed at the Maryland farm. Thomas Wentworth Higginson, *Contemporaries* at 233–34. "Annie Brown Adams to My Dear Friend (Richard Hinton)," October 6, 1894, Richard Hinton Papers, Kansas Historical Society.

18. Anne Brown Adams to Richard Hinton (undated), Hinton Papers, Kansas State Historical Society. Villard, *John Brown* at 259; Virginia Kennedy Cook Johnston interview, Villard Papers, Columbia University Library.

19. Reynolds, *John Brown* at 299; Oates, *Purge This Land* at 280; Carton, *Treason* at 286. The more anodyne description of Tidd's retreat derives from Richard Hinton, who quotes Anne Brown Adams's recollection that "Tidd got so warm . . . he left the farm and went down to Cook's dwelling 'to let his wrath cool off.'" Hinton, *JB's Men* at 258. This may have been another of Hinton's, and in this case Anne Brown's, efforts to scrub the record by minimizing the depth of dissent among Brown's men. Anne Brown Adams to Richard Hinton (undated), Hinton Papers, Kansas Historical Society. *New York Tribune*, October 29, 1859; see also *Virginia Calendar of State Papers*, vol. 11 at 347–49. In an 1860 conversation with Thomas Wentworth Higginson, Tidd related that objections to Brown's plan almost "broke up the camp" and that he "finally" agreed to rejoin the raiders only when Brown "consented" to an alteration in his plan, which in fact did not occur. Higginson notes, February 10, 1860, Rare Books and Manuscripts Collection, Boston Public Library; Higginson, *Yesterdays* at 228–29.

20. *Baltimore American*, November 11, 1859.

21. Annie Brown Adams to Richard Hinton, February 15, 1893, Hinton Papers, Kansas State Historical Society; *New York Tribune*, November 26, 1859. Unless otherwise noted, the details of Cook's meeting with Washington are taken from Lewis W. Washington testimony, *Senate Report* at 30–31. Washington testified on several other occasions, each time to the same effect.

22. Anne Brown Adams to Richard Hinton (undated), Hinton Papers, Kansas State Historical Society; "Statement of Annie Brown to Franklin Sanborn (November 1886), Frank Logan/John Brown Collection, Chicago History Museum.

23. Hinton, *JB's Men* at 257. *St. Louis Globe-Democrat*, April 8, 1886. Villard, *John Brown* at 408. Anne Brown Adams to Richard Hinton (undated), Hinton Papers, Kansas State Historical Society; "Statement of Annie Brown, Daughter of John Brown, Written November 1886," Frank Logan/John Brown Collection, Chicago History Museum.

24. *Richmond Enquirer*, November 4, 1859; Andrew Hunter testimony, *Senate Report* at 63; Cook, *Confession* at 11, 15. The purported statistical work was to

be published by "John Henri," a pseudonym for John Henry Kagi, who was Brown's second-in-command and also a legitimate journalist. See Ralph Plumb testimony, *Senate Report* at 179–80. There were several other reported sightings of Cook during the weeks before the Harper's Ferry raid. Simpson, *Southerner* at 206, 366.

25. Cook, *Confession* at 11, 15.

26. Ibid. at 11 (punctuation in original).

27. Ibid. at 11. Virginia Kennedy Cook Johnston interview, Villard Papers, Columbia University Library. Franklin Keagy to Frank Sanborn, March 24, 1891, Stutler Collection, West Virginia Archives; Keagy, "Ritner Boarding House," Stutler Collection, West Virginia Archives; Hinton, *JB's Men* at 266.

28. Hinton, *JB's Men* at 249, 482; Keeler, "Owen Brown's Escape" at 355. In 1836, Governor Ritner had given a historic address to the state legislature, in which he declared his "opposition to the admission into the Union of new slave-holding States, and opposition to slavery in the District of Columbia." Ritner, *Annual Message* at 291.

29. Lewis Washington testimony, *Senate Report* at 31; *St. Louis Globe-Democrat*, April 8, 1886.

CHAPTER 3. INSURRECTION

1. Anderson, *Voice* at 28.

2. Cook, *Confession* at 12.

3. Lewis Washington testimony, *Senate Report* at 30; Washington trial testimony, *American State Trials*, vol. 6 at 749.

4. *New York Tribune*, November 26, 1859.

5. Anderson escaped from Harper's Ferry and lived to write a memoir in which he also observed that Washington "stood 'blubbering' like a great calf" while held as a hostage at the Harper's Ferry Armory. Anderson, *Voice* at 34–35, 41. See also, Geffert, *Black Allies* at 591–610; DeCaro, *Cost of Freedom* at 91.

6. John H. Allstadt testimony, *Senate Report* at 41; John H. Allstadt (father) *American State Trials*, vol. 6 at 757; John T. Allstadt (son) *American State Trials*, vol. 6 at 758; Washington testimony, *Senate Report* at 32.

7. Washington testimony, *Senate Report* at 34.

8. Byrne testimony, *Senate Report* at 13–14.

9. *Baltimore American*, November 11, 1859. Byrne testimony, *Senate Report* at 16.

10. Currie testimony, *Senate Report* at 55–56.

11. Currie testimony, *Senate Report* at 57. Cook, *Confession* at 12.

12. Quoted in Hinton, *JB's Men* at 311.

13. Quoted in Reynolds, *John Brown* at 323.

14. Cook, *Confession* at 13; Cook to Redpath, December 11, 1859, Hinton Papers, Kansas State Historical Society.

15. *St. Louis Globe-Democrat*, April 8, 1886.

16. Cook, *Confession* at 14; Keeler, "Owen Brown's Escape" at 346. Hinton, *JB's Men* at 550.

17. *Richmond Enquirer*, October 21, 1859; Villard, *John Brown* at 469; *Harper's Weekly*, October 29, 1859. Cook, *Confession* at 14.

CHAPTER 4. ESCAPE

1. Hinton, *JB's Men* at 549. Two of Owen's surviving brothers lived in the Western Reserve, Jason in Akron and John, Jr., in Ashtabula. Keeler, "Owen Brown's Escape" at 365.

2. Affidavit of Lewis Washington, October 19, 1859, in *Calendar of Virginia State Papers*, vol. 11 at 71. *New York Tribune*, October 29, 1859.

3. *Indianapolis Journal*, October 25, 1859; *Indianapolis Journal*, October 25, 1859. *Richmond Enquirer*, October 21, 1859. *New York Tribune*, October 29, 1859. *Valley Spirit*, October 26, 1859. A. J. Nye to Henry A. Wise, December 5, 1859, Wise Family Papers, Library of Congress. *Indianapolis Journal*, October 27, 1859 (spelling original).

4. *Harper's Weekly*, October 29, 1859. Similarly, Raider William Leeman was shot to death when he tried to escape across the Potomac River, but local residents believed that the escape had really been at attempt at "conveying information to Cook." *Richmond Enquirer*, October 21, 1859. *Richmond Enquirer*, November 4, 1859; *Shepherdstown Register*, November 5, 1859; undated clipping, Villard Papers. *New York Herald*, October 26, 1859. Geffert, "They Heard His Call" at 34–35. As is often the case with storied criminals, numerous other crimes were "added to his name." In a letter to Governor Wise, for example, an Ohio man accused Cook of committing an 1856 robbery in Indianapolis. Benjamin Williamson to Henry A. Wise, November 21, 1859, Wise Family Papers, Library of Congress. Regarding the attribution phenomenon, see (or listen to) Woody Guthrie, "The Ballad of Pretty Boy Floyd" (1939).

5. The *Enquirer* also reported that "all the surviving leaders were arrested,

except John E. Cooke, who had escaped." *Richmond Enquirer*, October 21, 1859; *Richmond Enquirer*, October 22, 1859; *New York Tribune*, October 22, 1859. *Richmond Enquirer*, October 25, 1859. *Richmond Enquirer*, October 28, 1859; *New York Herald*, October 26, 1859. Mason also published a letter in the *Richmond Enquirer* on October 30, 1859, again naming only Cook among Brown's raiders. Mason, *Public Life* at 148.

6. *New York Times*, October 24, 1859.

7. Lee wrote to the War Department that "Cooke is the only man known to have escaped." "Col. R. E. Lee's Report to Adjutant General, October 19, 1859," Wise Family Papers, Library of Virginia; also published in *Virginia Magazine of History and Biography* (July 1902) at 22. *Harper's Weekly*, October 29, 1859; *The Locomotive*, October 22, 1859; *Indianapolis Journal*, October 20, 1859. *Richmond Enquirer*, October 21, 1859; *Indianapolis Journal*, October 19, 1859. *New York Tribune*, October 22, 1859. Willson, "Owen Brown's Escape" at 362.

8. "Col. R. E. Lee's Report to Adjutant General," October 19, 1859, Wise Family Papers, Library of Virginia; also published in *Virginia Magazine of History and Biography* (July 1902) at 22–23. Villard, *John Brown* at 470. A detachment of Maryland Volunteers also briefly "went on a scout" for Cook, but the mission ended as soon as the searchers discovered the schoolhouse weapons cache, which they hoped to keep for themselves. Colonel S. Mills to Secretary of War John Floyd, October 20, 1859, National Archives. Keeler, "Owen Brown's Escape" at 348–49.

9. Keeler, "Owen Brown's Escape" at 348. Reynolds, *John Brown* at 371–72; Hinton, *JB's Men* at 539, 549; Villard, *John Brown* at 421, 471; "John Brown and His Friends," *Atlantic Monthly*, July 1872 at 60.

10. Moses and Charlotte Varney to My Dear Friends Whipple and Tidd, May 10, 1858, *Calendar of Virginia State Papers*, vol. 11 at 289–92. Elizabeth is likely the same person as Emlen Varney, who wrote about her resentment of Cook's marriage to Virginia Kennedy.

11. "Statement of Annie Brown, Daughter of John Brown, Written November 1886," Frank Logan/John Brown Collection, Chicago History Museum.

12. Willson, "Owen Brown's Escape" at 366. Higginson notes on Tidd meeting, February 10, 1860, Rare Books and Manuscripts Collection, Boston Public Library. Villard, *John Brown* at 681. Keeler, "Owen Brown's Escape," at 346–47, 353. Hinton, *JB's Men* at 549, 551.

13. Keeler, "Owen Brown's Escape" at 351; Anderson, *Voice* at 48; Higginson notes on Tidd meeting, February 10, 1860, Rare Books and Manuscripts Collection, Boston Public Library.

14. Keeler, "Owen Brown's Escape" at 347.

15. Geffert, *Black Allies* at 597. McClure, *Lincoln* at 338; McClure, "Episode" at 281.

16. McClure, *Recollections* at 338–39.

17. Frederick Douglass, "John Brown," speech delivered at Storer College, Harper's Ferry, West Virginia, May 30, 1881, in Foner and Taylor, *Speeches* at 633; Stauffer, *Hearts of Men* at 259.

18. "Owen Brown's Story of His Journey from Hagerstown to Kennedy Farm, with Shields Green, a Colored Man," Horatio Nelson Rust Collection, Huntington Library.

19. McGlone, *Rescripting* at 1187.

20. Anne Brown Adams notation on Owen Brown to Dear Friends, Martha and Anna, November 27, 1859, Rust Collection, Huntington Library.

21. Keeler, "Owen Brown's Escape" at 348, 353.

22. Keeler, "Owen Brown's Escape" at 350–52.

23. The actual distance by road from Harper's Ferry to Chambersburg was only about sixty-five miles, but, as Tidd later estimated, the party's evasive path required them to hike at least twice as far. Higginson notes, February 10, 1860, Rare Books and Manuscripts Collection, Boston Public Library.

24. Keeler, "Owen Brown's Escape" at 353.

25. Keeler, "Owen Brown's Escape" at 354.

26. Keeler, "Owen Brown's Escape" at 354–55. Years later, Owen Brown claimed to have sent the Lafayette pistol back to Colonel Washington, requesting some of his father's effects in return. Washington did not respond, but in 1871 his widow sold to the Museum of New York one of the two "heavy horseman's pistols" that had been given to President Washington by Lafayette. *Valley Spirit*, November 2, 1859; Willson, "Owen Brown's Escape" at 366.

27. McClure, *Lincoln* at 340.

28. McClure, *Lincoln* at 340–42; Hinton, *JB's Men* at 476–77.

29. McClure, *Lincoln* at 343.

30. *Valley Spirit*, November 2, 1859.

31. McClure, *Lincoln* at 344–45; McClure, "Episode" at 279.

CHAPTER 5. JAILED

1. McClure, *Recollections* at 19; McClure, *Curtin Elected* at 102.

2. Nevin, *Men of Mark* at 410. McClure, *Lincoln* at 27; see Damon M. Laabs,

"McClure, Alexander Kelly"; Osborne and Gerencser, "Alexander Kelly McClure"; Gould, "Alexander Kelly McClure."

3. Torget and Ayers, *Two Communities* at 258. Bradley, *Simon Cameron* at 118, 149.

4. *Franklin Repository and Transcript*, May 4, 1859; *Franklin Repository and Transcript*, August 10, 1859.

5. McClure, *Recollections* at 19, 20. McClure, *Old Time Notes* at 361. *Franklin Repository and Transcript*, September 10, 1859. The *Valley Spirit* objected to Douglass's failure to appreciate "that the Creator Himself has made a distinction when he established the great and immovable barrier of color between the races." *Valley Spirit*, August 24, 1859.

6. *New York Tribune*, October 29, 1859. "This Merriam corresponds to a description of a man named J. Henrie." J. Lucius Davis to the Governor, October 23, 1859, *Calendar of Virginia State Papers*, vol. 11 at 78 (mistakenly asserting that F. J. Merriam and J. Henrie were one in the same person, and also attributing Merriam's "cutaneous disease" of the face to Henrie). Reynolds, *John Brown* at 306. Kagi was himself a lawyer, and he surely knew that two witnesses would have to be available in the event of a challenge to Merriam's will.

7. McClure, *Lincoln* at 336. "Boyle to Wise," October 21, 1859, *Calendar of Virginia State Papers*, vol. 11 at 75. McClure, *Old Time Notes* at 362.

8. McClure, *Lincoln* at 345.

9. Webb, *Life and Letters* at 368. *National Democrat*, October 31, 1859. In later versions of the story, the southern press magnified the proposed payoff to $20,000, which the "gallant Fitzhugh and Logan" were said to have declined as a matter of honor. *Virginia Free Press*, November 10, 1859.

10. *Franklin Repository and Transcript*, July 27, 1859; *Franklin Repository and Transcript*, August 3, 1859; *Franklin Repository and Transcript*, August 10, 1859.

11. McClure, *Lincoln* at 346.

12. McClure, *Lincoln* at 346–47. *Franklin Repository and Transcript*, December 28, 1859.

13. McClure, *Recollections* at 19; McClure, *Old Time Notes* at 367.

14. Although there were no written codes of attorney conduct in that era, it happens that Pennsylvania lawyers were central to the development of legal ethics as a unified discipline. In 1854, George Sharswood delivered a famous lecture on legal ethics to the law students at the University of Pennsylvania, which was

soon published as *A Compend of the Lectures on the Aims and Duties of the Profession of the Law*. Sharswood's principles would have been well known to McClure, and they are generally quite similar to the current rules in most American jurisdictions. In 1859, every Pennsylvania lawyer took an oath "to behave himself in the office of attorney according to the best of his learning and ability, and with all good fidelity, as well to the court as to the client; that he will use no falsehood, nor delay any man's cause for lucre or malice." According to Sharswood, the lawyer for an accused criminal was required to "exert all his ability, learning, and ingenuity, in such a defence, even if he should be perfectly assured in his own mind of the actual guilt of the prisoner." Needless to say, Sharswood would have excluded jailbreaks from the necessary scope of a lawyer's "ingenuity," and he also insisted that attorneys were required to disclose all conflicts of interest to their clients. Sharswood, *Lectures* at 10, 31, 48.

15. McClure, *Lincoln* at 340–47.

16. McClure, *Old Time Notes* at 368; McClure, *Lincoln* at 347.

17. DeWitt, *Life* at 24. McClure, *Lincoln* at 348.

18. McClure, *Lincoln* at 347–48; McClure, *Old Time Notes* at 365, 367.

19. McClure, *Lincoln* at 348–49.

20. *Valley Spirit*, June 15, 1859, page 5.

21. *Franklin Repository and Transcript*, October 12, 1859, page 3.

22. McClure, *Lincoln* at 349–50; McClure, *Old Time Notes* at 368–69. Regarding the 1833 case of Thornton and Lucie Blackburn, see Frost, *Glory Land* at 173–74.

23. Anderson, *Voice* at 53. The two men may have parted company for other reasons that Anderson chose not to reveal. Anderson wrote in his memoir that Hazlett "with his feet blistered and sore . . . declared it was impossible for him to go further, and begged me to go on" without him. But in fact, Hazlett was able to walk another fifteen miles from Chambersburg to Carlisle, eluding pursuers all the way, so he must not have been as badly disabled as Anderson later claimed. *Franklin Repository and Transcript*, October 12, 1859.

24. *Franklin Repository and Transcript*, October 26, 1859; *Carlisle American*, October 26, 1859; *The Locomotive*, October 29, 1859; Cress, "Cumberland County's Connection" at 49. *New York Times*, October 24, 1859. "Proclamation of Henry A. Wise," October 22, 1859, *Calendar of Virginia State Papers*, vol. 11 at 76–77 (capitalization original); *Carlisle American*, October 26, 1859; *New York Herald*, October 26, 1859.

25. Shearer, "Brown's Raid" at 5, quoted in Cress, "Cumberland County" at 49. *Franklin Repository and Transcript*, October 26, 1859; *New York Herald*, October 25, 1859. *New York Times*, June 22, 1901. Andrew Hunter to Governor Wise, October 23, 1859, *Calendar of Virginia State Papers*, vol. 11 at 78.

26. McClure, *Lincoln* at 350, 351; Hinton, *JB's Men* at 479.

27. *New York Tribune*, October 22, 1859; "The Harpers Ferry Affair," unidentified clipping, Stutler Collection, West Virginia Archives. A later edition of the *Tribune* carried a report from Baltimore, dated October 20, stating that Cook was "still in the mountains on the Virginia or Maryland side of the Potomac." *New York Tribune*, October 29, 1859. Franklin Keagy to Frank Sanborn, March 24, 1891, Stutler Collection, West Virginia Archives; Franklin Keagy, "Ritner Boarding House," February 2, 1891, Stutler Collection, West Virginia Archives.

28. William Boyle to the Governor (Henry Wise), October 21, 1859, *Calendar of Virginia State Papers*, vol. 11 at 76. Virginia Kennedy Cook Johnston interview, Villard Papers, Columbia University Library.

29. Franklin Keagy to Frank Sanborn, March 24, 1891, Stutler Collection, West Virginia Archives; Keagy, "Ritner Boarding House," Stutler Collection, West Virginia Archives. *New York Tribune*, November 7, 1859, at 7, quoting the *Harper's Ferry Independent Democrat* (undated). It appears, however, that Virginia's family in Harper's Ferry was never seriously suspected of participating in the conspiracy. Virginia's mother attended Brown's pretrial hearing in Charlestown on October 24, at a time when Cook was thought still to be at large "in the mountains near the Ferry." *New York Herald*, October 25, 1859. Following Cook's arrest, she was evidently free to travel as she pleased between Harper's Ferry and Charlestown, attending most sessions of the trial along with her son James and visiting Cook in jail.

30. Wm. H. Boyle, M.D., to the Governor, October 21, 1859, *Calendar of Virginia State Papers* at 75–76 (emphasis in original). Thrush, *Medical Men* at 79–80.

31. *Carlisle American*, October 26, 1859. *Valley Spirit*, October 26, 1859; *New York Herald*, October 25, 1859.

32. Franklin Keagy to Frank Sanborn, March 24, 1891, Stutler Collection, West Virginia Archives; Keagy, "Ritner Boarding House," Stutler Collection, West Virginia Archives. In fact, Virginia's "uncle" was Cook's brother-in-law Robert Crowley. Writing in mid-December 1859, a well-informed (if not gossipy) citizen of Harper's Ferry noted that "Cooks wife and child are with his sister Mrs. Crowley in New York." Mary E. Mauzy to Eugenia Burton, December 18, 1859, Stutler Collection, West Virginia Archives. In a "remarkable coincidence," Virginia's benefactor Franklin Keagy was a distant relative of Brown's adjutant

John Henry Kagi. Although they stayed at the same boardinghouse, the two men did not know each other at the time (John Kagi was then calling himself John Henrie), and Franklin did not learn until later of his cousin's connection to John Brown. Wayland, *John Kagi* at 93.

33. *Valley Spirit*, November 9, 1859. *New York Tribune*, October 29, 1859; "Arrest of Cooke," *Harper's Weekly*, November 5, 1859; *Virginia Free Press*, October 27, 1859. *New York Tribune*, October 29, 1859. *Valley Spirit*, November 2, 1859.

34. *Valley Spirit*, November 2, 1859. *Valley Spirit*, November 9, 1859. Logan claimed that he had easily subdued Cook, but several newspapers reported that Cook had put up "desperate resistance," only to be "overpowered by the superior strength of the two men." According to another source, Logan and Fitzhugh later claimed that "Cook sprang up like a wire [and] that both of them could hardly get him to the ground." Taken together, these reports support the claim that Cook had been roughed up and bloodied. *Carlisle American*, October 26, 1859; *National Democrat*, October 31, 1859; *Shepherdstown Register*, November 5, 1859; Webb, at 368. *New York Tribune*, November 5, 1859; "Arrest of Cooke," *Harper's Weekly*, November 5, 1859; *New York Herald*, October 28, 1859.

35. *Valley Spirit*, November 2, 1859. Affidavit of Joseph Mayo, Mayor of Richmond, Virginia, November 20, 1859, in *Calendar of Virginia State Papers*, vol. 11 at 92.

36. The *Valley Spirit* reported these events as "rumors," but most or all of the information could only have originated from Cook at that time. *Valley Spirit*, November 9, 1859 (punctuation and capitalization in original).

37. *Richmond Enquirer*, November 1, 1859; *New York Tribune*, November 5, 1859; *Indianapolis Journal*, November 8, 1859; *Richmond Enquirer*, November 4, 1859.

38. On November 5, 1859, Kelly and Hazlett departed Carlisle on the afternoon train. *Carlisle American*, November 9, 1859. Wise to Buchanan, November 13, 1859, reprinted in Douglass, *Life and Times* at 314. Frederick Douglass, "A Lecture on John Brown: Delivered at Harper's Ferry and Sundry Other Places," ca. 1890, Frederick Douglass Papers, Library of Congress. Hunter, "Brown's Raid" at 177; *St. Louis Globe-Democrat*, April 8, 1888.

39. *Valley Spirit*, November 9, 1859; *Richmond Enquirer*, November 4, 1859.

CHAPTER 6. CHARLESTOWN

1. Boteler, *Recollections* at 410.

2. Hunter testimony, *Senate Report* at 60. Regarding the inadmissibility of

involuntary confessions in the pre-*Miranda* era, see Smith, "Privilege," passim. For a short description of Henry Wise's career as a lawyer, see Downey, *Civil War Lawyers* at 326.

3. Other than as noted, quotations from Brown's interrogation are taken from: *New York Herald*, October 21, 1859; *Richmond Enquirer*, October 21, 1859; *Boston Traveler*, October 25, 1859; Hunter testimony, *Senate Report*. Summaries of the interrogation may be found in: Ruchames, *John Brown Reader* at 118–25; Lawson, *American State Trials*, vol. 6 at 711–16; and Shackleton, *Support* at 348–58.

4. *St. Louis Globe-Democrat*, April 8, 1886.

5. Hunter, "Brown's Raid" at 167.

6. "Col. R. E. Lee's Report to Adjutant General," October 19, 1859, Wise Family Papers, Library of Virginia; also published in *Virginia Magazine of History and Biography* (July 1902) at 24. "A. H. List of Insurgents" (undated 1859), Wise Executive Papers, Library of Congress; also printed in *Virginia Magazine of History and Biography* (January 1902) at 274–75. See also *Calendar of Virginia State Papers*, vol. 11 at 349. The other prisoners were evidently also questioned that day, but no record survives of their interrogations. Lee's official report does refer to "the statements of those now in custody," but it provides no details about Copeland, Coppoc, or Stevens. See M. Johnson to Andrew Hunter, November 15, 1859, Wise Family Papers, Library of Virginia, also printed in *Virginia Magazine of History and Biography* (January 1902) at 276–77.

7. Reynolds, *John Brown* at 349.

8. *American State Trials*, vol. 6 at 728n29.

9. *Richmond Enquirer*, October 25, 1859.

10. *New York Tribune*, October 29, 1859; *New York Herald*, October 26, 1859.

11. *American State Trials*, vol. 6 at 728n31.

12. McGinty, *JB's Trial* at 101.

13. *New York Herald*, October 26, 1859.

14. *New York Tribune*, October 29, 1859.

15. *St. Louis Globe-Democrat*, April 8, 1886; *American State Trials*, vol. 6 at 710n21. Tucker, "Virginia's Judges" at 16. McGinty, *JB's Trial* at 84, quoting Stutler, "Judge Parker" at 27–33.

16. Indictment of John Brown, et al., October 26, 1859. John Brown Papers, Circuit Court of Jefferson County.

17. *New York Herald*, November 10, 1859; *New York Tribune*, November 12, 1859.

18. The slaves were not as docile as Harding claimed. On the night Lewis Washington was taken prisoner, a free black man was visiting his wife on the plantation, and he observed the entire kidnapping. Although he was not taken in the wagon along with the other men, he refrained from raising an alarm, thus allowing the invasion to proceed unimpeded for the rest of the night. Even more directly, Washington's coachman, known only as Jim, "had joined the rebels with a good will" and was killed in the course of the insurrection. Jim's body was found with a pistol in his waistband and "his pockets filled with ball cartridges." *Richmond Enquirer,* November 4, 1859. "People may say what they please of the indifference of the negroes to the passing events, but it is not true," reported one journalist. "They burn with anxiety to learn every particular, but they fear to show it." *New York Tribune,* November 19, 1859. Geffert (with Libby), "Black Involvement," in McCarthy and Stauffer, *Prophets* at 165.

19. *New York Tribune,* November 19, 1859.

20. Hinton, *JB's Men* at 365–66; Villard, *John Brown* at 480–81. Hunter to Wise, October 28, 1859, quoted in Villard, *John Brown* at 485; Reynolds, *John Brown* at 352.

21. McGinty, *JB's Trial* at 127; Redpath, *Public Life* at 324–25.

22. Thomas Wentworth Higginson to Dear Friends (John Brown's Daughters), November 4, 1859, Stutler Collection, West Virginia Archive.

23. *New York Herald,* October 29, 1859.

24. John Brown to Dear Brother Jeremiah (Jeremiah Brown), November 12, 1859, in Ruchames, *JB Reader* at 134. McGinty, *JB's Trial* at 178.

25. *American State Trials,* vol. 6 at 766. McGinty, *JB's Trial* at 183.

26. *American State Trials,* vol. 6 at 792–94.

27. Barry, *Harper's Ferry* at 44.

28. *American State Trials,* vol. 6 at 801.

29. Andrew Hunter to Henry Wise, October 22, 1859, Wise Family Papers, Library of Virginia.

30. Ruffin, *Diary* at 366–67. Fellman, *God and Country* at 40. Phillips, *Speeches* at 272.

31. Reynolds, *John Brown* at 357, 367.

32. *New York Tribune,* November 5, 1859; *American State Trials,* vol. 6 at 802. Accounts of Brown's final speech that omit the criticism of his comrades include Carton, *Treason* at 327, Horwitz, *Midnight Rising* at 213, Reynolds, *John Brown*

at 354, Oates, *Purge this Land* at 327, McGlone, *JB's War* at 316, McGinty, *JB's Trial* at 226.

CHAPTER 7. CONFESSION

1. *Indiana State Sentinel*, November 9, 1859; *Richmond Enquirer*, November 1, 1859.

2. *Richmond Enquirer*, November 1, 1859; *Baltimore Sun*, October 29, 1859.

3. Willard had first been elected lieutenant governor in 1852, when he was only thirty-two. *National Cyclopedia* at 270. In siding with Buchanan, Willard broke decisively with the more moderate wing of the Democratic Party, which was led by Sen. Stephen Douglas of Illinois whom, as one Indiana newspaper reported, "Governor Willard don't like at all." *Indianapolis State Journal*, November 2, 1859. Woollen, "Willard" at 108, 112; Stampp, *Indiana* at 19. *Indiana State Sentinel*, November 24, 1858; *Indiana State Sentinel*, November 9, 1859; *Indianapolis Daily Journal*, October 24, 1859; *Indianapolis Daily Journal*, October 31, 1859.

4. Thornton, "Voorhees" at 355.

5. Ashbel Willard to the Governor (Henry Wise), October 29, 1859, *Calendar of Virginia State Papers*, vol. 11 at 88.

6. Wise to Hunter, November 6, 1859, in *Proceedings of the Massachusetts Historical Society* (February 1908) at 329.

7. Wise to Willard, October 30, 1859, *Calendar of Virginia State Papers*, vol. 11 at 88–89.

8. Kenworthy, *Tall Sycamore* at 21–22, 26, 44. Voorhees's own recollection was of meeting Lincoln in 1852, but in fact it was in autumn 1851. "Lincoln recommended Voorhees's admission to bar," October 23, 1851, http://www.lawpractice ofabrahamlincoln.org/Details.aspx?case=141344.

9. Bogardus, *Voorhees* at 95. Wilson, *Early Indiana* at 100. Kenworthy, *Tall Sycamore* at 33. Congressional Globe, 38th Cong., 2nd sess., January 9, 1865, pages 180–81. Jordan, "Voorhees" at 538, 540.

10. Rodgers, *Liberty* at 150.

11. "John Cook's description of four men," November 1, 1859, *Calendar of Virginia State Papers*, vol. 11 at 90; J. Lucius Davis to Dear Sir (Governor Henry Wise), November 1, 1859 (stating that "descriptions have been furnished by Cooke at the request of his brother in law Gov. Willard"), Wise Family Papers, Library of Congress.

12. "A Proclamation by the Governor," November 3, 1859, *Calendar of Virginia State Papers*, vol. 11 at 90. David Reynolds, for example, combined the separate reward offers, writing that "posters were widely distributed with descriptions of the fugitives and promises of $1000 reward for the capture of Cook and $2000 for Brown, Barclay, Tidd and Merriam." Reynolds, *John Brown* at 370–71. Richard Hinton appears to have intentionally obscured Cook's role by noting only that the reward was offered "after the arrest of Cook and Hazlett," and he additionally sanitized Merriam's description by omitting the reference to syphilis. Hinton, *JB's Men* at 548–49. More accurately, though rather tolerantly, Tony Horwitz writes, "Cook may have provided this information knowing that the men would be long gone by the time the notice circulated." Horwitz, *Midnight Rising* at 198. In fact, Cook began providing information about the other escapees at a time when they were still very much in the vicinity of Chambersburg.

13. "Affidavit of Jno. E. Cook," November 4, 1859, *Calendar of Virginia State Papers*, vol. 11 at 91.

14. Andrew Hunter to the Governor (Henry Wise), November 4, 1859, *Calendar of Virginia State Papers*, vol. 11 at 90–91. *Indianapolis American*, November 11, 1859 (dateline November 2, 1859); *Indiana State Sentinel*, November 9, 1859 (dateline October 31, 1859).

15. *Richmond Enquirer*, December 20, 1859. Galbreath, *Edwin Coppoc* at 448. *Baltimore Sun*, October 31, 1859; *New York Tribune*, November 12, 1859.

16. *American State Trials*, vol. 6 at 806.

17. *St. Louis Globe-Democrat*, April 8, 1886. *New York Tribune*, November 5, 1859. *New York Herald*, November 10, 1859. *Indianapolis Daily Journal*, November 2, 1859; *Indiana State Sentinel*, November 9, 1859.

18. *New York Tribune*, November 18, 1859; *New York Tribune*, November 12, 1859; *New York Tribune*, October 29, 1859.

19. John Brown to Andrew Hunter, November 22, 1859, Wise Family Papers, Library of Virginia; *New York Tribune*, November 12, 1859.

20. *Baltimore Sun*, October 31, 1859. *Indiana State Sentinel*, November 16, 1859.

21. Andrew Hunter to the Governor, November 4, 1859, *Calendar of Virginia State Papers*, vol. 11 at 91.

22. Wise to Willard, October 30, 1859, *Calendar of Virginia State Papers*, vol. 11 at 88 (emphasis in original).

23. Andrew Hunter to the Governor, *Calendar of Virginia State Papers*, vol. 11 at 91.

24. John E. Cook to My Ever Dear Wife and Son, November 6, 1859. The letter was thereafter published in the *New York Tribune*, the *Baltimore Sun*, and elsewhere. This iteration is taken from the *Indiana State Sentinel*, December 21, 1859 (italics original).

25. *New York Tribune*, November 12, 1859.

26. *New York Tribune*, November 12, 1859 (capitalization in original). The local newspaper was the *Spirit of Jefferson*, which was quoted at length in the *Tribune*.

27. *New York Tribune*, November 12, 1859 (capitalizations in original).

28. *Richmond Enquirer*, November 1, 1859; *New York Tribune*, October 29, 1859; *New York Tribune*, November 5, 1859; *New York Tribune*, November 12, 1859. According to the journalist and illustrator David Hunter Strother, Copeland was overwhelmed with fear and cowered before his interrogators. Historian Benjamin Quarles, however, discounts Strother's observation as the predictable report of a typical antebellum racist. Quarles, *Allies for Freedom* at 134. Andrew Hunter later claimed that he had also obtained a confession from Copeland, but no evidence of it was offered at trial. Hunter, *Brown's Raid* at 188.

29. *American State Trials*, vol. 6 at 811. According to another version of the confession, Copeland also implicated Charles Langston, one of the Oberlin rescuers and a leading black abolitionist in Ohio. Strother, "Copeland's Confession." Even some proslavery Democrats, however, considered Copeland's confession unreliable because it had been "wormed out of a negro scared almost to death at the prospect of the gallows." *Daily Cleveland Herald*, November 5, 1859.

30. *New York Tribune*, November 12, 1859.

CHAPTER 8. INTRIGUES

1. *New York Tribune*, November 12, 1859. Count One of the indictment charged treason against the Commonwealth of Virginia, Count Two charged conspiring with slaves to rebel, Count Three charged conspiring with others to induce slaves to rebel, Count Four charged murder in the first degree, and Count Five charged aiding and abetting murder. *Commonwealth of Virginia v. John E. Cooke*, Indictment in the Jefferson Circuit Court, November 7, 1859 (spelling original), John Brown Papers, Circuit Court of Jefferson County, Virginia.

2. *New York Tribune*, November 12, 1859. The dateline on the story was Sunday, November 6, which was the day before Cook was due back in court. Another observer "anticipated he will plead guilty and rely upon the Executive for mercy." Cleon Moore to David Hunter Strother, November 4, 1859, Stutler

Collection, West Virginia Archives. The Virginia press reported "that a plea of guilty will be entered, and that he will make certain revelations, upon the strength of which a commutation of sentence will be sought." *Richmond Enquirer*, November 8, 1859.

3. *Baltimore American*, November 9, 1859; *The Locomotive*, November 12, 1859.

4. *Baltimore American*, November 9, 1859; *Baltimore American*, November 10, 1859; *The Locomotive*, November 12, 1859.

5. *New York Tribune*, November 12, 1859.

6. Alfred Barbour to My Dear Sir (Governor Henry Wise), November 7, 1859, Wise Family Papers, Library of Congress.

7. *Baltimore American*, November 9, 1859; *The Locomotive*, November 12, 1859; *New York Tribune*, November 19, 1859.

8. *Baltimore American*, November 9, 1859.

9. *American State Trials*, vol. 6 at 817; *The Locomotive*, November 12, 1859; *New York Tribune*, November 19, 1859.*Baltimore American*, November 9, 1859; *The Locomotive*, November 12, 1859. The telegram was not offered in evidence, and there are consequently differing reported accounts of its precise language. Wise's handwritten draft read as follows (although it is possible that different language was transmitted by the operator or read aloud by Hunter): "You had better try Cooke & turn Stephens over to U.S. Court. Do that definitively." Wise to Hunter, November 7, 1859, Wise Family Papers, Library of Congress.

10. *Baltimore American*, November 9, 1859; *The Locomotive*, November 12, 1859; *New York Tribune*, November 19, 1859; *American State Trials*, vol. 6 at 817.

11. *New York Tribune*, November 19, 1859; *Baltimore American*, November 9, 1859; *The Locomotive*, November 12, 1859.

12. *Baltimore American*, November 9, 1859; *The Locomotive*, November 12, 1859; *New York Tribune*, November 19, 1859.

13. Perhaps due to his habitual inebriation, Harding caused one summons to be dated October 7 rather than November 7. The sheriff and the witnesses disregarded the obvious error. Summons to George F. Hoffmaster and Terrance Burns, misdated October 7, 1859, Helen Jones Campbell Collection, Virginia Historical Society; in fact issued on November 7, 1859 (spelling original). The other summonses were correctly dated and continued from day to day. Summons for Lewis W. Washington, John H. Allstadt, John T. Allstadt, John D. Starry, Lewis P. Starry, Daniel Phalen, Benjamin F. Beall, Lind F. Currie, George W. T. Reasley,

William Johnson, John E. P. Dangerfield, John Hutsen, Lieut. I. Green, to testify in *Commonwealth vs. John E. Cooke*, November 7, 1859 (spellings original), John Brown Papers, Circuit Court of Jefferson County. Summons for John T. Alstadt, Alexander Kelly, John Sturdy, John Steadman, Joseph A. Brown, Alfred M. Barbour, John Hutson, Terrence Burns, and John E. P. Dangerfield to testify in *Commonwealth of Virginia vs. John E. Cooke*, November 7, 1859 (spellings original), John Brown Papers, Circuit Court of Jefferson County.

14. *New York Tribune*, December 3, 1859.

15. *New York Tribune*, November 19, 1859.

16. *New York Tribune*, November 19, 1859. Defense counsel also moved to quash the other four counts of the indictment as improperly plead and therefore "not sufficient in law." *Commonwealth of Virginia v. John E. Cooke*, Motions to Quash, John Brown Papers, Circuit Court of Jefferson County.

17. *New York Tribune*, November 19, 1859.

18. *Commonwealth of Virginia v. John E. Cooke*, Venire Facias, November 8, 1859, John Brown Papers, Circuit Court of Jefferson County. *Richmond Enquirer*, November 11, 1859; *New York Tribune*, November 19, 1859. The quoted colloquy occurred during the aborted jury selection in Stevens's case, but it was widely reported that Parker used the same questions in every voir dire.

19. *Richmond Enquirer*, November 11, 1859. The twelve jurors named by the *Enquirer* were Charles T. Butler, Charles Hewett, Joseph Hout, Lorenzo Achinson, Thomas Chaplin, John Snyder, Henry Selby, William M. Leman, Jacob S. Sheetz, Martin Swimley, George Shovel, and Michael Hunsucker. Figures on slaveholding are from the 1850 and 1860 United States census reports.

20. *Baltimore American*, November 10, 1859.

21. *New York Herald*, November 9, 1859. Other sources also reported that the confession was twenty-five pages long: *Baltimore American*, November 10, 1859 ("The confession covers some twenty-five pages of manuscript, and is written in a smooth style"); *New York Tribune*, November 12, 1859 ("There were 25 foolscap pages of it"); *The Locomotive*, November 12, 1859 ("It is written by himself and fills twenty-five foolscap pages").

22. Andrew Hunter to Henry Wise, November 4, 1859, Wise Family Papers, Library of Congress.

23. *Baltimore American*, November 10, 1859; *Richmond Enquirer*, November 11, 1859. The *Virginia Free Press*, for example, did not publish the partial text of the confession until the beginning of December. *Virginia Free Press*, December 1, 1859. The *Shepherdstown Register* then published it a few days later. *Shepherds-*

town Register, December 3, 1859. *New York Tribune,* November 12, 1859. By the end of November, the *Tribune* had obtained and published the text of the confession.

24. The pamphlet was dated Wednesday, November 9, 1859, which was the second day of Cook's trial. It was recorded for the purpose of copyright on Friday, November 11. Cook, *Confession* (spelling original).

25. Andrew Hunter to the Governor, November 4, 1859, *Calendar of Virginia State Papers,* vol. 11 at 91.

26. *New York Tribune,* November 19, 1859.

27. Years later, Hunter would falsely claim that he had simply been given the confession by Voorhees and asked to "accept it," after which he "looked it over and . . . had no objection." *St. Louis Globe-Democrat,* April 8, 1886. The contemporaneous newspaper summaries of the confession are inconsistent with the pamphlet, providing additional evidence that Hunter read from a document different from the one that was ultimately published. *Richmond Enquirer,* November 15, 1859; *Baltimore American,* November 11, 1859; *Virginia Free Press and Farmers' Repository,* December 1, 1859.

CHAPTER 9. DEFENSE

1. *Baltimore American,* November 11, 1859.

2. *Baltimore American,* November 11, 1859.

3. Virginia Kennedy Cook Johnston interview, Villard Papers, Columbia University Library. Annie Brown Adams to Richard Hinton, May 23, 1893, Villard Papers, Columbia University Library.

4. *New York Tribune,* November 19, 1859.

5. *Baltimore American,* November 11, 1859; affidavit of Almira L. Steptoe, November 3, 1859, John Brown Papers, Circuit Court of Jefferson County.

6. *Baltimore American,* November 11, 1859; affidavit of Lucy A. Thompson, November 3, 1859, John Brown Papers, Circuit Court of Jefferson County. Lucy also visited Cook in jail, probably in the company of her grandmother.

7. *New York Times,* October 24, 1859; affidavit of John M. Stearns, November 3, 1859, Helen Jones Campbell Collection, Virginia Historical Society. *Richmond Enquirer,* October 25, 1859. *Baltimore American,* November 11, 1859.

8. *Baltimore American,* November 11, 1859. *Indiana State Sentinel,* November 14, 1859; *Indiana State Sentinel,* November 15, 1859.

9. Jordan, "Voorhees" at 553. Thornton, "Voorhees" at 363. The procedural rules in Indiana originally provided for only two rounds of final argument: first

the prosecution, then the defense. The legislature, however, added a prosecution rebuttal argument so that Voorhees and other defense lawyers would no longer have the advantage of the last word. Kenworthy, *Tall Sycamore* at 43.

10. *New York Tribune*, November 19, 1859. *American State Trials*, vol. 6 at 728.

11. *New York Tribune*, November 19, 1859. *Baltimore American*, November 11, 1859. *Indiana State Sentinel*, November 16, 1859.

12. *New York Tribune*, November 19, 1859.

13. *New York Tribune*, November 19, 1859. Except as noted, quotations from Voorhees's argument are taken from the pamphlet "Argument of Hon. D. W. Voorhees of Terre Haute, Indiana, Delivered at Charlestown, Virginia, November 8, 1859 (Daily State Sentinel). See also, Voorhees, *Oratory* at 379–402.

14. Bogardus, *Voorhees* at 95.

15. *Baltimore American*, November 11, 1859. Quoted in *Indiana State Sentinel*, November 23, 1859. Quoted in *Indiana State Sentinel*, November 30, 1859. *New York Tribune*, November 19, 1859.

16. *Virginia Free Press*, November 17, 1859. *Baltimore American*, November 11, 1859. A Republican newspaper in Indiana saw things slightly differently. "Mr. Voorhees made the jury cry," the reporter noted, "and he would have spoken till [they] did, if it had taken him till Christmas." *Indianapolis Daily Journal*, November 15, 1859.

17. *New York Tribune*, November 19, 1859. *Indianapolis Daily Journal*, November 15, 1859.

18. *Baltimore American*, November 11, 1859.

19. *Commonwealth of Virginia v. John E. Cooke*, Jury Instruction, John Brown Papers, Circuit Court of Jefferson County.

20. *Baltimore American*, November 11, 1859.

21. *Baltimore American*, November 11, 1859. Jury Verdict, *Commonwealth of Virginia v. John E. Cooke*, John Brown Papers, Circuit Court of Jefferson County; mislabeled "Indictment."

CHAPTER 10. REPENTANCE

1. Under Virginia law, the death penalty was mandatory upon conviction of murder in the first degree. Code of Virginia (1849), Chapter 191, Section 2. Multiple observers of Cook's trial, however, speculated that he might nonetheless be sentenced to imprisonment on the theory that Judge Parker would recommend executive commutation. *Virginia Free Press*, November 17, 1859; *Baltimore American*, November 12, 1859.

2. *Virginia Free Press*, November 17, 1859; *Baltimore American*, November 12, 1859. Coppoc's lawyer, Hiram Griswold, had long since departed Virginia. George Sennott, the attorney for Green and Copeland, had been in Charlestown as recently as the previous Monday, but there is no report of his presence at Thursday's sentencing.

3. *Virginia Free Press*, November 17, 1859; *Baltimore American*, November 12, 1859.

4. *Dawson's Daily Times*, November 19, 1859; *New York Tribune*, November 19, 1859.

5. *Virginia Free Press*, November 17, 1859.

6. *Virginia Free Press*, November 17, 1859 (use of neither/or in original).

7. *Dawson's Daily Times*, November 19, 1859. *Virginia Free Press*, November 17, 1859.

8. *Virginia Free Press*, November 17, 1859.

9. *New York Tribune*, November 19, 1859. For more on Brown's African-American supporters, see Jean Libby, *John Brown Mysteries*.

10. *Baltimore American*, November 12, 1859; *New York Tribune*, November 19, 1859. Death Warrants for John E. Cooke, Shields Green, and John Copeland, November 10, 1859, John Brown Papers, Circuit Court of Jefferson County. There was also a death warrant for Edwin Coppoc, but it has not survived in the records of the court.

11. *Baltimore American*, November 12, 1859.

12. *New York Tribune*, November 19, 1859.

13. *Indianapolis Journal*, November 2, 1859; *Indianapolis Journal*, November 4, 1859 (capitalization original).

14. *Indiana State Sentinel*, November 9, 1859.

15. *St. Louis Globe-Democrat*, April 8, 1886. *Shepherdstown Register*, December 3, 1859. *Richmond Enquirer*, November 11, 1859.

16. *New York Tribune*, November 19, 1859. *Baltimore American*, November 10, 1859.

17. *New York Tribune*, November 19, 1859. *New York Tribune*, December 3, 1859. American Anti-Slavery Society, *Anti-Slavery History* at 111–12.

18. *Baltimore American*, November 10, 1859; *Baltimore American*, November 15, 1859.

19. *Rochester Democrat*, October 31, 1859, reprinted in *New York Tribune*, November 12, 1859 (capitalization and italics original). Decades later, several of

Brown's surviving relatives claimed that Douglass had agreed to join the Harper's Ferry raid, only to back out at the last minute. DeCaro, *Fire* at 260–61. Such recollections are necessarily suspect, however, and they may well have been influenced by Cook's explosive accusation.

20. Scott, *Secret Six* at 301. *New York Tribune*, November 19, 1859.

21. *New York Tribune*, December 3, 1859.

22. Only in 1867 did Gerrit Smith feel free to make a public statement about his relationship to John Brown, and by then there "was no danger or even inconvenience from the fullest acknowledgement of such connection." Smith disclaimed any knowledge that Brown intended a general insurrection, and he made no mention of John Cook. Frothingham, *Gerrit Smith* at 253–55.

23. *St. Louis Globe-Democrat*, April 8, 1886.

24. Hitchcock, *Southern Unionism* at 66. Wise had won a resounding victory in 1855, routing the Know-Nothing candidate by over ten thousand votes. The Know-Nothings had expired as a political movement by 1859, as had the Whigs before them. Thus the only remaining political competition in Virginia was intra-Democratic, with the party soon to divide into "Constitutional Unionist" and secessionist factions. Shanks, *Secession Movement* at 48.

25. Horwitz, *Midnight Rising* at 228–29.

26. McGinty, *JB's Trial* at 241–48.

27. *Indiana State Sentinel*, November 9, 1859.

28. George Mauzy to My Dear Children (James and Eugenia Burton), December 3, 1859, Harpers Ferry National Historic Park Collection.

29. *Virginia Free Press*, November 10, 1859. *Virginia Free Press*, November 17, 1859. *Virginia Free Press*, November 18, 1859.

30. *Richmond Enquirer*, November 18, 1859. Quoted in *New York Tribune*, November 12, 1859.

31. *Indiana State Sentinel*, December 9, 1859.

32. Mrs. A. P. Willard to Governor Wise, November 24, 1859 (nonpunctuation original), Villard Papers, Columbia University Library. Kate C. Cook to Governor Wise, November 26, 1859 (punctuation original), Villard Papers, Columbia University Library. P. G. Cutler to Governor Wise, November 25, 1859, Villard Papers, Columbia University. Jane Pierce to His Excellency the Governor of Virginia, undated, Pierce Collection, Indiana State Library. The Indianapolis letter did not say whether Governor Willard had ever acceded to any of his wife's pleas for commutation.

33. Lewis Washington to Hon. H. A. Wise, November 7, 1859, Wise Family Papers, Library of Congress. Petition to Gov. Wise Not to Spare Cook's Life, November 17, 1859, Villard Papers, Columbia University Library. J. W. Ware to Governor Wise, November 13, 1859, Stutler Collection (punctuation and capitalization original).

34. *Indiana State Sentinel,* November 16, 1859.

35. *Indiana State Sentinel,* November 16, 1859 (capitalization original).

36. *Virginia Free Press,* December 8, 1859. *New York Times,* December 19, 1859 (italics, spelling, and capitalization original). Although published later, the letters to Cook's parents and wife were written on November 24 and 25, while Governor Wise was still considering the clemency petition.

37. *Richmond Enquirer,* November 25, 1859 (italics original). Cook's cooperation in providing descriptions had not been widely known, which further evidences Wise's hand in the editorial.

CHAPTER 11. ETERNITY

1. John Brown to Dear Brother Jeremiah, November 12, 1859, in Ruchames, *JB Reader* at 134. Oates, *Purge This Land* at 200.

2. "Words of Advice," quoted in Hinton, *JB's Men* at 587 and in Trodd and Stauffer, *Meteor of War* at 77–78. *New York Tribune,* November 19, 1859.

3. Annie Brown Adams to Richard Hinton, February 15, 1893, Villard Papers, Columbia University Library (emphasis original). *New York Tribune,* November 19, 1859.

4. Drew, *JB Invasion* at 36. Galbreath, *Edwin Coppoc* at 410.

5. John Copeland to Dear father & mother, November 26, 1859. Oberlin College Archive. Copeland also wrote to other friends and relatives in Ohio, as well as to the Oberlin Anti-Slavery Society, "absolving everyone other than himself from any blame for his having joined John Brown." Quarles, *Allies for Freedom* at 135–36.

6. Hinton, *JB's Men* at 490. Coppoc's letter was sent to friends in Iowa. He closed by assuring them that "J. E. Cook sends his love to all."

7. *New York Tribune,* December 3, 1859.

8. *Richmond Enquirer,* December 9, 1859.

9. *Baltimore Sun,* December 7, 1859.

10. *New York Tribune,* December 17, 1859.

11. Hunter, *Brown's Raid* at 188; *St. Louis Globe-Democrat,* April 8, 1886.

12. *Baltimore Sun*, December 13, 1859.

13. *New York Tribune*, December 17, 1859. The letter was published earlier in Baltimore and Richmond. Villard, *John Brown* at 570.

14. Thomas Winn to Mary Brown, January 13, 1860, Villard Papers, Columbia University Library. Winn, an Iowa Quaker, visited Coppoc in Charlestown and was present at his execution. *Cincinnati Gazette*, December 16, 1859, transcribed in Stutler Collection (spelling original). Edwin Coppock to My Dear Uncle (Joshua Coppock), December 13, 1859, Stutler Collection (spelling original); Edwin Coppock to My Dear Friend Thomas Winn, undated, Stutler Collection (spelling original); *Baltimore Sun*, December 13, 1859. Anne Brown believed that the fateful letter had been "written by Cook and dictated by Edwin Coppoc [and] that they were united in it." "Statement of Annie Brown, Daughter of John Brown, Written November 1886," Frank Logan/John Brown Collection, Chicago History Museum. "If Cook wrote it, the motive for not signing it himself, of course, would be that he thought Mrs. Brown would appreciate the letter more if it were not signed by him." Galbreath, *Edwin Coppoc* at 428.

15. Quoted in Villard, *John Brown* at 523. Some militant abolitionists—including Thomas Wentworth Higginson, Lysander Spooner, and Richard Hinton—had in fact explored various rescue schemes, but nothing ever came of their fanciful plotting. Brown himself discouraged all talk of a rescue. Reynolds, *John Brown* at 379, 389.

16. *New York Times*, December 3, 1859; Sanborn, *Life and Letters* at 625.

17. *New York Times*, December 3, 1859. *New York Tribune*, December 10, 1859. *Shepherdstown Register*, December 10, 1859. David Hunter Strother, "Eyewitness Account of the Execution of John Brown," unpublished manuscript, December 1859, Stutler Collection. According to the *New York Times*, Cook protested that Brown had told him "in Pittsburg" to come to Harper's Ferry. That is obviously inaccurate, as Cook had received his first instructions—whatever they were—in Chatham and proceeded to Virginia via Cleveland. Nonetheless, Brown's early biographers repeated the "Pittsburg" comment uncritically. DeWitt, *Life* at 100; Drew, *JB Invasion* at 67; Hinton, *JB's Men* at 484–85; Villard, *John Brown* at 554.

18. *New York Times*, December 3, 1859.

19. *New York Times*, December 3, 1859. John Brown to Aaron Stevens, December 2, 1859, Gilder Lehrman Collection, Gilder Lehrman Institute of American History. Horwitz, *Midnight Rising* at 248.

20. Reynolds, *John Brown* at 395; Ruchames, *JB Reader* at 167.

21. Ruffin, *Diary* at 370.

22. Quoted in Trodd and Stauffer, *Meteor of War* at 214. Quoted in Horwitz, *Midnight Rising* at 259. In nineteenth-century slang, a "ball" was a confrontation or battle, as in "the ball will open." And of course, rifles, pistols, and cannons fired balls. Thus, southerners would have understood "the Old Brown liberty-ball" to be a threat of violence. See, e.g., W. J. Srofe to Dear Mother, January 29, 1862, Civil War Letters of William J. Srofe, http://www.48ovvi.org/oh48wjs7.html; Post, *Soldiers' Letters* at 91.

23. *Anti-Slavery History* at 167. Garrison, *Reign of Terror* at 10. Reynolds, *John Brown* at 418.

24. Jefferson Davis, "Remarks to the U.S. Senate, December 8, 1859," quoted in Trodd and Stauffer, *Meteor of War* at 260.

25. Ruffin, *Diary* at 377.

26. Fellman, *God and Country* at 53. Thoreau also considered it a "great blunder" that Virginia had not hanged Brown's four followers along with him. By thus stretching out the drama, Brown's "victory was prolonged and completed." Henry Thoreau, *Anti-Slavery Papers* at 89.

27. Fellman, *God and Country* at 36. *New York Tribune*, December 3, 1859.

28. The Stauntons were accompanied by a Miss Hughes, who was said to be a cousin of Cook's. There were no Hugheses in Haddam, however, and further information about this cousin has not been found. *Indiana State Sentinel*, December 16, 1859; *Richmond Enquirer*, December 16, 1859.

29. *Indiana State Sentinel*, December 16, 1859; *New York Tribune*, December 17, 1859; *Indianapolis Journal*, December 16, 1859; *Richmond Enquirer*, December 16, 1859.

30. *Richmond Enquirer*, December 16, 1859; *Indianapolis Journal*, December 17, 1859; *Indiana State Sentinel*, December 16, 1859.

31. *New York Tribune*, December 17, 1859.

32. Gill interview, Hinton Papers, Kansas State Historical Society. Another observer said that "John E. Cook, unlike his captain [Brown], was not a religious man and . . . he uttered profane words." De Witt, *Life* at 23. *New York Tribune*, December 17, 1859.

33. *Indiana State Sentinel*, December 21, 1859.

34. Cook to Wm. Maxson & Family, December 15, 1859, Todd Collection, Iowa State Archives.

35. *Indiana State Sentinel*, December 21, 1859.

36. *Indiana State Sentinel*, December 21, 1859; *New York Tribune*, December 17, 1859.

37. *New York Tribune*, December 17, 1859.

38. *New York Tribune*, December 17, 1859; Winchester, Virginia, newspaper clipping (undated and untitled), Stutler Collection.

39. *New York Tribune*, December 17, 1859. *Indiana State Sentinel*, December 21, 1859. *Virginia Free Press*, December 22, 1859; *Richmond Enquirer*, December 20, 1859; *Shepherdstown Register*, December 24, 1859.

40. *New York Tribune*, December 17, 1859.

41. *Richmond Enquirer*, December 20, 1859; *Cincinnati Gazette*, December 16, 1859, transcribed in Stutler Collection.

42. *New York Tribune*, December 17, 1859; *Richmond Enquirer*, December 20, 1859. Cook may have been protecting someone else as well. According to Richard Hinton, Cook and Coppoc had arranged for assistance from Charles Lenhart, a free-state partisan from Kansas who had somehow infiltrated the Charlestown militia. I have my doubts about that story. Hinton also reported that Lenhart arrived in Charlestown before Brown's execution and had been at the gallows "in the same file as John Wilkes Booth." Hinton, *JB's Men* at 396, 401. Given the xenophobic hysteria that gripped Charlestown at the time, it seems unlikely that a Kansan could have remained incognito for so long, less likely that he could have successfully passed himself off as a Virginia militiaman, and even less likely that he could have arranged meetings with the imprisoned Cook and Coppoc. Nonetheless, Hinton's account of Lenhart has been accepted by many of Brown's later biographers, including Osward Garrison Villard, Jules Abels, and David Reynolds (who also reports paradoxically that Lenhart was killed in Kansas in 1856). There are no contemporary references to Lenhart's involvement in the Charlestown escape, but that might be because Cook shielded him so well at the time. Tony Horwitz relegates the Lenhart story to a footnote, and I have followed his wise example. Horwitz, *Midnight Rising* at 334.

43. Although Cook signed both prisoners' names to the letter, there is no evidence that Coppoc read or approved of it. The letter was mostly written in the first person singular, with references to Coppoc in the second person, such as "I urged Coppoc . . ."

44. *New York Tribune*, December 17, 1859; *Cincinnati Gazette*, December 16, 1859, transcribed in Stutler Collection; George Mauzy to Eugenia Burton, December 18, 1859 (capitalization original), Stutler Collection.

45. *Shepherdstown Register*, December 24, 1859.

46. *Shepherdstown Register,* December 24, 1859; *Richmond Enquirer,* December 20, 1859. In some accounts, the third minister is called either Lynch or Lehr.

47. *Richmond Enquirer,* December 20, 1859. Regarding the custom of the condemned prisoner's speech from the gallows, see Banner, *Death Penalty* at 24.

48. *Cincinnati Gazette,* December 16, 1859, transcribed in Stutler Collection; *Richmond Enquirer,* December 20, 1859. Governor Wise informed Copeland's father that a white man would be permitted to retrieve the corpse. Professor James Monroe of Oberlin agreed to undertake the mission, traveling to Virginia a few days after the execution. The Winchester medical students, however, refused to release the cadaver, and Monroe was forced to return empty-handed to Ohio. Monroe, *Oberlin Lectures* at 170–71.

49. *Shepherdstown Register,* December 21, 1859.

50. *New York Tribune,* December 17, 1859; *Shepherdstown Register,* December 21, 1859 (spelling original).

51. *Richmond Enquirer,* December 20, 1859; *New York Tribune,* December 17, 1859; *Cincinnati Gazette,* December 16, 1859, transcribed in Stutler Collection; *Shepherdstown Register,* December 21, 1859 (spelling original).

52. *New York Tribune,* December 17, 1859. Plans were later changed, and Coppoc was in fact buried near his birthplace in Ohio. Galbreath, *Edwin Coppoc* at 439. Jefferson County, Virginia, Register of Deaths, December 16, 1859, p. 20, line 28.

53. *Shepherdstown Register,* December 21, 1859 (spelling and emphasis original).

CHAPTER 12. FORGIVENESS

1. *New York Times,* December 19, 1859. *Cincinnati Gazette,* December 16, 1859, transcribed in Stutler Collection.

2. E. D. Culver to Rev. J. Young, December 18, 1859, Villard Papers, Columbia University Library. *New York Times,* December 19, 1859.

3. *New York Times,* December 19, 1859; *Richmond Enquirer,* December 23, 1859.

4. Webb, *Life and Letters* at 380. Cook to Dear Friends, August 10, 1859, Hinton Collection, Kansas Historical Society. On another occasion Cook wrote, "Through the dark gloom of the future I fancy I can almost see the dawning light of Freedom." Cook to My Dear Sisters, May 6, 1858, quoted in Richman, *Quakers* at 36. *New York Times,* December 19, 1859; *Richmond Enquirer,* December 23, 1859. Boyd B. Stutler to Harry Wade Hicks, August 24, 1939, Stutler Collection, West Virginia Archives.

The inscription on Cook's headstone reads (capitalization and spelling original):

CAPTAIN JOHN E. COOK

BORN MAY 12, 1829

DIED FOR THE CAUSE OF

EMANCIPATION AND HUMAN

LIBERTY WITH THE NOBLE

PATRIOT JOHN BROWN

AT CHARLESTON, VIRGINIA

DECEMBER 16, 1859

The reinterment took place on December 15, 1868, which explains the reference to John Brown as a noble patriot. It is improbable that anyone in the Cook family would have praised Brown at any time before the Civil War.

5. The quotations are from an editorial in the *Indiana State Sentinel*, which frequently spoke on behalf of Governor Willard. No other member of the extended Cook family appears to have publicly expressed a contrary sentiment in the aftermath of the execution. *Indiana State Sentinel*, December 21, 1859.

6. Higginson, *Contemporaries* at 234. Reynolds, *John Brown* at 377; Ruchames, *JB Reader* at 297. George Sennott to A. D. Stevens, December 5 and December 13, 1859, Villard Papers, Columbia University Library.

7. Barclay Coppoc was indicted in early 1860, in part based on information provided by Cook, but he had by then reached safety in Iowa where the antislavery governor refused to cooperate with Virginia's extradition request.

8. Abels, *Man on Fire* at 317; Oates, *Purge This Land* at 310; Reynolds, *John Brown* at 339, 340, 357, 362–63. Emerson's lecture, titled "Courage," was published in the *New York Tribune* on November 8, 1859, and subsequently in other newspapers around the country.

9. Anderson, *Voice* at 58. Higginson, *Contemporaries* at 234.

10. Peterson, *Legend Revisited* at 39. Redpath, *Public Life* at 8, 198, 286, 404–5 (non-hyphenation in original). The following year, in Dublin, Richard Davis Webb published another Brown biography, taking the same anodyne approach to John Cook. As did Redpath, Webb relied heavily on Cook's confession for details about Brown's recruiting and preparation, but he more or less cleansed the rest of the record, denying that Cook had made any "important revelations" and again omitting Brown's rebuke of Cook on execution day. Webb, *Life and Letters* at 371. Hinton, *JB's Men* at 484–85.

11. Boyd B. Stutler to Harry Wade Hicks, August 24, 1939, Stutler Collection.

12. "Statement of Annie Brown, Daughter of John Brown, Written November 1886," Frank Logan/John Brown Collection, Chicago History Museum.

13. Anne Brown Adams to Richard Hinton (undated), Hinton Papers, Kansas Historical Society.

14. Hinton considered Cook his comrade and he regarded "his errors . . . as matters of temperament" that did not detract from his "noble soul." Hinton, *JB's Men* at 483–87. In a magazine article published in London in 1890, Hinton praised Cook as a martyr who was "willing to be sacrificed for the weakest of his suffering countrymen," without even mentioning Cook's confession. Hinton, *Old John Brown* at 734.

15. C. D. Fitzhugh to My Dear Sir (Governor Henry Wise), November 21, 1859, Wise Family Papers, Library of Congress; Lewis Washington to Hon. H. A. Wise, November 7, 1859, Wise Family Papers, Library of Congress.

16. James Buchanan to Andrew Hunter, December 17, 1859, *Proceedings of the Massachusetts Historical Society* (December 1912) at 245.

17. Virginia Kennedy Cook Johnston interview, Villard Papers, Columbia University Library.

18. Virginia Kennedy Cook Johnston interview, Villard Papers, Columbia University Library. Although only two children are mentioned in the notes of the 1908 interview (John, Jr., and a daughter), both the 1900 and 1910 censuses list Virginia as the mother of five children, of whom four were alive in 1900 and three in 1910. It appears that Virginia was estranged from several of her children, not only John, Jr., for reasons unknown.

19. John E. Cook, Jr., to O. G. Villard, February 25, 1908, Villard Papers, Columbia University Library; Roland C. Cook to Oswald Garrison Villard, November 30, 1908, Villard Papers, Columbia University Library.

BIBLIOGRAPHY

ARCHIVES

Boyd B. Stutler Collection. West Virginia State Archives.

Calendar of Virginia State Papers.

Copeland, John A., Letters. Oberlin College Archive. Oberlin, Ohio.

The Dreer Collection. Historical Society of Pennsylvania.

Frank Logan/John Brown Collection. Chicago History Museum.

Frederick Douglass Papers. Library of Congress.

Gilder Lehrman Collection. Gilder Lehrman Institute of American History, New York, N.Y.

Governor's Office. Papers of Governor Henry A. Wise, 1856–1860. Library of Virginia. Richmond, Va.

Haddam Historical Society Collection, Haddam, Conn.

Harpers Ferry National Historic Park Collection.

Harriet Newby. Special Collection. Library of Virginia. Richmond, Va.

Helen Jones Campbell Papers. Virginia Historical Society.

Hinton Collection. Letters. Territorial Kansas Archive.

Horatio Nelson Rust. Papers. H. E. Huntington Library and Art Gallery. San Marino, Calif.

House Divided Archive. Dickinson College. Carlisle, Pa.

Jane Pierce Collection. Indiana State Library.

John Brown Papers. Circuit Court of Jefferson County, Charles Town, W.Va.

John Brown Papers. Manuscripts. Library of Congress.

John Todd Collection. Manuscripts. Iowa State Archives.

Law Practice of Abraham Lincoln. Abraham Lincoln Presidential Library and Museum.

Oswald Garrison Villard Papers. Columbia University Rare Book and Manuscript Library.

Richard Josiah Hinton Papers. Manuscripts. Kansas Historical Society Archives.

Thomas Wentworth Higginson Papers. Boston Public Library Rare Books and Manuscripts Collection.

The Valley of the Shadow Archive. Library of Virginia.

William J. Srofe's Civil War Letters. http://www.48ovvi.org/oh48wjs7.html.

Wise Family Papers, 1836–1928. Manuscripts. Library of Congress.

NEWSPAPERS AND MAGAZINES

Atlantic Monthly

Baltimore American

Baltimore Sun

Boston Traveler

Carlisle American (Pennsylvania)

Chicago Herald

Cincinnati Gazette

Cleveland Herald

Dawson's Daily Times (Ft. Wayne, Ind.)

Franklin Repository and Transcript (Chambersburg, Pa.)

Harper's Ferry Independent Democrat

Harper's Weekly

Hartford Courant

Indiana State Sentinel

Indianapolis American

Indianapolis Daily Journal

The Liberator

The Locomotive (Indianapolis)

National Democrat (Cleveland)

New York Herald

New York Times

New York Tribune

Philadelphia Press

Public Opinion (Chambersburg, Pa.)

Richmond Daily Whig

Richmond Enquirer

Rochester Democrat

Shepherdstown Register (Virginia)

Spirit of Jefferson (Charlestown, Va.)

St. Louis Globe-Democrat

Valley Spirit (Chambersburg, Pa.)

Virginia Free Press and Farmers' Repository (Charlestown, Va.)

BOOKS, MONOGRAPHS, AND ARTICLES

Abels, Jules. *Man on Fire: John Brown and the Cause of Liberty.* New York: MacMillan, 1971.

American Anti-Slavery Society. *The Anti-Slavery History of the John Brown Year; Being the Twenty-Seventh Annual Report of the American Anti-Slavery Society.* New York: Negro Universities Press, 1861.

Anderson, Osborne P. *A Voice from Harper's Ferry: A Narrative of Events at Harper's Ferry with Incidents Prior and Subsequent to Its Capture by Captain Brown and His Men.* Boston, 1861. Reprint, Freeport, N.Y.: Books for Libraries Press, 1972.

Applegate, Debby. *The Most Famous Man in America: The Biography of Henry Ward Beecher.* New York: Doubleday, 2007.

"Arrest of Cooke." *Harper's Weekly,* November 5, 1859.

Banner, Stuart. *The Death Penalty: An American History.* Cambridge: Harvard University Press, 2002.

Barry, Joseph. *The Annals of Harper's Ferry.* Martinsburg, W.Va.: Office of *The Berkeley Union,* 1872.

Bogardus, Frank Smith. "Daniel W. Voorhees." *Indiana Magazine of History,* June 1931.

Boteler, Alexander. "Recollections of the John Brown Raid." *The Century,* July 1883.

Bradley, Erwin Stanley. *Simon Cameron, Lincoln's Secretary of War: A Political Biography.* Philadelphia: University of Pennsylvania Press, 1966.

Cain, William E. *William Lloyd Garrison and the Fight against Slavery.* New York: Bedford/St. Martin's, 1994.

Calendar of Virginia State Papers and Other Manuscripts, January 1, 1836 to April 15, 1869. Vol. 11. Richmond, Va.: 1875–93. Reprint, New York: Kraus Reprint, 1968.

Carton, Evan. *Patriotic Treason: John Brown and the Soul of America.* New York: Free Press, 2006.

"Col. R. E. Lee's Report to Adjutant General." *Virginia Magazine of History and Biography,* July 1902.

Cook, John E. *Confession of John E. Cooke, Brother-in-Law of Gov. A. P. Willard of Indiana, and One of the Participants in the Harper's Ferry Invasion.* Charles Town, W.Va.: 1859.

Cress, Joseph D. "Cumberland County's Connection to John Brown's Raid at Harper's Ferry." *Cumberland County History*, 2009.

Davis, David Brion. *Inhuman Bondage: The Rise and Fall of Slavery in the New World*. New York: Oxford University Press, 2006.

DeCaro, Louis A., Jr. *"Fire From the Midst of You": A Religious Life of John Brown*. New York: New York University Press, 2002.

———— *John Brown: The Cost of Freedom*. New York: International Publishers, 2007.

DeWitt, Robert M. *The Life, Trial and Execution of Captain John Brown*. New York: 1859.

Dodd, Donald B. *Historical Statistics of the States of the United States: Two Centuries of the Census, 1790–1990*. Westport, Conn., 1993.

Douglass, Frederick. *The Life and Times of Frederick Douglass*. Boston: De Wolfe & Fiske, 1892.

Downey, Arthur T. *Civil War Lawyers: Constitutional Questions, Courtroom Dramas, and the Men behind Them*. Chicago: American Bar Association, 2010.

Drew, Thomas. *The John Brown Invasion*. Boston, 1860.

Etcheson, Nicole. *Bleeding Kansas: Contested Liberty in the Civil War Era*. Lawrence: University Press of Kansas, 2004.

"Extraordinary Insurrection at Harper's Ferry." *Harper's Weekly*, October 29, 1859.

Farrand, Max, ed. *Records of the Federal Convention of 1787*. 3 vols. New Haven: Yale University Press, 1986.

Fehrenbacher, Don. *The Dred Scott Case: Its Significance in American Law and Politics*. New York: Oxford University Press, 1981.

Fellman, Michael. *In the Name of God and Country: Reconsidering Terrorism in American History*. New Haven: Yale University Press, 2010.

Foner, Philip, and Yuval Taylor, eds. *Frederick Douglass: Selected Speeches and Writings*. Chicago: Lawrence Hill Books, 1999.

Frost, Karolyn Smardz. *I've Got a Home in Glory Land: A Lost Tale of the Underground Railroad*. New York: Farrar, Straus and Giroux, 2007.

Frothingham, Octavius Brooks. *Gerrit Smith: A Biography*. New York: Negro Universities Press, 1969.

Galbreath, C. B. "Edwin Coppoc." *Ohio History*, October 1921.

Garrison, William Lloyd. "Address to the Park Street Church." Lecture at Park Street Church, Boston, July 4, 1829.

————. *The New Reign of Terror in the Slaveholding States, for 1859–60*. New York: Arno Press, 1969.

Geffert, Hannah. "John Brown and His Black Allies: An Ignored Alliance." *Pennsylvania Magazine of History and Biography*, October 2002.

———. "Regional Black Involvement in John Brown's Raid on Harpers Ferry." With Jean Libby. In *Prophets of Protest: Reconsidering the History of American Abolitionism,* ed. Timothy Patrick McCarthy and John Stauffer, 165–82. New York: New Press, 2006.

———. "They Heard His Call." In *Terrible Swift Sword: the Legacy of John Brown,* ed. Peggy A. Russo and Paul Finkelman, 23–45. Athens: Ohio University Press, 2005.

Goodrich, Thomas. *War to the Knife: Bleeding Kansas, 1854–1861.* Mechanicsburg, Pa.: Stackpole Books, 1998.

Gould, Lewis L. "Alexander Kelly McClure." American National Biography Online. Accessed January 4, 2012. http://anb.org/articles/04/04–00676. html?a=1&n=alexander%20kelly%20mcclure&d=10&ss=0&q=1.

Gue, Benjamin F. *The Civil War.* Vol. 2. of *History of Iowa from the Earliest Times to the Beginning of the Twentieth Century.* New York: Century History, 1903.

———. "John Brown and His Iowa Friends." *Midland Monthly,* February 1897.

Guthrie, Woody. "The Ballad of Pretty Boy Floyd" on *Dust Bowl Ballads.* Buddha B00004TY8S, 2000, compact disc. Originally released in 1940.

Hamilton, James C. "John Brown in Canada." *Canadian Magazine,* December 1894.

"Henry Wise to Andrew Hunter, November 6, 1859." *Proceedings of the Massachusetts Historical Society,* February 1908.

Higginson, Thomas Wentworth. *Cheerful Yesterdays.* New York: Houghton Mifflin, 1900.

———. *Contemporaries.* Boston: Houghton Mifflin, 1899.

Hinton, Richard J. *John Brown and His Men.* New York: Arno Press, 1968.

———. "Old John Brown and the Men of Harper's Ferry." *Time* (London, England), July 1890.

Hitchcock, William S. "The Limits of Southern Unionism: Virginia Conservatives and the Gubernatorial Election of 1859." *Journal of Southern History,* February 1981.

Horwitz, Tony. *Midnight Rising: John Brown and the Raid that Sparked the Civil War.* New York: Henry Holt, 2011.

Hunter, Andrew. "John Brown's Raid." *Publications of the Southern History Association,* July 1897.

"James Buchanan to Andrew Hunter, December 17, 1859." *Proceedings of the Massachusetts Historical Society,* December 1912.

"John Brown and His Friends." *Atlantic Monthly.* July 1872.

Jones, Howard. *Mutiny on the Amistad: The Saga of a Slave Revolt and Its Impact on American Abolition, Law, and Diplomacy.* New York: Oxford University Press, 1987.

Jordan, Henry. "Daniel Wolsey Voorhees." *Mississippi Valley Historical Review*, March 1920.

Keagy, Franklin. "John Brown and His Men: Inmates of the Ritner Boarding House." *Public Opinion*, February 2, 1891.

Keeler, Ralph. "Owen Brown's Escape from Harper's Ferry." *Atlantic Monthly*, March 1874.

Kenworthy, Leonard S. *The Tall Sycamore of the Wabash: Daniel Wolsey Voorhees*. Boston: Bruce Humphries, 1936.

Laabs, Damon M. "McClure, Alexander Kelly." Cultural Heritage Map of Pennsylvania, Pennsylvania Center for the Book at Penn State University. Accessed January 4, 2012. http://www.pabook.libraries.psu.edu/palitmap/bios/McClure__Alexander_Kelly.html.

Langston, John Mercer. *From the Virginia Plantation to the National Capitol*. Hartford, Conn.: American Publishing, 1894. Reprint, North Stratford, N.H.: Ayer, 2002.

The Law Practice of Abraham Lincoln. "Lincoln recommended Voorhees's admission to bar." Accessed January 5, 2012, at http://www.lawpracticeof abrahamlincoln.org/Details.aspx?case=141344.

Lawson, John, ed. *1916*. Vol. 6 of *American State Trials*. St. Louis: Thomas Law Books, 1914–36.

Libby, Jean. *John Brown Mysteries*. With Hannah Geffert and Evelyn Taylor. Missoula, Mont.: Pictoral Histories Publishing, 1999.

Lloyd, Frederick. "John Brown among the Pedee Quakers." *Annals of Iowa*, July 1866.

Lovejoy, Julia Louisa. "Letter to the Editor, November 24, 1859." *Kansas Historical Quarterly* 16 (February 1948): 72–73.

Mason, Virginia. *The Public Life and Diplomatic Correspondence of James M. Mason*. New York: Neale Publishing, 1906.

Mayer, Henry. *All on Fire: William Lloyd Garrison and the Abolition of Slavery*. New York: St. Martin's Press, 1998.

McCarthy, Timothy Patrick, and John Stauffer, eds. *Prophets of Protest: Reconsidering the History of American Abolitionism*. New York: New Press, 2006.

McClure, Alexander. *Colonel Alexander K. McClure's Recollections of Half a Century*. Salem, Mass.: Salem Press, 1902.

———. "Curtin Elected Governor—1860." In *Andrew Gregg Curtin: His Life and Services*, ed. William H. Egle. Philadelphia: Avil Printing, 1895.

———. "An Episode of John Brown's Raid." *Lippincott's Magazine*, September 1883.

———. *Lincoln and Men of War-Times: Some Personal Recollections of War and Politics during the Lincoln Administration*. Philadelphia: Times Publishing, 1892.

———. Vol. 1 of *Old Time Notes of Pennsylvania*. Philadelphia: John C. Winston, 1905.

McGinty, Brian. *John Brown's Trial*. Cambridge: Harvard University Press, 2009.

McGlone, Robert. *John Brown's War against Slavery*. New York: Cambridge University Press, 2009.

———. "Rescripting a Troubled Past: John Brown's Family and the Harper's Ferry Conspiracy." *Journal of American History*, March 1989.

McPherson, James. *Battle Cry of Freedom: Civil War Era*. New York: Oxford University Press, 1988.

Monroe, James. *Oberlin Thursday Lectures, Addresses, and Essays*. Oberlin, Ohio: Edward J. Goodrich, 1897.

National Cyclopedia of American Biography. Vol. 13, s.v. "Ashbel P. Willard."

Nevin, Alfred. "Colonel Alexander Kelly McClure." In *Centennial Biography: Men of Mark of Cumberland Valley, Pa., 1776–1876*. Philadelphia: Fulton Publishing, 1876.

Oates, Stephen. *To Purge This Land with Blood: A Biography of John Brown*. New York: Harper & Row, 1970.

Osborne, John, and James Gerencser. "Alexander Kelly McClure." *Their Own Words*, Dickenson University. Last modified June 21, 2004. http://deila.dickinson.edu/theirownwords/author/McClureA.htm.

Peterson, Merrill D. *John Brown: The Legend Revisited*. Charlottesville: University of Virginia Press, 2002.

Phillips, Wendell. *Speeches, Lectures and Letters*. Boston: Lee and Shepard, 1872.

Plymouth Church. "Henry Ward Beecher." Accessed January 5, 2012. http://www.plymouthchurch.org/our_history_henry-wardbeecher.php.

Post, Lydia Minturn. *Soldiers' Letters, from Camp, Battle-field and Prison*. New York: Bunce & Huntington, 1865.

Quarles, Benjamin. *Allies for Freedom: Blacks and John Brown*. New York: Oxford University Press, 1974.

Rampersad, Arnold. *1902–1941*. Vol. 1 of *The Life of Langston Hughes*. New York: Oxford University Press, 1986–88.

Redpath, James. *The Public Life of Captain John Brown: With an Auto-Biography of His Childhood and Youth*. Boston: Thayer and Eldridge, 1860.

Reynolds, David S. *John Brown, Abolitionist: The Man Who Killed Slavery, Sparked the Civil War, and Seeded Civil Rights*. New York: Alfred A. Knopf, 2005.

———. *Mightier than the Sword: Uncle Tom's Cabin and the Battle for America*. New York: W. W. Norton, 2011.

Richman, Irving B. *John Brown among the Quakers and Other Sketches*. Des Moines: Historical Department of Iowa, 1897.

Ritner, Joseph. "Annual Message to the Assembly—1836." In *VI Pennsylvania Archives, 4th ser., Papers of the Governors, 1832–1845*, ed. George Edward Reed. Harrisburg, Pa.: State of Pennsylvania, 1902.

Rodgers, Thomas E. "Liberty, Will, and Violence: The Political Ideology of the Democrats of West-Central Indiana during the Civil War." *Indiana Magazine of History*, June 1996.

Ruchames, Louis. *A John Brown Reader: The Story of John Brown in His Own Words . . . .* London: Abelard-Schuman, 1959.

Ruffin, Edmund. *Toward Independence, October 1856–April 1861.* Vol. 1 of *The Diary of Edmund Ruffin.* Baton Rouge: Louisiana State University Press, 1972–89.

Sanborn, Franklin B. *The Life and Letters of John Brown, Liberator of Kansas and Martyr of Virginia.* 1885. Reprint, New York: Negro Universities Press, 1969.

Scott, Otto J. *The Secret Six: John Brown and the Abolitionist Movement.* New York: New York Times Books, 1979.

Select Committee of the Senate Appointed to Inquire into the Late Invasion and Seizure of the Public Property at Harper's Ferry. *Report.* 36th Cong., 1st sess., 1860.

Shackleton, Robert, Jr. "What Support Did John Brown Rely Upon." *Magazine of American History*, April 1893.

Shanks, Henry T. *The Secession Movement in Virginia, 1847–1861.* Richmond, Va.: Garrett and Massie, 1934.

Sharswood, George. *A Compend of the Lectures on the Aims and Duties of the Profession of the Law.* Philadelphia: T. & J. W. Johnson, 1854.

Shearer, W. J. "John Brown's Raid." Lecture presented at the Hamilton Library, Carlisle, Pa., January 17, 1905.

Simpson, Craig M. *A Good Southerner: The Life of Henry A. Wise of Virginia.* Chapel Hill: University of North Carolina Press, 1985.

Smith, Henry. "The Modern Privilege: Its Nineteenth Century Origins." In *The Privilege against Self-Incrimination*, ed. R. H. Helmholz, 145–80. Chicago: University of Chicago Press, 1997.

Stampp, Kenneth M. *Indiana Politics during the Civil War.* Indianapolis: Indiana Historical Bureau, 1949.

Stauffer, John. *The Black Hearts of Men: Radical Abolitionists and the Transformation of Race.* Cambridge: Harvard University Press, 2001.

Stewart, David O. *The Summer of 1787: The Men Who Invented the Constitution.* New York: Simon & Schuster, 2007.

Stewart, James Brewer. *Abolitionist Politics and the Coming of the Civil War.* Amherst: University of Massachusetts Press, 2008.

———. *Holy Warriors: The Abolitionists and American Slavery.* New York: Hill and Wang, 1976.

Strother, David Hunter. "Copeland's Confession." *Harper's Weekly*, November 12, 1859.

Stutler, Boyd B. "Judge Richard Parker." *Magazine of the Jefferson County Historical Society*. December 1953.

Sumner, Charles. "The Crime against Kansas." Cong. Globe, 34th Cong., 1st sess., 1856.

Thoreau, Henry David. *Anti-Slavery and Reform Papers*, ed. H. S. Salt. London: S. Sonnenschein, 1890.

Thornton, W. W. "Daniel W. Voorhees as Lawyer and Orator." *Green Bag* 14, no. 8 (1902): 355–63.

Thrush, Ambrose. *Medical Men of Franklin County, Pa., 1750–1925*. Chambersburg, Pa.: Medical Society of Franklin County, 1928.

Torget, Andrew J., and Edward L. Ayers. *Two Communities in the Civil War*. New York: W. W. Norton, 2007.

Trodd, Zoe, and John Stauffer, eds. *Meteor of War: The John Brown Story*. Maplecrest, N.Y.: Brandywine Press, 2004.

Tucker, John Randolph. "Reminiscences of Virginia's Judges and Jurists." *Virginia Law Register*, July 1895.

Van Gundy, John C. *Reminiscences of Frontier Life on the Upper Neosho in 1855 and 1856*. Topeka, Kans., 1925.

Villard, Oswald Garrison. *John Brown, 1800–1859: A Biography Fifty Years After*. New York: Houghton Mifflin, 1910.

Voorhees, Daniel Wolsey. "Defense of John E. Cook." In Vol. 2 of *Forty Years of Oratory: Daniel Wolsey Voorhees, Lectures, Addresses and Speeches*. 1898.

Wayland, John Walter. *John Kagi and John Brown*. Strasburg, Va.: Shenandoah Publishing House, 1961.

Webb, Richard Davis, ed. *The Life and Letters of Captain John Brown: Who Was Executed at Charlestown, Virginia, Dec. 2, 1859, for an Armed Attack upon American Slavery, With Notices of Some of His Confederates*. London: Smith, Elder, 1861.

Wells, Anna Mary. *Dear Preceptor: The Life and Times of Thomas Wentworth Higginson*. Boston: Houghton Mifflin, 1963.

Whittier, John Greenleaf. *The Complete Poetical Works of John Greenleaf Whittier*. New York: Houghton Mifflin, 1895.

Willson, Seelye A. "Owen Brown's Escape from Harper's Ferry." *Magazine of Western History*, February 1889.

Wilson, Henry Lane. "An Early Indiana Political Contest." *Indiana Magazine of History*, June 1928.

Woollen, William Wesley. "Ashbel Parsons Willard." In *Biographical and Historical Sketches of Early Indiana*, 104–12. Indianapolis: Hammond, 1883.

ACKNOWLEDGMENTS

For over a decade, Marcia Lehr, of the Northwestern University Law Library, has assisted me with reference requests. This may have been our most challenging project, but Marcia succeeded in locating obscure and arcane sources, often virtually overnight, and her resourcefulness seems to be without limit. Also seemingly boundless is the dedication and enthusiasm of Ann Nelson, whose editorial and other support have been essential to everything I have done in the past six years. I have had many excellent students at Northwestern, but Rebecca Felsenthal, NULS 2012, truly distinguished herself as my principal research assistant for *John Brown's Spy*. Her future clients will be lucky indeed to have such a diligent and creative attorney on their side.

It was my privilege to work with an outstanding, generous, and supportive editor—Christopher Rogers, of the Yale University Press. And it was my exceptional good fortune to be counseled by a gifted young literary agent—Katherine Flynn, of Kneerim & Williams.

It takes a long time to turn an idea into a book, and false starts are inevitable, so I am grateful for the early encouragement and good suggestions of Robert Warden, Joseph Margulies, Robert Burns, and Lea VanderVelde. The first versions of every manuscript are flawed by definition, so I am especially indebted to Brian McGinty, James Ford, Robert Clarke, and Sarah Lipton-Lubet, who patiently read, and helped improve, my initial drafts. Thanks also to Eliza Childs for carefully editing the final draft.

Primary source materials about John E. Cook are spread across the United States, and I could not have tracked everything down without the help of many fine independent researchers, archivists, and librarians. I am especially grateful to Cynthia Goetz, who lives in John Cook's childhood home in Haddam, Connecticut; Ceceile Kay Richter, who diligently investigated sources in the National Archives and Library of Congress; and Andrew Edwards, who assisted me in innumerable ways before returning to his hometown in Humboldt County, California, where he grew up hearing stories about Annie Brown. Thanks are also due for research and editorial assistance from Mimi Katz, Pegeen Bassett, Lynn Kincade, Jeffrey Sumner, Suzanne Mackenzie Salisbury, Eric Wakin, David Holmgren, Kim Baker, Donald Watts, James Ward, Julie Callahan, Olga Tsapina, Sabino Casella, Ann Hull, Matthew Pinsker, and Jennifer Born. Many others helped me in various ways as I worked on this project, including James Foody, Michael Dowling, Madhu Gorla, Richard Tye, Christel Bridges, Kurt Mitenbuler and the members of the Unicorn Roundtable. As always, I am deeply grateful for research support from the Spray Trust Fund of the Northwestern University School of Law.

There is enormous satisfaction in completing a book after years of hard work, but it still does not compare to the joy of sharing the years of my life with Linda, Natan, and Sarah.

INDEX